# HISPANIC PSYCHOLOGY YEARBOOK
# VOLUME 1

# HISPANIC PSYCHOLOGY YEARBOOK

Books in this series can be found on Nova's website under the Series tab.

E-books in this series can be found on Nova's website under the E-books tab.

HISPANIC PSYCHOLOGY YEARBOOK

# HISPANIC PSYCHOLOGY YEARBOOK
# VOLUME 1

CIRILO H. GARCÍA
EDITOR

Nova
Nova Science Publishers, Inc.
*New York*

For permission to use material from this book please contact us:
Telephone 631-231-7269; Fax 631-231-8175
Web Site: http://www.novapublishers.com



**LIBRARY OF CONGRESS CATALOGING-IN-PUBLICATION DATA**

Available upon request.

ISBN: 978-1-60741-786-6

*Published by Nova Science Publishers, Inc. ✢ New York*

# CONTENTS

# PREFACE

This compendium incorporates works of empirical research, derived from different conceptual models based on any psychological or psychosocial theory. It presents a global forum that exposes scientific studies on psychology, done principally by Spanish-speaking researchers from different countries. It includes the best academic efforts of research as an easy way of communication with non-Latin researchers, propitiating in this way a fertile exchange of knowledge and cooperation among scientists of psychology around the world.

Chapter 1 - In this paper the authors analyze the possible existence of policies for worker integration and promotion, according to gender, without taking into consideration the position held. The authors also validate an instrument for evaluating differences according to gender during the socialization process by following the Taormina's Model of Social Organization (1997). In this Model, four domains are proposed that coincide with the four subscales on the OSI Questionnaire (training, understanding, support of co-workers and future perspectives). In the same manner, the authors have designed a subscale that, in an abbreviated form, has been called the Gender Subscale for the Socialization Process. The degree of learning achieved in these domains is the main indicator of success in the socialization process. The study is composed of two transversal samples and a longitudinal sample. Data was gathered at two different times with approximately one year's difference between them. The first transversal sample contains 414 participants and the second transversal sample contains 396 participants. The longitudinal sample contains 118 participants. The authors can conclude that the statistical properties of this instrument for the Spanish sample, together with the items designed on this occasion, are appropriate and in accordance with the author's theoretical proposal, which insists on the relationship and inter-dependence between the different domains. In this paper, the authors discuss the relationship between the newly created gender variable of socialization and satisfaction and commitment. In the same manner, it the authors show how gender differences are an additional domain in the socialization process and how this is reflected in increased learning.

Chapter 2 - Recent research incorporates correspondence training procedures as an example of stimuli control. Lattal and Doepke (2001) state that correspondence and conditional discrimination procedures are homologous due to the fact that both contain behavioral relations in different temporalities and because the relationship between two or more stimuli or behaviors in both procedures is a distinctive feature. This paper attempts to explore the functional correspondence between the participants' reports of the rule and their performance on a task of matching to sample during training and transference tests. Five experimental groups were exposed to a do-report procedure, where the temporal distance from requesting the general rule of execution and the inclusion of incomplete sentences with different semantic properties were manipulated. Results were analyzed according to correspondence and non-correspondence between execution on transfer tests and the rule of execution reported. This analysis showed important group differences. The authors propose a methodological matrix that allow integrate research in the area of evaluation and training in doing-reporting in conditional discrimination tasks.

Chapter 3 - The Learning Styles and Motivational Orientation Inventory (EDAOM, according to its initials in Spanish) is a viable instrument for evaluating learning strategies and motivation for study. Castañeda and Ortega (2004) stated that the reliability of this inventory is high, as well as its concurrent validity. It is known that any instrument of measurement has to have acceptable levels of reliability and validity and, for that reason the object of this paper was to carry out an evaluation of the reliability of the EDAOM with a student sample from Iztacala FES, in order to verify the initial index and establish the inventory's subscale index. The results obtained confirm the level of reliability; however, in this application in order to preserve the validity of the instrument, some items were eliminated because they had negative correlations. The data is discussed in the context of the psychometric characteristics of an instrument and items and response choices were proposed.

Chapter 4 - Studying family-home inter-relationships from the environmental psychology perspective implies tackling several epistemological and methodological aspects. In this paper some preliminary answers concerning the same are provided. In the first place, it is proposed that home-family inter-relationships be approached as a *system* composed of biological, psychological and socio-cultural components. The *family-housing system contemplates objective aspects* (daily activities) and *subjective aspects* (appreciation and affection). Aimed at including the notion of development in the analysis, the reconsideration of life cycles from developmental psychology and the classification of family life cycles from systemic theory are proposed. A proposal is made to reformulate both classifications in the framework of environmental psychology and, consequently a system to analyze dynamic diachronic and synchronic inter-relations in the housing-family system.

Chapter 5 - The objective of the study was to determine the semantic content associated to being married, considering the sample as a social group, as well as to delimit sub-groups of subjects and characterize them by comparing them in psychometric measures related to marital adjustment. A self-reporting questionnaire was administered to a sample of 100 married couples. The questionnaire was formed by a free association test, questions concerning socio-demographic data, sexual relations and nine scales (dyadic adjustment, marital satisfaction, sexual dissatisfaction, alexithymia, state-trait anxiety, depression, positive and negative affect, social desirability and marital aggrandizement). An analysis of thematic content was applied to data from the free association test. Fifteen specific categories were defined as well as a residual category with an initial average inter-rater reliability of .81 and a final one of .93. The central nucleus of social representation is formed by couple and family obligations and functions, positive feelings emphasizing love, fidelity values, a family formed by parents and children, as well as values for living together; that is to say, the image of a united, happy family that struggles for its stability through fidelity, and living together in peace and harmony. The 200 subjects, with basis on a cluster analysis concerning the 15 specific semantic categories, were classified into 4 groups: 1) being married because of children, 2) being married for the company of his/her spouse, 3) being married for conjugal and family duties and 4) being married for love. The group married because of love is closer to the nucleus of social representation and reports better adjustment and marital satisfaction.

Chapter 6 - This cross-sectional study was carried out with the main objective to assess the specific role of stress-related situations as predictors of adherence-to-medication behavior in 225 women with type 2 diabetes living in Hermosillo, Mexico, whom responded to a self-administered questionnaire evaluating stress-related situations in three modalities: making decision, tolerance to ambiguity, and tolerance to frustration. A multiple regression analysis (stepwise method) was performed to identify which of those situations predicted the adherence-to-medication behavior. This analysis showed that the stress-related situation in the modality of making decision was a predictor for adherence-to-medication behavior ($F[1, 207] = 6.041$; $p = 0.015$). The results point out that experiencing low levels of stress related to making decision facilitate the practice of adherence-to-medication behavior in women with type 2 diabetes and also support the recommendation to monitor psychological well-being related to experiencing stress in patients with type 2 diabetes.

Chapter 7 - The purpose of this study was to adapt two discipline scales (Papaioannou, 1998) to the Spanish educational context. The authors investigated construct validity and reliability of the instruments designed to measure pupils' reasons to be disciplined in the classroom and perceptions of strategies used by the teacher to maintain discipline in the physical education class. Participants were 356 Spanish pupils aged between 14 and 16. Results obtained from principal components analysis with varimax rotation revealed the existence of (a) five factors for the Reasons for Discipline Scale (RDS), that is: identified reasons, intrinsic reasons, introjected reasons, amotivation and caring reasons for behaving, and (b) four factors for the Strategies to Sustain Discipline Scale (SSDS), that is: caring and responsibility reasons, intrinsic reasons, introjected and external reasons and teacher's indifference to maintaining discipline. The alphas varied between .86 and .58 for the first scale and between .88 and .70 for the second. In addition, the results showed suitable predictive validity. More studies are necessary to corroborate the results found with different populations and cultures.

Chapter 8 - The objective of this study is to determine if the Intervention Program for Young Adults with Social Phobia/Intervención en Adultos Jóvenes con Fobia Social – IPYASP/ IAJFS- (Olivares and Rosa, 2005), is good and effective in treating this disorder. To carry it out, 20 adults, from 18 to 20 years old were selected (average: 18.8, DT: 0.83) who were randomly distributed between two experimental conditions: 1) IPYASP/ IAJFS, and 2) control group - standby. The evaluation was applied before, after and on six and twelve months after the treatment finished. The results show the program efficiency in short and medium terms of all the measurements that directly evaluate anxiety and social avoidance, as well as the correlation of self-esteem, adaptation and social abilities; on the contrary, control group subjects did not have significant statistical improvement in any of the variables measured.

Chapter 9 - To evaluate the effect of the difference in response morphology emitted to sample (SS1 and SS2) and comparison stimuli (COS1 and COS2) on the accuracy index, four groups of university students participated in a successive symbolic matching to sample task. The groups were unequal among them by the morphological difference of the response to SS and COS stimuli. The results showed than in the conditions of similarity between SS1-COS1 and SS2-COS2, but with differences between SS1-SS2 and COS1-COS2, the participant's accuracy was greatly enhanced as opposed to any other type of difference between the stimuli. Results are discussed by the analysis of the role of the difference in the contingency structures in the development of conditional stimulus control.

Chapter 10 - This paper employs a quasi-experimental ABA design to analyze the implementation of Communicative Restructuring (CR) in 15 cases of couple therapy. A semi-structured interview format with a guide was used to measure family dysfunction (FD) before and after the application of the CR. Even though the therapy only targeted the marital holon, the effects of CR seem to have influenced family structure at large, since the degree of FD decreased significantly after the implementation of the technique. The affected boundaries changed from the diffuse to the clear or partially clear, and conflicts tended to disappear. The paper also emphasizes the importance of the systemic principle of totality (if an element in the system is modified this will alter or affect the other elements) and the need to take it into account.

Chapter 11 - In this chapter, the authors will analyze the strategies for HIV/AIDS prevention, especially on young people, since they are the riskiest group to be infected, due to their life style and practices in today's situations and contexts. From the experience of working with young people in the promotion of health, the authors propose a model for HIV/AIDS prevention, based on psychological competencies development and strengthening, which, at a time, is based on the following: (1) to transmit clear and true information concerning HIV/AIDS and preventions methods; (2) to develop high motivation for the use of prevention methods; (3) to develop the necessary abilities to handle risky situations and to put them into practice when necessary; and (4) to confront the environments that favor or block young people from practicing prevention. To undertake these aspects, it is necessary to evaluate the development state of young people's psychosocial competencies; to understand and intervene from young culture's point of view, and to tackle the dynamics of living with health and illness processes, incorporating prevention as an academic course, as well as parent education.

Chapter 12 - This study describes and explains how the interest of companies in paying performance bonus (PPB) and information of the current process has an impact on the payment objectives' effectiveness (POE). The research was carried out between 419 persons who are executives (11.5%); managers (41.1%), and administrators (47.5%), from which 213 do receive performance bonus (50.8%), and 206 do not receive it (49.2%). Regarding sex, the sample is divided into 66.6% male and 33.4% female. Concerning age, 202 persons are under 30 years old; 141 persons are between 31 and 40 years old, and the other 76 are over the age of 40. The object of the article is to find out if POE shows significant differences between people who do receive the PPB and those who do not. By using variance analyses, there were found significant statistical differences between variables. In addition, to test the hypotheses presented, the results obtained are analyzed from their management's point of view.

Chapter 13 - A sample of 192 university students was divided into two groups. The first group (experimental) comprised those individuals with the highest scores on the "Fear of negative evaluation" (FNE, Watson and Friend, 1969) and the "Social avoidance and distress" scales (SAD, Watson and Friend, 1969). The second group (control) consisted of students who had obtained the lowest scores in both scales. Both groups were required to participate in one affective priming study in order to compare automatic valence recognition latencies using stressful word pairs related to social fear and social phobia, as well as positive, negative, and neutral words. Only the experimental group showed affective priming for social fear and social phobia. The control group showed no priming effect for any experimental condition.

These results are discussed in terms of their implications for an integral diagnostic system of social anxiety disorder that takes into account automatic and controlled emotional appraisal of social stressful events.

Chapter 14 - The term burnout refers to a feeling of failure and to an exhausted or used-up existence, and it is considered as a three-dimensional syndrome in which feelings of emotional exhaustion, depersonalization, and lack of personal accomplishment are present. This phenomenon has become a public health concern and may turn into a menace for teams of professionals whose objective is to help others, as it is the case for the education professionals. An instrument with the aims of knowing, describing and correlating some of the models related to the presence of the burnout syndrome in primary school teachers who work in public schools, was applied in this study. This instrument was a questionnaire directed to the teachers in 123 public primary schools in the municipality of San Nicolas de los Garza, Nuevo Leon, México. The results did not evidence the presence of the syndrome in its three dimensions in the studied sample. However, it is relevant the lack of personal accomplishment in the male teachers (33.61%), while the female teachers manifested as relevant the emotional exhaustion (44.33%). The analysis of this investigation gives us an idea of the importance of preventing the burnout syndrome in teachers.

In: Hispanic Psychology Yearbook Volume 1
Ed: Cirilo H. García pp. 1-17

ISBN: 978-1-60741-786-6


*Chapter 1*

# DEVELOPMENT OF A SCALE TO STUDY DIFFERENCES IN GENDER IN ORGANIZATIONAL SOCIALIZATION PROCESSES*

***Ana Lisbona Bañuelos and Francisco J. Palací*** [1]
Universidad Nacional de Educación a Distancia (UNED) and
Esteban Agulló Tomás, Universidad de Oviedo

## ABSTRACT

In this paper we analyze the possible existence of policies for worker integration and promotion, according to gender, without taking into consideration the position held. We also validate an instrument for evaluating differences according to gender during the socialization process by following the Taormina's Model of Social Organization (1997). In this Model, four domains are proposed that coincide with the four subscales on the OSI Questionnaire (training, understanding, support of co-workers and future perspectives). In the same manner, we have designed a subscale that, in an abbreviated form, has been called the Gender Subscale for the Socialization Process. The degree of learning achieved in these domains is the main indicator of success in the socialization process. The study is composed of two transversal samples and a longitudinal sample. Data was gathered at two different times with approximately one year's difference between them. The first transversal sample contains 414 participants and the second transversal sample contains 396 participants. The longitudinal sample contains 118 participants. We can conclude that the statistical properties of this instrument for the Spanish sample, together with the items designed on this occasion, are appropriate and in accordance with the author's theoretical proposal, which insists on the relationship and inter-dependence between the different domains. In this paper, we discuss the relationship between the newly created

* A version of this chapter was also published in the *International Hispanic Psychology Journal, Volume 1 Issue 1*, published by Nova Science Publishers, Inc. It was submitted for appropriate modification in an effort to encourage wider dissemination of research.

[1] Address for correspondence: fpalaci@psi.uned.es, Telephone: 34 : 913986264, Fax: 34 913986215. Francisco José Palaci Descals, Department of Social Psychology and Organizations in the School of Psychology of the UNED, C/ Juan del Rosal, 10. 28040, Madrid, Spain.

gender variable of socialization and satisfaction and commitment. In the same manner, it we show how gender differences are an additional domain in the socialization process and how this is reflected in increased learning.

**Keywords**: socialization process, organizations, gender differences, validation.

## RESUMEN

En este trabajo deseamos analizar si las empresas difieren en las políticas de integración y promoción laboral de sus trabajadores, en función de su género y con independencia del puesto que ocupen. Tambien se procede a la validación de un instrumento que evalúa las diferencias en función del género durante el proceso de socialización.

Siguiendo el modelo de Socialización Organizacional de Taormina (1997) se proponen 4 dominios, que coinciden con las cuatro subescalas del Cuestionario OSI (entrenamiento, comprensión, apoyo de los compañeros y perspectivas de futuro). Asimismo, hemos diseñado una subescala, que, de manera abreviada, se ha venido denominando Subescala de Género del Proceso de Socialización El grado de aprendizaje logrado en estos dominios es el principal indicador del éxito del proceso de socialización. El estudio se compone de dos muestras transversales y una muestra longitudinal. Se han recogido datos en dos momentos temporales con aproximadamente un año de diferencia entre los dos tiempos. La primera muestra transversal se compone de 414 participantes. Y la segunda muestra transversal de 396 participantes. La muestra longitudinal se compone de 118 participantes.

Podemos concluir que las propiedades estadísticas de este instrumento para la muestra española, junto con los ítems diseñado en esta ocasión, son apropiadas y, se ajustan a la propuesta teórica de autor, que insiste en la relación e interdependencia de los distintos dominios.

En el trabajo se discuten las relaciones entre la variable de nueva creación de socialización en función del genero con la satisfacción y el compromiso.

Asimismo, se muestra como las diferencias en función del género son un dominio más en el proceso de socialización y se refleja en un aumento del aprendizaje.

Palabras clave: proceso de socialización, organizaciones, diferencias de género, validación.

## INTRODUCTION

Social changes in the role of women during the XX century cannot be questioned. Thus, the massive entrance of women into the workplace involves one of the farthest reaching transformations in contemporary society. However, numerous studies show evidence of constantly present inequality between men and women in pay, in conditions for access to jobs or in the possibility of professional development, among others. Thus, according to data gathered by the Spanish National Statistical Institute (INE) in a survey among the working population of Spain during the last quarter of 2006, the unemployment rate among women was 11.36% compared to 6.06% for men. In the same manner, the percentage of women directors in companies with more than 10 employees was only 22.09%. These persistent forms of discrimination are explained in social sciences by the survival of beliefs known as stereotypes (e.g., López-Sáez, Morales and Lisbona, in the press) and the inter-relationship between numerous factors that are frequently referred to as the "glass ceiling" (Segerman-Peck, 1991; Powell, 1991; Davidson and Cooper, 1992), which is an invisible but unsurpassable wall of procedures, structures and beliefs that make it very difficult for women to have access to decision-making positions or to fully develop their potential.

In the same manner, from the perspective of socialization, studies have been done on how people learn and internalize socio-cultural elements from their social environment, under the influence of experience and significant social agents, in an attempt to adapt themselves to the social context where they must exist (Rocher, 1990). From this perspective, we are confronted with a profuse and complex investigative task that allows us to reveal how the processes of academic socialization, family socialization, socialization of peers and socialization of means of communication have influenced the configuration of guidelines for differential behavior in accordance to gender and which, at the same time, reinforces discrimination of women.

However, the question concerning how aspects of the employing organization affect the socialization of employees by maintaining gender differences has barely been studied in an empirical manner. In other words, we find that authors who attempt to analyze job discrimination among women according to socialization have not paid attention to the effect of that process on the context of organizations; while studies carried out to reveal the factors forming the glass ceiling have touched on organizational aspects such as culture or leadership style but they have not paid attention to socialization within the organization itself.

Nevertheless, we agree with Agulló (2003) who indicates that once the academic-educational-formative stage is over, after the family environment and society has provided the elements necessary for individuals to effectively remain in their setting, companies become another significant agent of socialization for adapting people to the social environment. In this sense, we feel that socialization factors in labor can also be converged and their knowledge and analysis can contribute to explaining the inequality of job opportunities for men and women.

Specifically, in this paper we wish to do an analysis to find out if companies use--in a more or less subtle manner--different forms of socialization and promotion with their workers, depending on their gender. Within those different strategies of socialization, different types of training can be mentioned as well as possible inequality in treatment by co-workers and supervisors when attempting to promote integration and adjustment of men and women within the organization.

For this reason, the main objective of this study is to prove to what extent companies in our sample differ in policies for integration and promotion of their workers, according to gender and without taking into consideration the position held. In the same manner, an analysis will be made of the perception of the men and women in our sample of different possible integration and professional promotion techniques practiced by their companies in the socialization process of new members of the same or those used for promoting workers to new positions within the same. We will also validate an instrument for evaluating gender differences during the socialization process.

# ORGANIZATIONAL SOCIALIZATION

Job incorporation is done by labor organizations. For that reason, together with the job socialization process, we find ourselves faced with a process of organizational socialization. The organizational socialization process is concealed by the general socialization process of individuals and, in an arbitrary manner, we can establish that it begins when people decide to apply for a position, when he/she sends in his/her curriculum vitae to the organization when applying for a job and when he/she goes to an interview. There are organizations that even begin their "socializing work" beforehand.

Definitions of the organizational socialization construct are very diverse. One concept with high consensus among authors is that organizational socialization is considered to be a process by which persons learn the values, abilities, expectations and behaviors that are important for taking on determined organizational roles and for participating as active members in the organization (Louis, 1980; Van Maanen and Schein, 1979). It must be pointed out that since the decade of the eighties, the majority of studies on the process of incorporating persons within organizations have taken on a conceptual formula in which the active role of both parties stands out. Faced with very passive worker concepts in which the labor of building an organization was very much like that of a sculptor creating a sculpture from a piece of inert marble—according to the Van Maanen metaphor (1978).

Taormina (1997, 2000, 2004) emphasizes the idea that socialization is not only the process by which people learn to work in an specific organization, but it also leads them to accept and believe in the most appropriate manner of behavior within the organization. Thus, one measurement of socialization must indicate if employees accept the different characteristics of the organization. In the same way that socialization in society consists of learning about a variety of new roles (as people mature from infancy to adolescence, youth and adult life) socialization is a long term process and can be measured not only for new employees but for employees that have been with the organization for a long time.

The majority of today's bibliography on the topic of socialization states that learning is its essential component (Thomas and Anderson, 2005). In the same manner, this concept fits the theories of reduction in uncertainty (e.g. Falcione and Wilson, 1988; Morrison, 1993) and theories of developing meaning (e. g., Louis, 1980). Since the theory of reduction in uncertainty was developed, some authors have emphasized the fact that the fundamental component for the behavior of a new employee is the search for information (Miller and Jablin, 1991; Morrison, 1993; Ostroff and Kolzowski, 1992).

That search for information allows him/her to reduce uncertainty, to understand, predict and control his/her environment; and in the same manner it will help him/her to occupy and fulfill the position correctly and integrate himself/herself to the work group and to the organization, making his/her permanence in the same more probable (Morrison, 1993). In relation to these theories, there is empirical evidence showing that learning by new employees is associated with better results (Chao, O'Leary-Kelly, Wolf, Klein and Gardner,1994; Bauer Morrison, and Callister, 1998). In our study, as will be seen below, following Taormina's socialization model (1997), we share the opinion that learning is a central element of that process.

With the idea that learning is an essential component in the socialization process, the authors present questions related to the content of that learning. Chao, et al. (1994) and

Taormina (1994, 1997) have each presented models and instruments about the content of socialization and those models have important similarities. Taormina (2004) has made an effort to compare his proposal to that of Chao and collaborators and, for that reason, we will comment on Taormina's contribution and this focus will be the one followed by us throughout our paper.

Chao et al. (1994) and Taormina (1994) each created evaluation instruments for their proposals on organizational socialization called CAS (Measurement of Content Areas of Socialization) and OSI (Organizational Socialization Inventory), respectively.

In Taormina's model (1997), 4 domains are proposed that coincide with the four subscales on the questionnaire (training, understanding, support of co-workers and future perspectives) and each one of them includes various content areas and, at the same time, each of them operates in a continuous and concurrent manner with the others. Those domains are part of a continuous process of organizational socialization. The theory suggests that the domains are superimposed on each other and they are adjusted within a global process. They are not totally independent and they are not exclusive. According to Taormina, each domain can be understood as a sphere of influence or activity, similar to a conceptual field. Dimensions or factors are found in these domains that are found in the research on organizational socialization, although on different levels.

The model also suggests that although the four processes take place continuously and simultaneously, they occur on a variety of levels and/or quantities for different employees and it suggests that the levels or amounts vary over time. We define the four domains proposed by Taormina as follows:

## Training

This refers to the development of skills and abilities required to carry out the job. This domain was already explicitly indicated by Wanous (1980), Feldman (1989) and Fisher (1986). A person's competence, expressed in terms of knowledge, abilities, aptitudes and skills when compared to job requirements such as work load, complexity and other demands by the organization, is essential for adequate productiveness and integration of new employees (Wamous, 1992; Hontangas and Peiró, 1996).

Taormina defines training as an act, process or method by which an ability or functional skill is acquired that is required to carry out a specific position. This definition allows us to clearly delimit what training is and separate it from the other domains that will be used by us in this paper, following Taormina's theory.

## Understanding

The term understanding is used by Taormina in a form that is similar to that which other researchers have call "learning" or "search for information" (e.g., Fisher, 1986; Ostroff and Kozlowski, 1992). This behavior allows employees to learn about the organization, how to behave and why things are the way they are. It refers to the ability to explain the nature, meaning and what happen in the workplace. It also refers to knowing how to explain the way things are in an organization and why things are done in a specific manner.

## Support of Co-Workers

This is a fundamental role of co-workers, bosses and supervisors in this learning process. Taormina defines this domain as the emotional, social or instrumental support provided, in addition to economic compensation, by other employees in the organization. Numerous studies consistently indicate that relationships with the supervisor and co-workers can have long-term consequences on the development of employee careers (Jablin, 1987: Wolf, 1989; Eisenberger, Fasolo, and Davis-LaMastro, 1990; Staw, Sutton, and Pelled, 1994; Randall, Cropanzano, Bormann, and Birjulin 1999).

## Future Perspectives

Future perspectives refer to the degree in which employees expect opportunities for promotion and other types of rewards for their permanence in the organization they have joined.

Taormina justifies including future perspectives as a domain of socialization in different sources. On one hand, the authors who proposed models for stages already dealt with this dimension, at least implicitly. Specifically, the models developed by Buchanan (1974), Feldman (1976, 1981) and Nelson (1990) included aspects such as the expectation of rewards or the possibility of promotion, training, or permanence when referring to anticipated socialization and they feel that a pre-visualization of a future in the organization must be achieved during this stage.

The results of socialization probably depend on employee interpretation of the perception of gender differences, whether it is premeditated or not, and that organizations may be treating their employees in different manners according to their gender. There are probably significant differences between men and women in the perception of the training received, future perspectives, social support. In the same manner, men and women may differ in their subjective evaluation concerning whether others consider them to be newcomers or veterans. Thus, in this paper, together with the socialization domains proposed by Taormina, a new Gender subscale is considered.

With basis on Taormina's proposal for evaluating the socialization process, we have designed an abbreviated subscale that has been called the Gender Subscale of the Socialization Process. We evaluate the perception by employees of a difference between men and women in this process. For us it is of extreme importance to analyze not only socialization contents, but if these contents are different according to gender, to add them to Taormina's proposal.

The last result of the socialization process, as far as gender is concerned, is to learn about different or equal treatment within the organization. In some manner, employees learn how they are expected to behave in the workplace if they are men or if they are women. Learning is the first indicator of success in the socialization process. According to Taormina's model (1997), the level of training, comprehension, support of co-workers and future perspectives achieved are the result of socialization. To that we will add that the level of learning about differences in a specific organization as far as gender is concerned is another result of socialization. However, other aspects have traditionally been considered to be the result of socialization. For example, reference is made to the degree of satisfaction reached with respect to the job position and its conditions. Other aspects considered are commitment or production. These results are as beneficial to organization as they are to individuals.

Different studies carried out by Taormina (2000, 2004) have found that the four domains of socialization were significant variables for predicting affective commitment and satisfaction. In these studies, the Allen and Meyer (1990) scale of affective commitment was used which we have also used in our study. In the same manner, Bauer (2000) finds that the four domains of socialization were able to predict affective commitment, while future perspectives also predicted commitment to standards and to continuation with the organization.

In the same manner, Bravo, Gómez-Jacinto and Montalbán (2004) have found that the four domains of socialization were significant variables for predicting affective commitment and satisfaction. Job satisfaction is part of the dimension of attitude and it occupies a central place in the consideration of experience of people towards their job. Job satisfaction has been defined as a set of positive attitudes and emotional reactions that the individual has towards his job, constructed from the comparison between the results expected and those that have been effectively obtained for that job (Oshagbemi, 1999).

As far as the second result of socialization is concerned: organizational commitment, the perspective of Meyer and Allen (1997) has been adopted as well as their instrument for evaluating the same. These authors defend a model of organizational commitment that contains three factors: affective commitment that refers to the employee's emotional ties and his/her identification and sense of belonging to the organization; the commitment to standards that reflects a sense of obligation to continue within the organization and, lastly, the commitment to continue, based on Meyer and Allen's (1997) perception of costs associated with abandoning the organization.

## Hypotheses

First hypothesis: To validate the newly created scale on socialization as far as gender is concerned, appropriate reliability and factorial structure will be analyzed. Thus, it is expected that the new scale will constitute the fifth factor of the OSI Scale.

Second hypothesis: It is expected that this newly created scale will be related to the classical results of socialization and will increase the predictive ability of the four original socialization scales.

Third hypothesis: This refers to the main result of the socialization process: learning. Thus, we expect that differences related to gender are one more domain in the socialization process and this will be reflected in increased learning.

In an exploratory manner, an analysis will be made to find out if there are gender differences in different dimensions of the socialization process.

# METHOD

## Participants

The study is composed of two transversal samples and one longitudinal sample. Data has been gathered at two different times with approximately one year's difference between them. The first transversal sample contains 414 participants and the second transversal sample has 396 participants. The longitudinal sample contains 118 participants.

The first transversal sample was gathered from 22 organizations and the second sample was gathered from 15 organizations from the first sample and from 7 different organizations. The companies are located in different parts of Spain: Ibi (Alicante), Madrid, Tarragona, Valladolid and Zaragoza and they pertain to different sectors of activity. In addition, the companies are different sizes, including multi-national companies and small family businesses 55.08% of the participants in first sample gathered are men and 40.6% are women. The average age is 31.53 years with a standard deviation of 8.46. The youngest person was 17 years old and the two oldest people were 57 years old.

The second time data was gathered, the participants were 50.67% men and 44.34% women. The average age is very similar to the first data sample: 32.27 with a standard deviation of 8.97. In this case, ages vary between 18 and 65 years.

## Procedure

As far as the procedure is concerned, questionnaires were administered in each of the companies through a contact person in the organization or by sending a researcher to hand out questionnaires and collect them.

## Instruments

To measure the content of the socialization process, the OSI (Organizational Socialization Inventory) was used, as proposed by Taormina (1994) and it was translated into Spanish and validated by Bravo et al. (2004). In this questionnaire the author proposes four dimensions: training, understanding, support of co-workers and future perspectives which correspond to the four theoretical domains mentioned by the author. Each one of these dimensions is composed of 5 items with a Likert-type response scale (1= completely disagree to 5=completely agree). In addition, a scale was designed to evaluate gender differences during the socialization process. This constitutes the fifth dimension of the organizational socialization inventory, composed of 3 items.

To evaluate job satisfaction, a scale was used that was composed of 4 items referring to aspects related to the job and to the socialization process (Topa, Lisbona, Palací and Alonso, 2004; Lisbona, Morales and Palací, 2006 and Lisbona, 2007). It has a Likert-type response scale (1=Dissatisfied to 5= Very satisfied). Organizational commitment was evaluated by the Meyer and Allen (1997) sub-scales for affective commitment and normative commitment with 6 items contained in the affective scale and 4 items in the normative dimension. The response scale is equal to that used for the OSI. The subscale for commitment to continuing has not been used since other studies have been unreliable (see Lisbona, Morales and Palací, 2006).

## RESULTS

First, information was gathered for two tables with descriptive statistics and correlations between the different scales used, respectively.

The reliability of the new socialization scale for gender is adequate (Alpha= .883 and .890 for each of the two transversal samples). In addition, it was expected that the new dimension of socialization, gender difference, would behave as an additional factor within the factor structure of the socialization inventory. To contrast this hypothesis, an exploratory factor analysis has been performed with the first transversal sample, through the method of principal components and with varimax rotation and its matrix of rotated components appears as follows.

Five factors were obtained that explain 61.39% of the variance. The first factor gathers the five items from the first dimension: training and one item from the understanding dimension and it explains 28.18% of the variance. The second corresponds to the five items in the dimension of support of co-workers and it explains 10.42% of the total variance. The third factor groups together four items from the dimension of understanding. The fourth factor groups together three items that compose the dimension that has been called gender. Lastly, the fifth factor groups three of the five items from the dimension of future perspectives. See table 3.

**Table 1. Descriptive statistics**

| VARIABLES | 1st Transversal | | | 2nd Transversal | | |
|---|---|---|---|---|---|---|
| | Alpha | Mean | ED | Alpha | Mean | ED |
| OSI training | .883 | 2.76 | 1,03 | .924 | 2.88 | 1,14 |
| OSI understanding | .776 | 3.40 | .745 | .816 | 3.40 | .807 |
| OSI support of co-workers | .796 | 3.51 | .762 | .826 | 3.56 | .842 |
| OSI future perspectives | .659 | 3 | .709 | .700 | 2.99 | .751 |
| OSI gender differences | .883 | 3.46 | 1,03 | .890 | 3.42 | 1,10 |
| Satisfaction | .709 | 3.33 | .781 | .688 | 3.30 | .801 |
| Affective Commitment | .815 | 3.47 | .834 | .828 | 3.47 | .856 |
| Normative Commitment | .878 | 2.89 | .911 | .818 | 2.87 | .943 |

**Table 2. Correlations**

| T1 | OSI Training | OSI Understanding | OSI Co-workers support | OSI Future prospects | OSI Gender | Satisfaction | Affective commitment | Normative commitment |
|---|---|---|---|---|---|---|---|---|
| OSI Training | - | ,525** | ,364** | ,381** | ,190** | ,436** | ,384** | ,353** |
| OSI Understanding | | - | ,343** | ,549** | ,098* | ,493** | ,409** | ,401** |
| OSI Co-workers support | | | - | ,284** | ,159** | ,239** | ,304** | ,189** |
| OSI Future prospects | | | | - | ,138** | ,507** | ,530** | ,464** |
| OSI Gender | | | | | - | ,164** | ,229** | ,130** |
| Satisfaction | | | | | | - | ,592** | ,530** |
| Affective commitment | | | | | | | - | ,656** |
| Normative commitment | | | | | | | | - |

| T2 | OSI Training | OSI Understanding | OSI Co-workers support | OSI Future prospects | OSI Gender | Satisfaction | Affective commitment | Normative commitment |
|---|---|---|---|---|---|---|---|---|
| OSI Training | - | ,565** | ,371** | ,431** | ,301** | ,370** | ,403** | ,417** |
| OSI Understanding | | - | ,415** | ,539** | ,250** | ,522** | ,483** | ,457** |
| OSI Co-workers support | | | - | ,274** | ,247** | ,254** | ,352** | ,290** |
| OSI Future prospects | | | | - | ,081 | ,474** | ,474** | ,501** |
| OSI Gender | | | | | - | ,141** | ,197** | ,168** |
| Satisfaction | | | | | | - | ,592** | ,530** |
| Affective commitment | | | | | | | - | ,656** |
| Normative commitment | | | | | | | | - |

It must be pointed out that except for one item from dimension of understanding and two items from the dimension of future perspectives, the factor structure obtained with the first sample of data collected is very similar to the theoretical structure proposed by Taormina (1994).

A confirming factor analysis has also been carried out with a different sample, the one in the second transversal sample. The model of four of Taormina's OSI factors was tested and compared with the adjustment to a confirming factor model of second order that assumes that all of the items saturate a latent dimension. The hypothesized model of 5 factors was also tested and it includes the new scale of gender differences during the socialization process. Lastly, to improve the models, errors were correlated, according to modification indexes, between items in the same subscale.

In Table 4, adjustment indexes for each of the models are gathered as follows. We see that the model including gender, the dimension developed for the study, always has a better adjustment than the model with four dimensions proposed by Taormina. Lastly, the model correlating the five dimensions between themselves is better adjusted when compared to the model that assumes a factor structure of second order for the socialization dimension.

**Table 3. Factor structure of the OSI Scale**

| | Factor 1 28,18 % | Factor 2 10,42% | Factor 3 9,11% | Factor 4 8,50% | Factor 5 5,12% |
|---|---|---|---|---|---|
| Training 1. | .830 | | | | |
| Training 2. | .803 | | | | |
| Training 3. | .834 | | | | |
| Training 4 | .828 | | | | |
| Training 5. | .631 | | | | |
| Understanding 1. | .526 | | | | |
| Understanding 2. | | | .584 | | |
| Understanding 3 | | | .697 | | |
| Understanding 4. | | | .727 | | |
| Understanding 5. | | | .640 | | |
| Co-worker support 1. | | .528 | | | |
| Co-worker support 2 | | .619 | | | |
| Co-worker support 3. | | .829 | | | |
| Co-worker support 4. | | .845 | | | |
| Co-worker support 5 | | .706 | | | |
| Future perspectives 1 | | | | | .765 |
| Future perspectives 2. | | | | | .658 |
| Futuer perspectives 3 | | | | | .729 |
| Gender 1. There are differences in which the professional trajectory is set for men and women. | | | | .891 | |
| Gender 2. There are differences in the type of tasks assigned men and women. | | | | .881 | |
| Gender 3. There are differences in the way professional promotion is defined for men and women. | | | | ,907 | |

We conclude that the statistical properties of this instrument for the Spanish sample, together with the items designed on this occasion are appropriate and they are adjusted to the theoretical proposal of the author, who insists on the relationship and interdependence of different domains.

As far as the second hypothesis is concerned, a regression analysis has been made with the first transversal sample. In the regression equation in which we attempt to predict the score for affective commitment using the socialization domains, the results were exactly as we expected in our hypothesis and these relations are positive and significant for all domains, except for understanding, a domain in which relationships are not significant. Upon introducing the gender domain, an increase in the explained variance has been significant.

This indicates that the employee's perception of no gender differences during socialization is related to greater affective employee commitment. *See table 5.*

**Table 4. Goodness of fit indexes by means of confirmatory factor analysis in socialization domains**

| Model | $\chi^2$ | *df* | *p* | *GFI* | *AGFI* | *RMSEA* | *NFI* | *CFI* | *IFI* | *TLI* |
|---|---|---|---|---|---|---|---|---|---|---|
| 4 factors | 968.02 | 164 | .000 | .824 | .774 | .104 | .811 | .837 | .838 | .811 |
| 5 factors | 1081.88 | 220 | .000 | .826 | .782 | .093 | .824 | .853 | .854 | .831 |
| Factorial 2nd Time 4 factors | 971.20 | 166 | .000 | .823 | .776 | .103 | .810 | .837 | .837 | .813 |
| Factorial 2nd Time 5 factors | 1103.69 | 225 | .000 | .822 | .781 | .093 | .820 | .851 | .851 | .832 |
| Factorial 2nd Time 5 factors improved | 543.851 | 194 | .000 | .907 | .868 | .063 | .911 | .940 | .941 | .922 |
| 5 factors improved | 534.71 | 189 | .000 | .909 | .867 | .063 | .913 | .941 | .942 | .921 |

The procedure has been repeated with the normative commitment variable. In the regression equation in which we attempt to predict the score in normative commitment starting with socialization domains, the relationships found have not been significant except for future perspectives, in which relationships have been as expected. Upon introducing the gender domain, an increase in the explained variance has been significant but negative. Surprisingly, not establishing gender differences during socialization are related to a lower normative commitment. *See table 6.*

**Table 5. Hierarchical regression for variables predicting affective commitment**

| Variable | | b | Standard error | Beta |
|---|---|---|---|---|
| Step 1 | | | | |
| | OSI training | .127 | .035 | .160* |
| | OSI understanding | .078 | .053 | .071 |
| | OSI co-worker support | .110 | .043 | .103* |
| | OSI future perspectives | .451 | .051 | .388* |
| Step 2 | | | | |
| | OSI training | .111 | .035 | .140* |
| | OSI understanding | .087 | .052 | .079 |
| | OSI co-worker support | .096 | .043 | .090* |
| | OSI future perspectives | .438 | .051 | .377* |
| | OSI gender | .101 | .029 | .128* |

$R^2$ = .318 for step 1.$\Delta R^2$= ,016 (p<.05).
*p<.05.

**Table 6. Hierarchical regression for variables predicting normative commitment**

| Variable | | b | Standard error | Beta |
|---|---|---|---|---|
| Step 1 | | | | |
| | OSI training | .054 | .047 | .060 |
| | OSI understanding | -.057 | .071 | -.046 |
| | OSI co-worker support | -.005 | .058 | -.004 |
| | OSI future perspectives | .178 | .069 | .136* |
| Step 2 | | | | |
| | OSI training | .072 | .047 | .081 |
| | OSI understanding | -.068 | .071 | -.055 |
| | OSI co-worker support | .011 | .058 | .009 |
| | OSI future perspectives | .193 | .068 | .148* |
| | OSI gender | -.121 | .040 | -.136* |

$R^2$ = ,020 for step 1.$\Delta R^2$= ,018 (p<.05).
*p<.05.

In order to find an explanation for this result, the analysis has been repeated, but separately for men and women. While it was not significant for women, it was significant for men. See table 7.

**Table 7. Hierarchical regression for men and women for OSI gender and normative commitment when first collecting data**

| Variable | | b | Standard error | Beta |
|---|---|---|---|---|
| Gender | Men | -.210 | .055 | -.221* |
| | Women | .026 | .053 | .034 |

*p<.00.

**Table 8. Hierarchical regression for variables predicting satisfaction**

| Variable | | b | Standard error | Beta |
|---|---|---|---|---|
| Step 1 | | | | |
| | OSI training | .153 | .033 | .202* |
| | OSI understanding | .222 | .050 | .211* |
| | OSI co-worker support | .005 | .041 | .005 |
| | OSI future perspectives | .338 | .048 | .305* |
| Step 2 | | | | |
| | OSI training | .146 | .033 | .193* |
| | OSI understanding | .225 | .050 | .215* |
| | OSI co-worker support | -.002 | .041 | -.002 |
| | OSI future perspectives | .333 | .048 | .301* |
| | OSI gender | .044 | .028 | .059 |

$R^2$ = ,341 for step 1.$\Delta R^2$= ,003 (p>.05).
*p<.05.

As far as the regression equation is concerned in which we try to predict the satisfaction score in socialization domains, the relationships found have been meaningful and in accordance to the hypotheses formulated, except for the dimension of support of co-workers. With the introduction of the gender domain, the increase in thenormative explained variance was not significant.

A “t” test was carried out to prove the existence of differences between the scores obtained the first and second times with the longitudinal sample.

As proposed in the third hypothesis, it is expected that the learning process will have a higher score in the different socialization domains the 2nd time with respect to the 1st time. The results confirm this hypothesis.

**Table 9. Student test. T1 and T2 gender socialization domains.**

| Gender | Weighted Mean | t | df | p |
|---|---|---|---|---|
| T1 | 2,6724 | -6,053 | 115 | .000 |
| T2 | 3,3736 | 106,823 | 488 | .000 |

The fourth and last hypothesis, of an exploratory nature, was analyzed by carrying out an ANOVA. It attempted to prove the existence or non-existence of gender differences in different dimensions of the socialization process.

Differences have only been statistically significant for support of co-workers, with women scoring higher than men in this dimension.

**ANOVA OSI Table on Gender Differences**

| | df | F | p |
|---|---|---|---|
| Training | 501 | 1,665 | .198 |
| Understanding | 503 | 1,469* | .226 |
| Co-worker Support | 500 | 5,463* | .020 |
| Future Perspectives | 500 | 2,172 | .141 |
| Gender | 494 | .579 | .447 |

## Discussion

It has been found that psychometric properties of the OSI for the Spanish sample, together with the gender differences scale is appropriate and it adjusts itself to the author’s theoretical proposal which insists on the relationship and interdependence of different domains.

When carrying out the confirming factor analysis we find that the model including the gender differences scale is better adjusted than Taormina’s proposed model with four dimensions.

The perception that no gender differences are established in socialization is related to greater affective commitment, with lower normative commitment and there is no relationship between the perception of gender differences and satisfaction. This relationship is difficult to explain. The lack of the establishment of gender differences is probably related to emotional socialization factors linked to affective commitment.

For that reason, knowledge and learning that the organization does not establish differences in socialization appears as a domain that is separate from socialization.

The perception that there is no gender difference is probably related to organizational justice. From this perspective the knowledge that the organization does not establish gender differences would be a central aspect of the perception of organizational justice and, more specifically, of the justice of procedures and interaction.

The perception of gender differences causes something that has been called distributive justice. This occurs when the results distributing something or when compensations are consistent with certain implicit norms such as equity (Adams, 1965; Deutsch, 1975; Leventhal, 1980).

However we calculate that gender differences will be more related to procedural justice and to justice of interaction (Leventhal, 1980; Thibaut and Walter, 1975). Decision-making processes are characterized by procedural justice when the opinion of the other party involved is heard, when this party has some influence on the outcome or when the criteria of justice is followed such as consistence, the absence of bias or correction. It has been suggested that the construct of the justice of interaction (Bies and Moag, 1986) is closely related to this. This type of justice is defined as the perception that people have been treated with justice during interactions when a decision-making process takes place. It is achieved when those who have to make the decision treat people with respect and sensitivity and they explain the reasons for their decision.

Research has shown that distributive justice is related to results referring to people, such as satisfaction with their salary and procedural justice is more related to results related to the organization, such as organizational commitment (Folger and Konovsky, 1989; Sweeney and McFarlin, 1993).

Gender differences in the domains of socialization have only been statistically meaningful for support of co-workers, with women scoring higher than men in this dimension. In other words, men and women perceive the content of socialization in similar ways; however, when fewer differences are established as far as gender is concerned, there is greater affective commitment. The central result of socialization is learning and as the third hypothesis proposed, there is a higher score in different socialization domains the 2$^{nd}$ time in comparison to the 1$^{st}$ time. The results confirm this hypothesis.

Relationships between the domains of socialization and job satisfaction have been in accordance to that expected in the Taormina model. For that reason, these results support the idea of the model that success with socialization is learning, which at the same time is related to other indicators such as satisfaction. However, in this case no significant relationship has been found for the gender differences scale.

## References

Adams, J. (1965). Inequity in social exchange. In Berkowitz (ed.), *Advances in experimental social psychology* (pp. 267- 299). New York: Academic Press.

Agulló, E. (2003). Un lugar en la empresa, un espacio en la sociedad. Más allá del empleo de los jóvenes. . In F. J. Palací and J. A. Moriano (eds.), *El nuevo mercado laboral. Estrategias de inserción y desarrollo profesional*. Madrid: Cuadernos de la UNED.

Bauer, T.N., Morrison, E.W., and Callister, R. R. (1998). Organizational socialization: A review and directions for future research. *Research in Personnel and Human Resource Management*, 16, 149-214.

Bies, R. J., and Moag, J. F. (1986). Interactional justice: Communication criteria of fairness. In R. Lewicki y B. Shepard and M. Bazerman (eds.), *Research on negotiations in organizations* (Vol. 1, pp. 43- 55). Greenwich: JAI Press.

Chao, G.T. O'leary-Kelly, A.M., Wolf, S., Klein, H. J., and Gardner, P.D. (1994). Organizational socialization: its content and consequences. *Journal of Applied Psychology*, 79, (5), 730-743.

Cooper-Thomas, H.D., and Anderson, N. (2005). Organizational socialization: A field study into socialization success and rate. *International Journal of Selection and Assessment,* 13,.2.

Davidson, M.J., and Cooper, C. L. (1992). Shattering the glass ceiling: The woman manager. Paul Chapman Publishing.

Deutsch, M. (1975). Equity, equality and need: What determines which value will be used as the basis of distributive justice? *Journal of Social Issues, 31*, 137- 149.

Leventhal, G. S. (1980). What should be done with equity theory? New approaches to the study of fairness in social relationships. In K. Gergen, M. Greenberg and R. Willis (eds.), *Social exchange: Advances in theory and research.* (pp. 27-55). New York: Plenum Press.

Leventhal, G. S., Karuza, J., and Fry, W. R. (1980). Beyond fairness: A theory of allocation preferences. In G. Mikula (ed.), *Justice and social interaction* (pp. 167- 218). New York: Springer- Verlag.

Falcione, R.L., and Wilson, C. E. (1988). Socialization processes in organizations. In G.M. Golhaber and G.A. Barnett (eds.), *Handbook of organizational communication:* 151-169. Norwood, NJ: Ablex.

López-Sáez, M., Morales, J. F., and Lisbona, A. (2007). Indicadores de estereotipia de género en España. Rasgos y roles. *Submitted for review and eventual publication.*

Louis, M. R. (1980). Surprise and sense-making: What newcomers experience in entering unfamiliar organizational settings. *Administrative Science Quarterly, 25,* 226-251.

Miller,V. D., and Jablin, F. M. (1991). Information seeking during organizational entry: influences, tactics, and a model of the process. *Academy of Management Review,* 16, 1, 92-120.

Morrison, E. W. (1993). Longitudinal study of the effects of information seeking on newcomer socialization. *Journal of Applied Psychology*, 78, 173- 183.

Ostroff, C., and Kolzowski, S. W. (1992). Organizational socialization as a learning process: The role of information acquisition. *Personnel Psychology,* 45, 849-874.

Powell, G. N. (1991). Women and men in management. Los Angeles: Sage.

Rocher, G. (1990). *Introducción a la sociología general.* Barcelona: Herder.

Segerman-Peck, L. M. (1991). *Networking and mentoring. A woman's guide.* London: Judy Piatkus Ltd.

Sweeney, P. D., and McFarlin, D. B. (1993). Workers' evaluations of the "ends" and the "means": An examination of four models of distributive and procedural justice. *Organizational Behavior and Human Decision Processes*, 55, 23-40.

Taormina, R.J. (1994). The Organizational Socialization Inventory, *International Journal of Selection and Assessment*, 2: 133–45.

Taormina, R.J. (1997). Organizational socialization: A multidomain, continuous process model. *International Journal of Selection and Assessment*, 5, 29–47.

Taormina, R.J. (2004). Convergent validation of two measures of organizational socialization. *International Journal of Human Resource Management*, 15, 76-94.

Thibaut, J., and Walker, L. (1975). *Procedural justice: A psychological analysis.* Hillsdale: Erlbaum.

Van Maanen, J. (1978). People processing: Strategies of organizational socialization. *Organizational Dynamics*, 7, 18-36.

Van Maanen, J., and Schein, E.H. (1979). Towards a theory of organizational socialization. In B. M. Staw (ed.), *Research in Organizational Behavior,* 1, 209-264. Greenwich, Conn.: JAI Press.

Wanous, J. P. (1992). Organizational entry: Recruitment, selection, orientation and socialization Newcomers. Reading, MA: Addison-Wesley (second edition).

In: Hispanic Psychology Yearbook Volume 1
Ed: Cirilo H. García pp.19-33
ISBN: 978-1-60741-786-6


*Chapter 2*

# ANALYSIS OF THE CORRESPONDENCE BETWEEN REPORTING AND DOING IN A TASK OF MATCHING TO SAMPLE*

***Hortensia Hickman[1], Diana Moreno, Olivia Tena, Patricia Plancarte, Rosalinda Arroyo and María Luisa Cepeda***
Facultad de Estudios Superiores Iztacala
Universidad Nacional Autónoma de México

## ABSTRACT

Recent research incorporates correspondence training procedures as an example of stimuli control. Lattal and Doepke (2001) state that correspondence and conditional discrimination procedures are homologous due to the fact that both contain behavioral relations in different temporalities and because the relationship between two or more stimuli or behaviors in both procedures is a distinctive feature. This paper attempts to explore the functional correspondence between the participants' reports of the rule and their performance on a task of matching to sample during training and transference tests. Five experimental groups were exposed to a do-report procedure, where the temporal distance from requesting the general rule of execution and the inclusion of incomplete sentences with different semantic properties were manipulated. Results were analyzed according to correspondence and non-correspondence between execution on transfer tests and the rule of execution reported. This analysis showed important group differences. We

---

* A version of this chapter was also published in the *International Hispanic Psychology Journal, Volume 1 Issue 1*, published by Nova Science Publishers, Inc. It was submitted for appropriate modification in an effort to encourage wider dissemination of research.
1 Address for correspondence: Hortensia Hickman Rodríguez, UNAM, Iztacala, Escuela de Estudios Superiores-Iztacala,, Avenida de los Barrios # 1, Los Reyes Iztacala, Tlalnepantla, Edo. Mex. C.P. 54090, México. Phone-fax: 01 (55) 56231298l. Email address: hortensiahickman@gmail.com. This paper was done under the auspices of the Program of Support of Professors in the Field (PAPCA ).

propose a methodological matrix that allow integrate research in the area of evaluation and training in doing-reporting in conditional discrimination tasks.

**Keywords:** correspondence, matching to sample, verbal behavior, non verbal behavior, transference tests.

## Resumen

Investigaciones recientes incorporan a los procedimientos en entrenamiento en correspondencias como una instancia del control de estímulos. Lattal y Doepke (2001) sostienen que la correspondencia y los procedimientos en discriminación condicional son homólogos en tanto involucran una relación entre acciones en tiempos distintos. El presente trabajo evaluó las correspondencias funcionales entre los reportes de la regla de los participantes y su ejecución en una tarea de igualación a la muestra durante entrenamiento y pruebas de transferencia. Se trabajó con cinco grupos experimentales en un procedimiento de hacer – reportar, variando la distancia temporal de solicitud de la regla general de ejecución y diferentes tipos de enunciados incompletos con diferente contenido semántico. Este análisis mostró diferencias entre los grupos. Se propone una matriz metodológica que permite integrar la investigación en el área de evaluación y entrenamiento del hacer-reportar en tareas de discriminación condicional.

*Palabras claves:* correspondencia, igualación a la muestra, conducta verbal, conducta no verbal, pruebas de transferencia.

One of the central concerns that has guided the work of behavioral analysts in the area of conditional discrimination and/or stimuli equivalence over the last few decades of the past century has been the possible link between execution in conditional relationships and language or verbal behavior (Sidman, 1971; Sidman and Tailby, 1982; Roche, Barnes and Smeets, 1997; Wulfert and Hayes, 1988; Lipkens, Hayes and Hayes, 1993; Devany, Hayes and Nelson, 1986; O´Donnell and Saunder, 2003). And although the use of conditional discrimination procedures and the evaluation of emerging relationships have allowed for systematic approach with respect to the phenomena traditionally classified as mental—the formation of concepts, private verbal behavior, formulation of rules, thought, etc.-, to date there is no conceptual consensus with respect to the role that language plays in this type of phenomenon. We have Sidman's position (1994) as an example, concerning the fact that language would not be a fundamental and necessary element for the configuration of emerging relationships which contrasts with the bi-directional hypothesis of language proposed by Hayes (1991) and, more recently, with Horne and Lowe's (1996) naming hypothesis.

In spite of the fact that the data gathered to date in this field does not conclusively validate the primacy of one model over another, investigators who adhere to the hypothesis of language or of naming or any of its variants, have used distinct methodological strategies to explain the functional relationship between verbal and non-verbal behavior. Among these are examples of post-session questionnaires or interviews; protocol analysis with the goal of teaching subjects to think out loud during training and tests (Wulfert, Dougher and Greenway, 1991; Wulfert, Greenway and Dougher, 1994); and self-reports with respect to restricted topographies executed during training and testing (Critchfield, 1996; Walker and Branch, 1996 and Plancarte et al. 2000; Hickman et al. 2001). One of the main characteristics of these studies is the analysis of the possible functional correspondence – not necessarily morphological or topographical – existing between language and the emergence of new relationships.

In relation to this, attempts have recently been made to include procedures in correspondence as an instance of stimuli control. Lattal and Doepke (2001), sustain that the procedures in correspondence and in conditional discrimination (matching to sample and/or classes of equivalence) are homologous since they involve a relationship between actions at different times. For those authors the defining characteristic of both procedures lies in the relationship that is established between two or more stimuli or actions. For example, to give feedback on correct selection between two comparative stimuli in accordance to the type of sample stimulus by the participant; or to give feedback for correspondence between the action and the subsequent report after this (do-report) or between a statement and the action carried out at a later time (say-do).

The central element in conditional discrimination as in correspondences is that the effective response is the product of a functional relationship between two actions, more than morphological or topographical actions, allowing one to include the correspondence as an instance of control of conditional stimuli, whose substantial axis is the configuration of two temporarily different responses.

On the other hand, it is undeniable that the study of correspondences by behavioral analysts is directly linked to the relationship between verbal and non-verbal behavior. For example, Lloyd (2002) mentions that training in correspondence has been analyzed by some authors, in the terms of behavior governed by rules (Deacon and Konarski, 1987; Ward and Stare, 1990), which has allowed them to explain maintenance and generalization in different sequences of training. We could therefore state that the relationship between verbal and non-verbal conduct constitutes a bridge between the area of investigation of conditional discrimination and the area of investigation in training in correspondences. All points to the need to explore methodologies derived from the field of conditional relationships more systematically with those from the field of procedures in correspondences.

In this study the functional correspondence between the report of participants and their execution in a procedure of first order matching to sample is analyzed. Five experimental groups were worked differentiated among them by the temporal distance required to report the rule, as well as by the type of semantic content of sentences to be completed. In three of the five groups the effect was evaluated for acquisition and transference, for semantic complexity of the sentences maintaining a constant temporal distance for asking for the report; while in the other two groups, the temporal distance varied without exposure to incomplete sentences. That previously mentioned was in order to do a possible functional analysis of the correspondences and non-correspondences between verbal and non-verbal behavior.

# METHOD

## Participants

25 students majoring in Psychology in the Iztacala School of Higher Studies in the UNAM, Mexico, participated and they had an average age of 20. These obtained a maximum of two correct answers out of 36 possible questions on the pre-test and they were assigned to five groups with five participants each.

## Instruments and Experimental Situation

Programming (instructions, arrangement of stimuli corresponding to the experimental tasks and transference tests) and a record of responses was carried out by computer systems, using a program designed in the Toolbook 1.53. Incomplete sentences and the trans-situational test were taken on sheets of paper. The training and test sessions were carried out individually in five soundproof cubicles.

## Conditions of Stimulus, Training and Tests

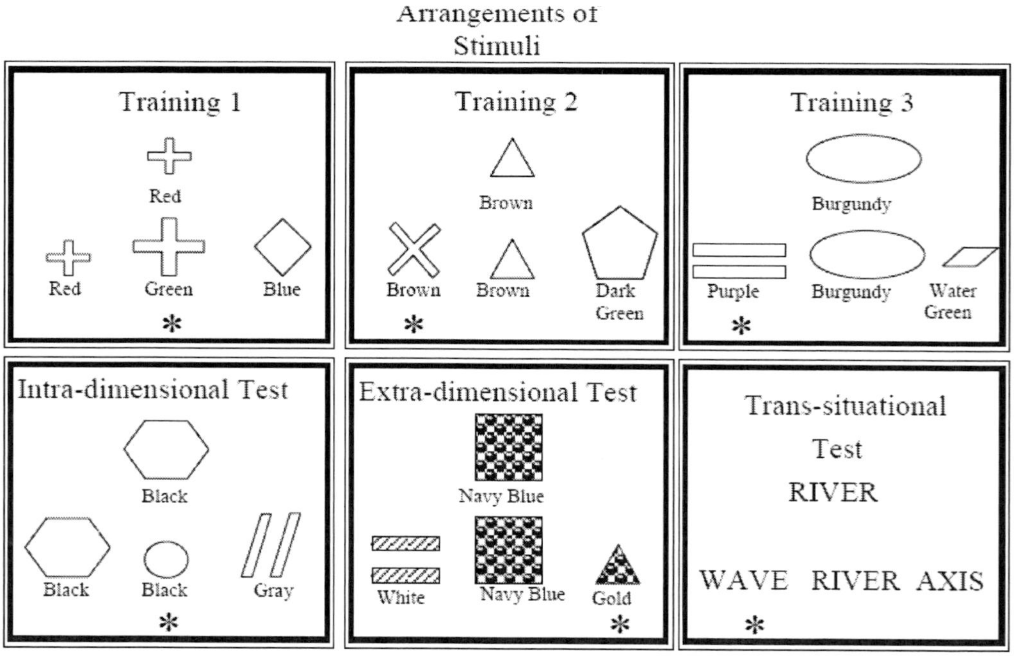


Figure 1. Shows experimental arrangements and instances of stimulus employed for each training and testing condition. The asterisk indicates the correct comparative stimulus according to the criteria of similarity.

Each session consisted of 36 tests of matching to sample under the criteria of similarity. Each test was composed of presentation of the sample stimulus in the upper part of the monitor together with three comparative stimuli in the lower part, one was identical, one was different and another one was similar to the sample. With their mouse, participants selected one of the three comparative stimuli. If the selection was correct, a message appeared in the lower part of the monitor for two seconds with the word *correct,* as well as an intermittent sound; if the answer was incorrect, the word *error* appeared and there was a continuous sound. At the end of the session, the total score was presented. Different colors and figures were used (three stimuli per dimension) for each phase of training. The criterion used for finishing the training phase was a score of 90% of the correct answers during three consecutive sessions or a maximum of ten sessions.

Conditions for the testing sessions were similar to the training sessions, except that they were only informed concerning the total score at the end of the session. In addition, colors and figures were used that were different from those used during the training phases. Figure 1 shows the stimuli used during training conditions and during the transference tests.

## Procedure

Five groups were formed according to: 1) the semantic content of the sentences and, 2) the temporal location requesting the general rule of execution (see Table 1).

*Group 1. Relationship between sample and comparative stimuli and a rule per phase.* At the end of each training session, participants in this group were requested to complete four sentences in writing. The semantic content of these alluded to the relationship between the stimuli. In addition, they were required to write the general rule of execution at the end of each training phase and at the end of each transference test.

*Group 2. Relationship between stimuli and responses and a rule per phase.* For this group, the semantic content of the sentences alluded to relationships between the matching stimuli and the subject's response. The description of the general rule of execution was requested at the end of each training and testing phase.

*Group 3. Relationship between responses and consequences and a rule per phase.* In this group the semantic content of the sentences emphasized the relationships between the subject's responses and the consequences of these. In the same manner the request for the general rule occurred at the end of each training and testing phases.

*Group 4. Without sentences and a rule per phase.* The training and testing conditions were similar to those of the previous groups, except that no incomplete sentences were presented and only the general rule of execution was requested at the end of each training and testing phases.

*Group 5. Without sentences and a rule per session.* For this group, the description of the general rule of execution was requested at the end of each training and testing session, without requiring incomplete sentences.

*Pre-test and post-test.* The pre-test was used as a way to select participants as well as for an evaluation of their entrance level and the post-test evaluates their exit level with respect to the task. In these tests the correct response was matched to something similar (size, form, color or pattern) and there was no feedback. At the end of the test the number of correct answers was reported.

**Table 1. Types of incomplete sentences and moments upon requesting the rule**

| GROUPS | INCOMPLETE SENTENCES | TEMPORAL DISTANCE OF THE REQUEST OF THE RULE |
|---|---|---|
| Group 1 | 1. If the figure above is __ the correct figure below is ____<br>2. The figures above can have traits in common with those below.<br>3. The figures above can be different from those below in ___<br>4. Of the three figures below, the correct one is always the one that has ____ in common with that above. | Rule at the end of each training and testing phase. |
| Group 2 | 1. The figure that I always choose has ___ in common with the one above.<br>2. When the figure above is ____, I choose ____<br>3. To select the correct figure, I am certain that the figure is ____<br>4. I do not choose the figure that ___ | Rule at the end of each training and testing phase. |
| Group 3 | 1. My response is correct whenever I choose.<br>2. My response is incorrect whenever I choose.<br>3. To assure that my response is correct, I must be certain that __<br>4. Whenever I choose _______they tell me that my response is ___ | Rule at the end of each training and testing phase |
| Group 4 | No sentences | Rule at the end of each training and testing phase. |
| Group 5 | No sentences | Rule at the end of each training and testing SESSION. |

Before beginning the first training session, participants were requested to read on the computer's monitor, the general instructions concerning how to use the *mouse*, how to select the stimuli and the description of contingencies. Once they indicated that there were no doubts as far as the task was concerned, the session began and the researcher left the experimental classroom.

*Training 1.* During this phase there was training on the relationship of similarity in form and the participant had to select the comparative stimulus similar in form but different in color and size.

*Training 2.* During this phase, out of the total number of trials, 80% corresponded to trials in which the correct response was that of similarity in color and 20% corresponded to similarity in form.

*Training 3.* During this phase, out of the total number of trials per session, 60% corresponded to trials in which the correct response was the relationship of similarity in size, 20% was similarity in form and the other 20% was similarity in color.

*Tests on intra-dimensional and extra-dimensional transference..* At the end of training, the emergence of new dimensions in the relationship of similarity was evaluated, without feedback. In the intra-dimensional test, trials were mixed in which the correct relationship for similarity could be in color, form or size – 33% of trials corresponded to each one of the three dimensions to be evaluated.

The extra-dimensional test evaluated if the relationship of similarity was maintained with a new dimension for the stimulus: pattern. In this test a mixture of geometric figures and colors used during the training were used as instances of stimulus.

*Test for trans-situational transference.* This test evaluated the emergence of the relationship of similarity considering textual words. Words that made sense were used as instances of stimuli. The arrangements were formed by four words with four letters, each as a sample stimulus and three as comparative stimuli. One of these was identical to the sample word, another was different and one had one letter that was similar. In this test a correct answer consisted of indicating the word that shared only one of the four letters with the stimulus. There was no feedback.

## RESULTS

Individual data was obtained in the terms of the percentage of correct answers per session in training and testing conditions, as well as the number of sessions required by each participant to reach the criterion for acquisition.

Table 2 shows the average percentage of correct answers and the number of sessions during the acquisition phase for each participant in each group. As can be observed, the majority of participants reached the criterion for acquisition in an average of three sessions for training 1 and training 2, while they needed an average of four and five sessions for the third training.

On the other hand, the types of correspondence and non-correspondence were analyzed between the execution of tests and the description of the general rule of execution. This analysis was selected since the tests allowed for measurement of the transference of participants to new dimensions of stimuli, thus constituting an evaluation tool of possible linguistic functioning. It must be stated that the criterion for satisfactory transference was when participants obtained 80% of more correct responses during each of the testing sessions.

The following was analyzed: a) *positive correspondence* between doing and reporting (D-R), that is, a score of 80% or more of correct responses and an adequate report on the general rule of execution; b) *negative correspondence (D-R)*, a score of less than 80% for correct answers and an incorrect report on the rule; c) *non-correspondence* between doing and reporting (D-R), that is, a score of 80% or higher for correct responses and an erroneous report on the general rule of execution and d) *non-correspondence* between doing and reporting (D-R), understood as a score of less than 80% of transference of correct answers and a correct report on the general rule of execution.

Figure 2 shows the percentage of correct answers per participant during three transference tests (intra-dimensional, extra-dimensional and trans-situational) and the types of correspondence and non-correspondence obtained from the analysis of verbal reports and execution.

**Table 2. Data on individual percentages and group percentages in training phases**

| GROUPS | Subjects | TRAINING 1 | | TRAINING 2 | | TRAINING 3 | |
|---|---|---|---|---|---|---|---|
| | | % of correct answers | # of sessions | % of correct answers | # of sessions | % of correct answers | # of sessions |
| Grupo 1 (E-E, R x F) | S1 | 97 | 4 | 99 | 3 | 95 | 3 |
| | S2 | 98 | 3 | 100 | 3 | 93 | 4 |
| | S3 | 97 | 3 | 94 | 4 | 92 | 4 |
| | S4 | 98 | 3 | 100 | 3 | 86 | 10 |
| | S5 | 97 | 3 | 98 | 3 | 90 | 5 |
| | $\bar{X}$ | 97,4 | 3,2 | 98,2 | 3,2 | 91,2 | 5,2 |
| Group 2 (E-R, R x F) | S6 | 99 | 3 | 99 | 3 | 87 | 4 |
| | S7 | 97 | 3 | 98 | 3 | 85 | 7 |
| | S8 | 98 | 3 | 100 | 3 | 100 | 3 |
| | S9 | 96 | 3 | 100 | 3 | 94 | 4 |
| | S10 | 99 | 3 | 100 | 3 | 96 | 3 |
| | $\bar{X}$ | 97.8 | 3 | 99.4 | 3 | 92.4 | 4/2 |
| Group 3 (R-C, R x F) | S11 | 100 | 3 | 100 | 3 | 94 | 3 |
| | S12 | 96 | 3 | 97 | 4 | 97 | 3 |
| | S13 | 96 | 3 | 100 | 3 | 96 | 4 |
| | S14 | 91 | 3 | 96 | 3 | 95 | 4 |
| | S15 | 100 | 3 | 100 | 3 | 96 | 4 |
| | $\bar{X}$ | 96,8 | 3 | 98,6 | 3,2 | 95,6 | 3,6 |
| Group 4 (Without txt, R x F) | S16 | 96 | 3 | 100 | 3 | 51 | 10 |
| | S17 | 93 | 4 | 98 | 3 | 99 | 3 |
| | S18 | 96 | 4 | 96 | 4 | 81 | 8 |
| | S19 | 100 | 3 | 97 | 3 | 95 | 4 |
| | S20 | 99 | 3 | 93 | 4 | 98 | 3 |
| | $\bar{X}$ | 96,8 | 3,4 | 96,8 | 3,4 | 84,8 | 5,6 |
| Group 5 (Without txt, R x S) | S21 | 98 | 3 | 100 | 3 | 70 | 8 |
| | S22 | 99 | 3 | 90 | 4 | 99 | 3 |
| | S23 | 97 | 3 | 99 | 3 | 99 | 3 |
| | S24 | 100 | 3 | 99 | 3 | 97 | 4 |
| | S25 | 98 | 3 | 97 | 3 | 77 | 5 |
| | $\bar{X}$ | 98,4 | 3 | 97 | 3,2 | 88,4 | 4,6 |

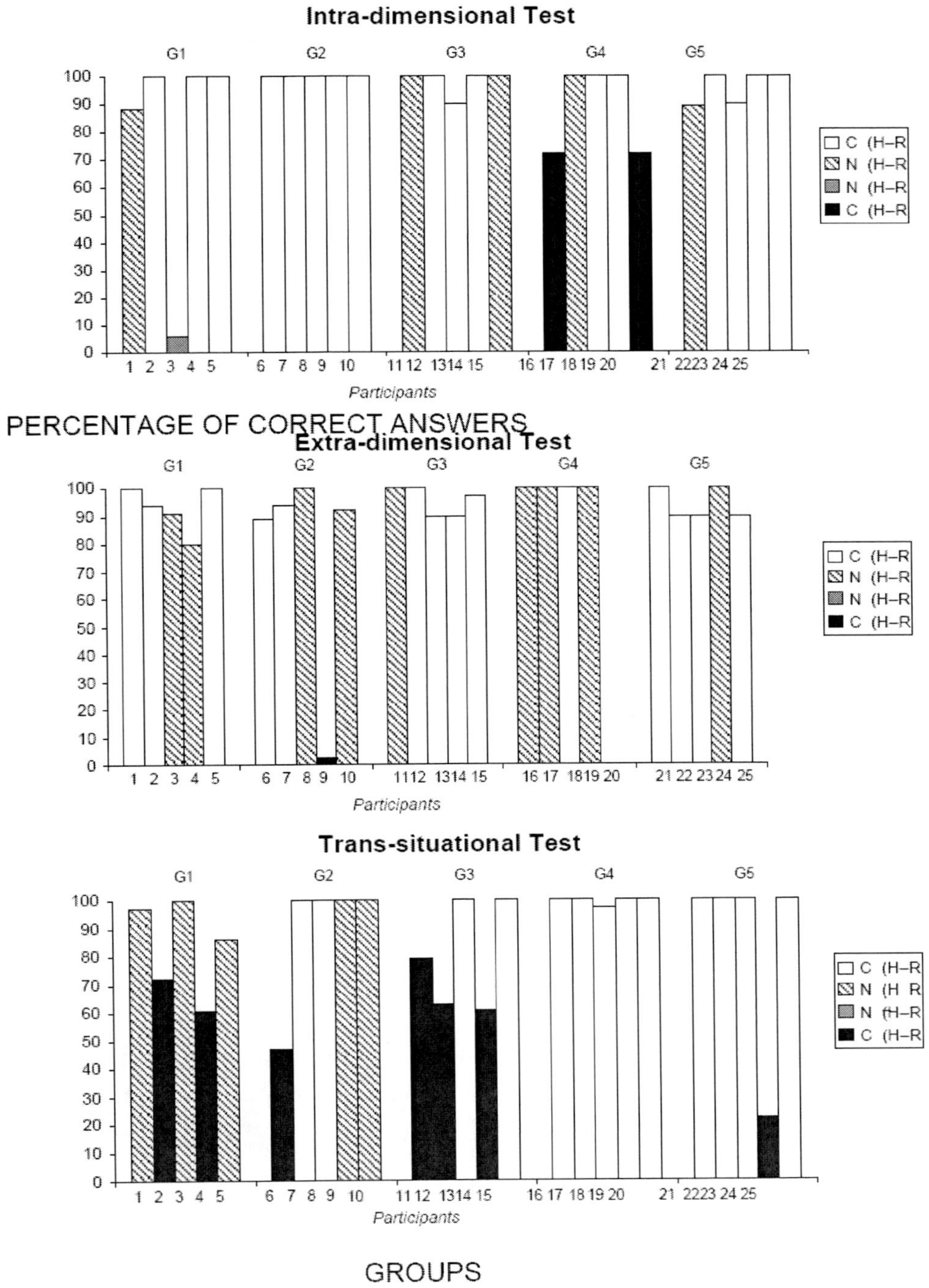


Figure 2. Percentage of correct answers and type of correspondence per person or per group during the three tests of transference.

On the intra-dimensional test (graph on top in Figure 2), the majority of participants showed positive correspondences (D-R), that is, percentages of correct answers higher than 80% and a correct report on the general rule of execution. For participants 1, 11, 15, 16 and

22, in spite of showing high percentages of transference, they had an incorrect report on the general rule and, for that reason they were evaluated as non-corresponding (D). It is important to point out two findings: First, all of the participants in group 2 showed positive correspondence between doing and reporting and second, participants 21 and 25 – both in group 4-, were the only ones who had a negative correspondence (~~D-R~~). That is to say, their execution was below 80% and there was an incorrect report on the rule. The type of non-correspondence by participant 3 seemed to be a special case, since his execution on this test was a score of approximately 10% of correct answers, and he gave an adequate report on the general rule (R).

The central graph of Figure 2 shows correspondences during the extra-dimensional test. As with the previous test, the majority of participants showed positive correspondences (D-R); however, there were more participants (3, 4, 8, 10, 11, 19, 21 and 22) who in spite of having reached levels of transference above 80%, had an incorrect report on the general rule. That is to say that there was no correspondence between doing and reporting (D); especially in three of the five participants in group 4. As far as the negative correspondences were concerned, only participants 9 and 20 were evaluated in that type, since their executions did not surpass 3% of the correct answers with an incorrect reference to the general rule.

Finally, the analysis of correspondences by participants in the trans-situational test (bottom graph in Figure 2) showed clear differences in each one of the groups. In the first place positive correspondences were observed (D-R) in the five participants in group 4, as well as four in group 5. The non-correspondence of the doing and not reporting type (D), were observed in participants 1, 3 and 5 belonging to group 1; and in participants 9 and 10 of group 2. In the same manner it is important to indicate that contrary to intra-dimensional and extra-dimensional tests, a greater concentration of negative correspondences was observed that is to say, levels of transferal below 80% and an incorrect report on the general rule in participants 2, 4, 6, 11, 12, 13 and 19. This datum appears to suggest that the stimuli (in this case, words) made the transference of the relationship difficult in non-trained contexts and, for that reason, the correct formulation of the general rule was more difficult.

## Discussion

We feel that the analysis of types of correspondences between non-verbal and verbal behavior (do-report) as far as the temporal distance of request of the general rule is concerned, was suggestive for discussion of emerging behaviors such as those evaluated during the transferal tests.

With respect to this, it was found that upon varying the semantic quality of the sentences (Group 1, 2 and 3) there was greater variability in the types of correspondences analyzed, especially during the trans-situational test. This could point towards a possible interference by the texts concerning the evaluation of the correspondences, specifically under the terms of correct or incorrect reference to the general rule of execution. In previous studies we have explored the relationships between execution and selection of incomplete sentences (Cepeda, Hickman, Moreno, Peñalosa and Ribes, 1991; Ribes, Moreno and Martínez, 1995); the relationship between transference and semantic complexity of the references (Moreno, Hickman, Cepeda, Tena and Plancarte, 1997; Hickman et al. 2001); the effects between the density of presentation of sentences and the quality of references (Morales, Hickman, Tena, Cepeda and García, 1992). However, it seems that systematic training in the correspondences would be necessary, not only the evaluation of the same as a supplementary measurement, as has been done traditionally in this type of study.

The inclusion of training procedures in correspondences such as an instance of conditional stimuli control, exactly as is indicated by Lattan and Doepke (2001), would allow us to describe those procedures in terms of behavior governed by rules and thus establish a conceptual link between these rules and those generated in the field of conditional discrimination; since "all elements necessary for the development of behavior governed by rules are found in procedures for training in correspondences" (Deacon and Konarski, 1987, p. 399).

Thus, we consider it important to develop investigations that systematically train and not only evaluate the correspondences between verbal and non-verbal behavior. In the following paragraph we present some methodological possibilities of training.

## Devices for Training in Correspondences in Complex Tasks

Tables 3 and 4 present some forms for using procedures for matching to sample and the stimuli equivalence, training and/or evaluating correspondences.

Table 3 represents training in which there would be no indispensable requirement for feedback, the emission of corresponding behaviors. In *Case 1* feedback is circumscribed only towards the emission of non-verbal behavior (Doing), in spite of the quality or verisimilitude of verbal behavior (Reporting). These relationships represent the majority of field studies on conditional discrimination and/or stimuli equivalence where verbal behavior is evaluated or measured in a supplementary manner.

This Case is subdivided into two types (Type 1 and Type 2) that allude to the moments in which non-verbal behavior would receive feedback. In Type 1, the participant would issue his non-verbal response, which would or would not receive feedback in accordance to a correct or incorrect selection and the report would later be requested. As far as Type 2 is concerned, the report followed by non-verbal behavior would be requested, maintaining the same feedback requirements.

*Case 2* represents training that would only be circumscribed by feedback on the report or by verbal behavior, after execution (Type 1) or before execution (Type 2). At least in the review of literature made by us, we have not found investigations that explore the effect of feedback on the verbal dimension or investigations in which the non-verbal dimension acquires a supplementary role.

Contrary to the two previously mentioned cases, *Case 3 and Case 4* (see Table 4) describe training in *correspondences* and not only the evaluation or analysis of the same. It is notable that the great majority of investigations related to the study of conditional discrimination and/or emerging behavior have been centered on– with some exceptions – training in the instrumental dimension of behavior, leaving verbal behavior as a supplementary measure.

**Table 3. Cases in which the correspondence is not a necessary requirement and execution is given in feedback – Doing – or the report from the subject – Saying.**

| | | | | |
|---|---|---|---|---|
| **CASE 1. FEEDBACK TO DO** | | | | |
| **Type 1** | | | | |
| Doing | ⟶ | $E^r$ | ⟶ | Reporting |
| *Example* | | | | |
| I.M. correct | ⟶ | $E^r$ | ⟶ | Reporting |
| I.M. incorrect | ⟶ | No $E^r$ | ⟶ | Reporting |
| No I.M. | ⟶ | No $E^r$ | ⟶ | Reporting |
| **Type 2** | | | | |
| Reporting | ⟶ | Doing | ⟶ | $E^r$ |
| *Example* | | | | |
| I will choose *x* or *y* | ⟶ | I.M. correct | ⟶ | $E^r$ |
| I will choose *x* or *y* | ⟶ | I.M. incorrect | ⟶ | No $E^r$ |
| Not reported | ⟶ | I.M. correct | ⟶ | $E^r$ |
| Not reported | ⟶ | I.M. incorrect | ⟶ | No $E^r$ |
| **CASE 2. FEEDBACK TO REPORT** | | | | |
| **Type 1** | | | | |
| Doing | ⟶ | Reporting | ⟶ | $E^r$ |
| *Example* | | | | |
| I.M. | ⟶ | Correct report | ⟶ | $E^r$ |
| I.M. | ⟶ | Incorrect report | ⟶ | No $E^r$ |
| I.M. | ⟶ | No report | ⟶ | No $E^r$ |
| **Type 2** | | | | |
| Reporting | ⟶ | $E^r$ | ⟶ | Doing |
| *Example* | | | | |
| I will choose *x* | ⟶ | $E^r$ | ⟶ | Selection of IM*x* |
| I will choose *x* | ⟶ | $E^r$ | ⟶ | Selection of IM*y* |
| I will choose *y* | ⟶ | $E^r$ | ⟶ | Selection of IM*y* |
| I will choose *y* | ⟶ | $E^r$ | ⟶ | Selection of IM*x* |
| No report | ⟶ | No $E^r$ | ⟶ | Selection of IM*x* or *y* |
| IM= Task of matching the sample<br>$E^r$= Feedback<br>No $E^r$ = No feedback | ⟶ Indicates the sequence between the elements. | | | |

**Table 4. Cases in which there is training in the correspondence between doing and reporting or reporting and doing**

| | | | | |
|---|---|---|---|---|
| **CASE 3. TRAINING IN DO-REPORT CORRESPONDENCE** | | | | |
| Doing | - - - - - - - -▶ | Reporting | ——————▶ | $E^r$ |
| *Example* | | | | |
| IM*x* | - - - - - - - -▶ | I did *x* | ——————▶ | $E^r$ |
| | | | | |
| IM*x* | - - - - - - - -▶ | I did *y* | ——————▶ | No $E^r$ |
| **CASE 4. TRAINING IN REPORT-DO CORRESPONDENCE** | | | | |
| Reporting | - - - - - - - -▶ | Doing | ——————▶ | $E^r$ |
| *Example* | | | | |
| I will choose *x* | - - - - - - - -▶ | IM*x* | ——————▶ | $E^r$ |
| | | | | |
| I will choose *x* | - - - - - - - -▶ | IM*y* | ——————▶ | No $E^r$ |
| IM= Task of matching sample<br>$E^r$= Feedback<br>No $E^r$ = No feedback | | ——▶ Indicates the sequence between elements.<br>- - -▶ Indicates the dependence between elements | | |

Thus, Case 3 describes the training in correspondences between non-verbal and verbal behavior (Doing-Reporting). For this, the correspondence between both behaviors would be necessary for feedback. As far as Case 4 is concerned, temporality would be invested in the two types of behavior, since in the first case the participant would be requested to give the report with respect to what he will do and he would later be exposed to the selection of the instrumental and non-verbal component.

Methodological devices are proposals that do not describe each and every one of the possible variables to be investigated between the components in a accurate manner and that form the cases; but that place an accent on the need to explicitly train relationships corresponding to verbal and non-verbal behavior and their temporal links. Thus, for example, there could be training in correspondences under the terms of the qualities of the references of participants in an oral or textual manner, the effects on acquisition and transference of training in correspondences when the report is requested before or after non-verbal behavior; training in the preciseness of verbal or non-verbal correspondences, just to mention a few possibilities. We feel that the previously mentioned examples could constitute a heuristic tool tending to explore the function between that done and that reported in the framework of behavioral analysis.

## References

Cepeda, M. L., Hickman, H., Moreno, D., Peñalosa, E., and Ribes, E. (1991). The effect of prior selection of verbal descriptions of stimulus relations upon the performance in condicional discrimination in human adults. *Revista Mexicana de Análisis de la Conducta, 17*, 53-79.

Critchfield, T. S. (1996). Self-reports about performance under time pressure: Bias and discriminability. *The Psychological Record, 40*, 541-554.

Deacon, J. R., and Konarski, E. A. (1987). Correspondence training: An example of rule-governed behavior?. *Journal of Applied Behavior Analysis, 20* (4), 391-400.

Devany, J. M., Hayes, S. C., and Nelson, R. O. (1986). Equivalence class formation in language-able and language-disabled children. *Journal of the Experimental Analysis of Behavior, 46* (*3*), 243-257.

Hayes, S. C. (1991). A Relational control theory of stimulus equivalence. In L. J. Hayes and P. N. Chase (Eds,), *Dialogues on verbal behavior* (pp. 19-41). Reno, NV: Context Press.

Hickman, H., Tena. O., Moreno, D., Cepeda, M. L. Plancarte, P., and Larios, R. M. (2001). Análisis de autodescripciones en relación con el comportamiento complejo, *Revista Latina de Pensamiento y Lenguaje, 9* (*1*), 105-122.

Horne, P. J., and Lowe, C. F. (1996). On the origins of naming and other symbolic behavior. *Journal of the Experimental Analysis of Behavior, 65*, 185-241.

Lattal, K. A., and Doepke, K. J. (2001). Correspondence as conditional stimulus control: Insights from experiments with pigeons. *Journal of Applied Behavior Analysis, 34*, 127-144.

Lipkens, R., Hayes, S. C., and Hayes, L. J. (1993). Longitudinal study of the development of derived relations in an infant. *Journal of the Experimental Child Psychology, 56*, 201-239.

Lloyd, K. E. (2002). A review of correspondence training: Suggestions for a revival. *The Behavior Analyst, 25* (*1*), 57-73.

Morales, F., Hickman, H., Tena, O., Cepeda, M. L., and García, R. (1992). Interacción entre la ejecución en tareas de discriminación compleja y descripciones textuales en adultos. Paper read it in the *Primer Congreso Internacional sobre el Conductismo y las Ciencias de la Conducta.* Guadalajara: México.

Moreno, D., Hickman, H., Cepeda, M. L., Tena, O., and Plancarte, P. (1997). Descriptions function on complex behavior. Paper read it in the *23 Annual Convention of the Association for Behavior Análisis.* Chicago: USA.

O´Donnell, J. and Saunder, K. J. (2003). Equivalence relations in individuals with language limitations and mental retardation. *Journal of the Experimental Analysis of Behavior, 80* (*1*), 131-157.

Plancarte, P., Hickman, H., Tena, O., Moreno, M. L., Cepeda, M. L., and Larios, R. M. (2000). Correspondence of verbal descriptions and matching performance of Mexican children. *Behavior Development Bulletin, 9*, 26-29.

Ribes, E., Moreno, D., and Martínez, C. (1995). Efecto de distintos criterios verbales de igualación en la adquisición y transferencia de una discriminación condicional de segundo orden en humanos. *Acta Comportamentalia, 3*, 27-54.

Roche, B., Barnes, D. and Smeets, P. M. (1997). Incongruous stimulus pairing and conditional discrimination training: Effects on relational responding. *Journal of the Experimental Analysis of Behavior, 68*, 143-160.

Sidman, M. (1971). Reading and auditory-visual equivalences. *Journal of Speech and Hearing Research, 14*, 5-13.

Sidman, M. (1994). *Equivalence relations and behavior: A research story.* Boston: Authors Cooperative.

Sidman, M., and Tailby, W. (1982). Conditional discrimination vs matching to sample: An expansion of the testing paradigm. *Journal of the Experimental Analysis of Behavior, 37*, 5-22.

Walker, D. J., and Branch, (1996). Effects of cocaine on briefly signaled versus completely signaled delays to reinforcement. *Journal of the Experimental Analysis of Behavior, 65* (*2*), 375-388.

Ward, W., and Stare, S. W. (1990). The role of subject verbalization in generalized correspondence. *Journal of Applied Behavior Analysis, 23*, 129-136.

Wulfert, E.,and Hayes, S.C. (1988). Transfer of a conditional ordering response though conditional equivalence classes. *Journal of the Experimental Analysis of Behavior, 50*, 125-144.

Wulfert, E., Dougher, M. J., and Greenway, D.E. (1991). Protocol analysis of the correspondence of verbal behavior and equivalence class formation. *Journal of the Experimental Analysis of Behavior, 56* (*3*), 489-504.

Wulfert, E., Greenway, D. E., and Dougher, M.J. (1994). Third-order equivalence classes. *The Psychological Record, 44*, 411-439.

In: Hispanic Psychology Yearbook Volume 1
Ed: Cirilo H. García pp. 35-46

ISBN: 978-1-60741-786-6


*Chapter 3*

# ASSESSMENT OF RELIABILITY OF INVENTORY ON LEARNING STYLES AND MOTIVATIONAL ORIENTATION (EDAOM)*

***Zaira Vega Valero*[1]*, Eduardo Peñalosa Castro, Patricia Landa Durán and Carlos Nava Quiroz***

Facultad de Estudios Superiores Iztacala,
Universidad Nacional Autónoma de México

## ABSTRACT

The Learning Styles and Motivational Orientation Inventory (EDAOM, according to its initials in Spanish) is a viable instrument for evaluating learning strategies and motivation for study. Castañeda and Ortega (2004) stated that the reliability of this inventory is high, as well as its concurrent validity. It is known that any instrument of measurement has to have acceptable levels of reliability and validity and, for that reason the object of this paper was to carry out an evaluation of the reliability of the EDAOM with a student sample from Iztacala FES, in order to verify the initial index and establish the inventory's subscale index. The results obtained confirm the level of reliability; however, in this application in order to preserve the validity of the instrument, some items were eliminated because they had negative correlations. The data is discussed in the context of the psychometric characteristics of an instrument and items and response choices were proposed.

**Keywords:** learning strategies, motivation for study, reliability, validity, psychometrics.

---

* A version of this chapter was also published in the *International Hispanic Psychology Journal, Volume 1 Issue 1*, published by Nova Science Publishers, Inc. It was submitted for appropriate modification in an effort to encourage wider dissemination of research.

[1] This paper was financed by PAPCA 2006. Address for correspondence: Cynthia Zaira Vega Valero, Bosques de Vincenes 4 casa 15,Bosques del Lago, Cuautitlán Izcalli, Edo. de Méx. CP 54760, E-mail: czaira.vega@correo.unam.mx, Eduardo Peñalosa Castro: eduardo.penalosa@gmail.com, Patricia Landa Durán: patl@servidor.unam.mx, Carlos Nava Quiroz: canaqi@servidor.unam.mx

## RESUMEN

El Inventario de Estilos de Aprendizaje y Orientación Motivacional (EDAOM), es una propuesta viable para evaluar las estrategias de aprendizaje y la motivación al estudio. La fiabilidad presentada por Castañeda y Ortega (2004) de este inventario es alta, así como la validez concurrente. Se sabe que cualquier instrumento de medida tiene que contar con niveles de fiabilidad y validez aceptables, por lo que el objetivo de este trabajo fue realizar una evaluación de la fiabilidad del EDAOM en una muestra de estudiantes de la FES Iztacala, para verificar el índice inicial y establecer el de las sub escalas del inventario. Los resultados obtenidos confirman el nivel de fiabilidad, sin embargo, en esta aplicación se eliminaron reactivos por resultar negativos en su correlación, pues esta situación ponía en riesgo la validez del instrumento. Los datos se discuten bajo las características psicométricas de un instrumento proponiéndose reactivos y alternativas de respuesta.


*Palabras clave*: estrategias de aprendizaje, motivación al estudio, fiabilidad, validez, psicometría.

## INTRODUCTION

Learning styles as motivational orientation for study are very important aspects for understanding processes by which students learn in the classroom, and its measurement is not of less importance since it has been demonstrated that this type of characteristics in students is related to high levels of academic performance (Castañeda, 2004; Weinstein, 1998; Pintrich, 2000). The Learning Styles and Motivational Orientation Inventory (EDAOM) is a viable proposal for evaluating the previous constructs. Although this instrument has been made reliable and validated with a sample of 1500 students on the national level (Castañeda and Ortega, 2004), what we present in this paper is a study on reliability that complements the EDAOM in a sample of first semester students studying psychology in the Iztacala School of Higher Studies (Facultad de Estudios Superiores of Iztacala) of the UNAM.

It is known that any instrument of measurement has to have acceptable levels of reliability and validity. In essence, the reliability referred to the non-existence of errors in measurement instruments known as exactness and precision of the measurement procedures (Kerlinger, 1981; Silva, 1992; Coolican, 1997; Namakforoosh, 2000). On the other hand, the validity is the degree to which the test measures what one really wishes to measure. Validity is respect for the instrument and what is required for this is the certainty that it fulfills the purpose for which it was created (Coolican, 1997; Namakforoosh, 2000; Kerlinger and Lee, 2002).

The possession of reliable and valid instruments allows for the most adequate explanation of the psychological phenomena of interest. In particular, in the field of education there are different strategies for the evaluation of learning by the student (Winne and Perry, 2000). Many of those strategies consist of inventories that evaluate student learning abilities, motivation, values, goals, different types of knowledge, among others.

However, a considerable number of measurement instruments in this area were developed in other languages, under cultural, social, political and ideological logic that is different from ours. For example, Roces, González-Pineda, Nuñez, González-Pumariega, García and

Alvarez (1999) translated, checked the reliability and validated the instrument *Motivated Strategies for Learning Questionnaire* (MSLQ) developed by Pintrich, Smith, García and Mckeachie (1991). The translation and adaptation of the instrument into Spanish is called "Cuestionario de Estrategias de Aprendizaje y Motivación (CEAM)". It is a self-information questionnaire that measures student motivational factors and learning strategies. Roces and collaborators (op cit) report that in the original (MSLQ) instrument items were grouped into six motivational scales and nine strategies. The factorial analysis carried out with the Spanish version revealed the existence of six motivational scales and seven learning strategies. However, with the CEAM inventory results were obtained that were similar to those reported by Pintrich and colleagues (op cit) for the relationship between motivation, learning strategies and achievement, on different academic levels.

Unfortunately, one does not have access to the CEAM since publications to that respect only report the analysis of reliability and factorial analysis but not the translation of the complete inventory. In addition, it is difficult to find studies with extensive use of the same.

Since understanding mechanisms responsible for efficient learning continue to be of utmost importance, the Evaluation of Learning Strategies and Motivational Orientation Inventory (EDAOM) (Castañeda, 2004), is a viable alternative for researchers and evaluators in the field of education, not only because it was constructed by and for a Mexican population, but also because it justly evaluates learning strategies and the motivational orientation for studying, which are variables identified as relevant for explaining strategic learning; it has been affirmed that upon understanding this area, this would imply more successful students (Zimmerman and Martínez Pons, 1988), with orientation to better defined goals (Zimmerman and Martínez-Pons, 1986) and with a better designed environment of study (Dembo, Junge and Lynch, 2004).

The EDAOM was published by Castañeda (2004) who reported the results of its application on 2995 students and he obtained 0.94 index of reliability. The concurrent validity was evaluated with respect to the general grade average, which resulted in a score of 0.67 and with diverse academic tasks, it was 0.89. In the same manner, he commented that in order to establish the validity of the converging and diverging construct of the subscales, a confirming factorial analysis was carried out with a MRMM co-variance matrix. He found that *traits* were represented by learning styles and self-regulation of students and *methods* by the types of processing used in the strategies that make up the styles.

Thus, the EDAOM is an instrument that fulfills the desired measurement characteristics of reliability and validity; however, and since it represents a valuable option for investigators in this field, it is convenient to analyze some additional aspects. It is well-known that the measurement characteristics of an instrument are not affected by the particularities of the sample, by its size, by the time it was given, by the investigator who used it, etc. In this case, the study in which the EDAOM was published did not include the report on the indexes of reliability of the sub-scales, an aspect that we consider to be of extreme importance to establish complete reliability.

In a preliminary study, the EDAOM was taken by a sample of new undergraduate students registered with a major in psychology at the Iztacala FES – UNAM (Vega, Peñalosa and Landa, 2006) and it was found that the reliability was similar to that reported by Castañeda. However, some inconsistencies were found, such as negative or very little correlation between the items, especially in the section that evaluates the perceived quality of strategies. Due to this, our study's objective is to report on the results of a study of reliability carried out to evaluate EDAOM's initial index as well as the subscales.

# METHOD

## Participants

134 students who were in the first semester of their freshman year with a major in psychology at the Iztacala School of Higher Studies, UNAM.

## Scenario

The instrument was taken in a classroom provided by the school.

## Instrument

Learning Styles and Motivational Orientation Inventory (EDAOM) (Castañeda, 2004) was applied, which was designed to identify the self-evaluation that students in middle higher and higher education had concerning their learning strategies and motivational orientation to study. The self-evaluations are measured in three areas: a) the frequency with which they use an extensive variety of learning strategies and motivational orientations in their studies; b) the ease or difficulty with which they do it and c) the quality that they report to have with their results.

The inventory is formed by 91 Likert type items. For each item, frequency, ease and quality are evaluated and for that reason upon carrying out the analysis of reliability there are 273 items. This inventory contains items that are scored positively, but there are also items that are scored negatively, and instead of adding them, they are subtracted from the score. Those items are: 49, 53, 60, 61, 62, 63, 69, 70, 75, 80, 83, 86 and 90. The response options and scoring are presented in table 1 as follows.

On the other hand, the EDAOM is composed of four general scales and 13 subscales. The *Styles for Acquiring Information* scale evaluates learning strategies on two levels: *Selective Acquisition,* which includes superficial processing strategies of what is being learned and *Generative Acquisition,* which considers strategies for deep processing of the information to be acquired.

The second scale, *Styles for Recovery of Information Learned* evaluates two contexts: *before* different academic tasks and *during* the exams.

The third scale, *Processing Styles*, contemplates two types: the *converging style* – reproduces the information to be learned – and the *diverging style* – where students create innovative productions and critically think about that learned.

Finally, the *Metacognitive and Metamotivational Self-regulation Styles* scale is formed by three components: the *personal dimension* that evaluates the efficiency perceived, internal contingency, perceived autonomy and orientation to external approval; *the task dimension* that evaluates the orientation of the task itself and that of the achievement of goals and the *materials dimension.*

**Table 1. Response options for any item and score**

| | A | | | B | | C | |
|---|---|---|---|---|---|---|---|
| | Frequency done by me | | | Ease with which I do it | | Quality | |
| "X" Ítem | Always or most of the time | Half of the time | Never or almost never | Easily | With difficulty | Very good/positive | Very poor/negative |
| | 2 | 1 | 0 | 2 | 1 | 2 | 1 |

## Procedure

The application of the inventory was during one single 30 minute session. The three persons in charge of applying the instrument received training that consisted of the adequate reading of items and the solution of any doubt concerning the inventory. The tests were applied to a group in a classroom.

## Dependent Variable and Analysis of Results

Each one of the items was scored. The Cronbach alpha was calculated in order to obtain reliability and at the same time, descriptive statistics were obtained.

## Analysis of Results

The sample consisted of 106 women and 28 men. The instrument in general obtained a high level of reliability, while that for the subscales were from moderately high to high.

The analysis of results considered the evaluation of two of the columns of the EDAOM: that of frequency and that of ease. The third column evaluating quality was discarded for this study, since a great number of items with negative correlations or correlations under .20 and levels of reliability very similar to those reported by Castañeda.

The first analysis of reliability of the inventory gave a Cronbach alpha store of .9360, which means that the instrument is 93% reliable. In this first analysis we eliminated 11 items in both columns to obtain a negative correlation or less than .20. These were: 16, 53, 61, 62, 73, 82, 83, 84, 87, 88 and 89.

**Table 2. Cronbach General Alpha from the EDAOM Inventory**

| Ítem | Alpha | Ítem | Alpha | Ítem | Alpha | Ítem | Alpha |
|---|---|---|---|---|---|---|---|
| 1.1 | .9487 | 21.2 | .9485 | 41.1 | .9482 | 64.2 | .9486 |
| 1.2 | .9486 | 22.1 | .9485 | 41.2 | .9484 | 65.1 | .9485 |
| 2.1 | .9486 | 22.2 | .9484 | 42.1 | .9484 | 65.2 | .9487 |
| 2.2 | .9487 | 23.1 | .9490 | 42.2 | .9485 | 66.1 | .9482 |
| 3.1 | .9486 | 23.2 | .9485 | 43.1 | .9478 | 66.2 | .9485 |
| 3.2 | .9487 | 24.1 | .9484 | 43.2 | .9482 | 67.1 | .9487 |
| 4.1 | .9492 | 24.2 | .9485 | 44.1 | .9483 | 67.2 | .9487 |
| 4.2 | .9488 | 25.1 | .9486 | 44.2 | .9486 | 68.1 | .9486 |
| 5.1 | .9486 | 25.2 | .9487 | 45.1 | .9489 | 68.2 | .9487 |
| 5.2 | .9490 | 26.1 | .9488 | 45.2 | .9486 | 69.1 | .9482 |
| 6.1 | .9483 | 26.2 | .9486 | 46.1 | .9491 | 69.2 | .9486 |
| 6.2 | .9485 | 27.1 | .9489 | 46.2 | .9487 | 70.1 | .9487 |
| 7.1 | .9492 | 27.2 | .9486 | 47.1 | .9484 | 70.2 | .9491 |
| 7.2 | .9488 | 28.1 | .9486 | 47.2 | .9486 | 71.1 | .9484 |
| 8.1 | .9485 | 28.2 | .9486 | 48.1 | .9487 | 71.2 | .9489 |
| 8.2 | .9486 | 29.1 | .9488 | 48.2 | .9488 | 72.1 | .9481 |
| 9.1 | .9482 | 29.2 | .9487 | 49.1 | .9492 | 72.2 | .9486 |
| 9.2 | .9486 | 30.1 | .9487 | 49.2 | .9490 | 74.1 | .9482 |
| 10.1 | .9488 | 30.2 | .9488 | 50.1 | .9486 | 74.2 | .9484 |
| 10.2 | .9489 | 31.1 | .9489 | 50.2 | .9489 | 75.1 | .9490 |
| 11.1 | .9490 | 31.2 | .9490 | 51.1 | .9490 | 75.2 | .9491 |
| 11.2 | .9488 | 32.1 | .9486 | 51.2 | .9490 | 76.1 | .9489 |
| 12.1 | .9492 | 32.2 | .9489 | 52.1 | .9486 | 76.2 | .9486 |
| 12.2 | .9489 | 33.1 | .9480 | 52.2 | .9486 | 77.1 | .9485 |
| 13.1 | .9486 | 33.2 | .9484 | 54.1 | .9483 | 77.2 | .9484 |
| 13.2 | .9488 | 34.1 | .9490 | 54.2 | .9485 | 78.1 | .9486 |
| 14.1 | .9488 | 34.2 | .9489 | 55.1 | .9485 | 78.2 | .9488 |
| 14.2 | .9486 | 35.1 | .9479 | 55.2 | .9491 | 79.1 | .9482 |
| 15.1 | .9478 | 35.2 | .9484 | 56.1 | .9484 | 79.2 | .9487 |
| 15.2 | .9482 | 36.1 | .9490 | 56.2 | .9486 | 80.1 | .9482 |
| 17.1 | .9487 | 36.2 | .9489 | 57.1 | .9488 | 80.2 | .9488 |
| 17.2 | .9489 | 37.1 | .9490 | 57.2 | .9489 | 81.1 | .9480 |
| 18.1 | .9483 | 37.2 | .9489 | 58.1 | .9484 | 81.2 | .9484 |
| 18.2 | .9489 | 38.1 | .9491 | 58.2 | .9484 | 85.1 | .9493 |
| 19.1 | .9487 | 38.2 | .9490 | 59.1 | .9489 | 85.2 | .9490 |
| 19.2 | .9490 | 39.1 | .9489 | 59.2 | .9490 | 86.1 | .9488 |
| 20.1 | .9487 | 39.2 | .9486 | 60.1 | .9488 | 86.2 | .9490 |
| 20.2 | .9486 | 40.1 | .9487 | 60.2 | .9491 | 90.1 | .9483 |
| 21.1 | .9485 | 40.2 | .9488 | 63.1 | .9488 | 90.2 | .9487 |
| | | | | 63.2 | .9488 | 91.1 | .9482 |
| | | | | 64.1 | .9479 | 91.2 | .9486 |

In the second alpha analysis the result was .9656, which implies that it increased its percentage of reliability. On this occasion, no item was eliminated. The final reliability of the inventory was high and the instrument consisted of 80 items that evaluate the frequency and ease of learning strategies and motivational orientation to study. The alpha of the items in the general instrument was higher than .94 (see table 2).

The alpha for the selective subscale was .7025 and for the items in this area it was greater than .67. The items that form the selective area are: 2, 5, 13, 17, 25 y 52 (see table 3). For the generative subscale, the reliability was .6274 and for items it was greater than .55 (see table 4). The items in this area are: 20, 23, 26, 55, 56 and 78.

**Table 3. Cronbach Alphas for the Selective Acquisition Subscale**

| Ítem | Alpha | Ítem | Alpha |
|---|---|---|---|
| 2.1 | .6795 | 17.1 | .7025 |
| 2.2 | .6854 | 17.2 | .6955 |
| 5.1 | .6750 | 25.1 | .6639 |
| 5.2 | .6843 | 25.2 | .6564 |
| 13.1 | .6705 | 52.1 | .6733 |
| 13.2 | .6820 | 52.2 | .6854 |

**Table 4. Cronbach Alphas for the Generative Acquisition Subscale**

| Ítem | Alpha | Ítem | Alpha |
|---|---|---|---|
| 20.1 | .6092 | 55.1 | .6057 |
| 20.2 | .5865 | 55.2 | .6246 |
| 23.1 | .5886 | 56.1 | .5680 |
| 23.2 | .5754 | 56.2 | .5819 |
| 26.1 | .6050 | 78.1 | .5563 |
| 26.2 | .6077 | 78.2 | .5770 |

For the recovery of diverse tasks subscale, the alpha result was .6639 and for the items it was greater than .62 (see table 5). The items in this area are: 3, 7, 28, 31, 34, 79 and 90. For the recovery on exams subscale the reliability was .7145 and for items it was greater than .66 (see table 6). The items in this area are: 14, 29, 59, 64, 65 and 91.

**Table 5. Cronbach Alphas for the Subscale of Recovery of Different Tasks**

| Ítem | Alpha | Ítem | Alpha |
|---|---|---|---|
| 3.1 | .6129 | 34.1 | .6782 |
| 3.2 | .6324 | 34.2 | .6503 |
| 7.1 | .6599 | 79.1 | .6042 |
| 7.2 | .6511 | 79.2 | .6184 |
| 28.1 | .6136 | 90.1 | .6324 |
| 28.2 | .6389 | 90.2 | .6299 |
| 31.1 | .6413 | | |
| 31.2 | .6432 | | |

Regarding the convergent subscale, alpha was .7472 and for the items it was greater than .72 (see table 7). The items in this area are: 6, 8, 15, 19, 72, 74 and 75.

For the divergent subscale, the reliability was .7314 and for the items it was greater than .68 (see table 8). The items for this area are: 4, 22, 27, 33, 66 and 70.

**Table 6. Cronbach Alphas for the Recovery of Exams Subscale**

| Ítem | Alpha | Ítem | Alpha |
|---|---|---|---|
| 14.1 | .6951 | 64.1 | .6640 |
| 14.2 | .6822 | 64.2 | .6858 |
| 29.1 | .6877 | 65.1 | .6551 |
| 29.2 | .6715 | 65.2 | .6693 |
| 59.1 | .6975 | 91.1 | .6807 |
| 59.2 | .6958 | 91.2 | .6918 |

**Table 7. Cronbach Alphas for the Convergent Subscale**

| Ítem | Alpha | Ítem | Alpha |
|---|---|---|---|
| 6.1 | .7418 | 19.2 | .7457 |
| 6.2 | .7473 | 72.1 | .7260 |
| 8.1 | .7342 | 72.2 | .7423 |
| 8.2 | .7416 | 74.1 | .7240 |
| 15.1 | .7269 | 74.2 | .7414 |
| 15.2 | .7373 | 75.1 | .7507 |
| 19.1 | .7326 | 75.2 | .7648 |

**Table 8. Cronbach Alphas for the Divergent Subscale**

| Ítem | Alpha | Ítem | Alpha |
|---|---|---|---|
| 4.1 | .7195 | 33.1 | .6928 |
| 4.2 | .7093 | 33.2 | .7031 |
| 22.1 | .6938 | 66.1 | .6811 |
| 22.2 | .7013 | 66.2 | .6998 |
| 27.1 | .7203 | 70.1 | .7359 |
| 27.2 | .7068 | 70.2 | .7630 |

**Table 9. Cronbach Alphas for the Perceived Efficiency Subscale**

| Ítem | Alpha | Ítem | Alpha |
|---|---|---|---|
| 1.1 | .7785 | 32.2 | .7916 |
| 1.2 | .7875 | 35.1 | .7679 |
| 9.1 | .7711 | 35.2 | .7741 |
| 9.2 | .7812 | 54.1 | .7737 |
| 24.1 | .7686 | 54.2 | .7783 |
| 24.2 | .7763 | 59.1 | .7862 |
| 32.1 | .7904 | 59.2 | .7873 |

**Table 10. Cronbach Alphas for the Internal Contingency Subscale**

| Ítem | Alpha | Ítem | Alpha |
|---|---|---|---|
| 37.1 | .5722 | 67.2 | .6103 |
| 37.2 | .5879 | 68.1 | .6241 |
| 38.1 | .5934 | 68.2 | .6044 |
| 38.2 | .6091 | 85.1 | .5837 |
| 39.1 | .5728 | 85.2 | .5807 |
| 39.2 | .5776 | 86.1 | .6140 |
| 67.1 | .5930 | 86.2 | .6274 |

**Table 11. Cronbach Alphas for the Preceived Autonomy Subscale**

| Ítem | Alpha | Ítem | Alpha |
|---|---|---|---|
| 30.1 | .7389 | 42.2 | .7313 |
| 30.2 | .7402 | 58.1 | .7378 |
| 40.1 | .7377 | 58.2 | .7437 |
| 40.2 | .7434 | 63.1 | .7546 |
| 41.1 | .7360 | 63.2 | .7490 |
| 41.2 | .7291 | | |
| 42.1 | .7180 | | |

**Table 12. Cronbach Alphas for the Achievement of Goals Subscale**

| Ítem | Alpha | Ítem | Alpha |
|---|---|---|---|
| 47.1 | .6470 | 50.2 | .6750 |
| 47.2 | .6556 | 71.1 | .6386 |
| 48.1 | .6672 | 71.2 | .6695 |
| 48.2 | .6574 | 76.1 | .6446 |
| 49.1 | .7068 | 76.2 | .6546 |
| 49.2 | .6932 | 77.1 | .6241 |
| 50.1 | .6656 | 77.2 | .6463 |

**Table 13. Cronbach Alphas for the Task Itself Subscale**

| Ítem | Alpha | Ítem | Alpha |
|---|---|---|---|
| 10.1 | .6813 | 44.2 | .6695 |
| 10.2 | .6779 | 45.1 | .6893 |
| 21.1 | .6831 | 45.2 | .6849 |
| 21.2 | .6836 | 46.1 | .6998 |
| 43.1 | .6554 | 46.2 | .6896 |
| 43.2 | .6631 | 60.1 | .7125 |
| 44.1 | .6817 | 60.2 | .7117 |

Concerning the efficiency perceived subscale the alpha resulted in .7913 and for the items it was greater than .76 (see table 9). The items for this area are: 1, 9, 24, 32, 35, 54 and 59.

Considering the internal contingency subscale the reliability was .6322 and for the items it was greater than .57 (see table 10). The items in this area are: 37, 38, 39, 67, 68, 85 and 86. Regarding the perceived autonomy subscale the alpha was .7626 and for items it was greater than .71 (see table 11). The items in this area are: 30, 40, 41, 42, 58 and 63. It was found a negative correlation among the items regarding the external approval subscale.

Concerning the subscale for the achievement of goals, the alpha was .6984 and for the items it was greater than .62 (see table 12). The items in this area are: 47, 48, 49, 50, 71, 76 and 77. For the Task Itself subscale, the reliability was .7161 and for the items it was greater than .65 (see table 13). The items of this area are: 10, 21, 43, 44, 45, 46 and 60.

Finally, for the materials dimension subscale, the alpha was .5969 and for the items it was greater than .52 (see table 14). The items in this area are: 11, 12, 18, 36, 57, 80 and 81.

**Table 14. Cronbach Alphas for the Materials Dimension Subscale**

| Ítem | Alpha | Ítem | Alpha |
|---|---|---|---|
| 11.1 | .5570 | 36.2 | .5904 |
| 11.2 | .5489 | 57.1 | .5931 |
| 12.1 | .5956 | 57.2 | .5725 |
| 12.2 | .5928 | 80.1 | .5918 |
| 18.1 | .5582 | 80.2 | .6112 |
| 18.2 | .5923 | 81.1 | .5230 |
| 36.1 | .5955 | 81.2 | .5452 |

In the beginning EDAOM instrument was composed of 91 items, with three columns of evaluation: frequency, facility and quality. After the analysis of reliability, the quality column was completely eliminated, upon discarding many items by negative correlation. From the frequency and facility columns, only 11 items were eliminated, for the same reasons, and the final version was composed of a total of 80 items.

From the four general scales: Acquisition of Information (×= 37.56, s = 5.03) Administration of Memory Resources (×= 34.84, s = 5.93), Information Processing (×= 25.89, s = 6.85), and Self-Regulation, this containing at the same time the person dimension (×= 48.06, s = 6.98), task dimension (×= 31.32, s = 6.11), and materials dimension (×= 16.04, s = 6.24), it was found that for all cases the averages implied that students need to reinforce learning strategies or motivational orientation, although they still do not defect.

## Discussion

In general, the EDAOM had a high level of reliability and a moderately high to high level for the different subscales. The average score indicates that students need to reinforce their learning strategies, as well as their motivation.

After the replication of the study of the metric qualities of the EDAOM we obtained levels of reliability similar to those reported by Castañeda (2004). In contrast to that reported by the author, the column that evaluated the quality that students perceived concerning their strategies had to be eliminated, since they do not fulfill the metric criteria necessary to assure reliability, perhaps due to the lack of congruency between the wording of the item and the response option offered: Very good/positive or Very poor/negative. It is probable that since the items are not congruent with the response options, they are difficult to understand and make selection difficult by the person surveyed, causing the internal consistency of the item to decrease and doubtful accuracy in the results (Cadoche, Stegmayer, Burioni, Bernandez, 1998).

Eleven items were eliminated from the instrument, four of these belong to the items that are scored negatively, it is probable that the manner in which they are worded and the corresponding choice is not correct. On the other hand, the items eliminated were from different subscales of the instrument, and for that reason it did not affect just one subscale.

Due to the differences found in the reliability of the inventory of this study and that reported by Castañeda, some modifications are suggested to assure reliability and validity of the same. For example, the response options to evaluate quality could be: "I do very well", "I do average", "I do very poorly".

On the other hand, it would be very convenient to develop questions that evaluate metacognitive and metamotivational self-regulation, since this area does not at present form part of the inventory and its evaluation is important since it is medullar in the Pintrich and Zimmerman model. For that reason we propose the following items:

1. In order to better focus myself on my studies, I set my own learning goals.
2. I continuously review to see if I am fulfilling the goals that I have set.
3. When I realize that I am not achieving a goal, I try to convert it into smaller goals to achieve it.
4. When I study I try to do tasks or exercises to be aware of what I am learning.
5. I normally take notes to better understand what I am studying.
6. I do summaries, outlines, diagrams or synopses.
7. The notes I take are clear and understandable.
8. I write down pending activities and homework in an agenda.
9. I check in the agenda to be sure that I have done my tasks.

Finally, we feel that the EDAOM is a useful instrument for identifying variables in students that are critical in their study process, and even when some modifications are proposed in this study to use it within our population, it is important to indicate that it provides us with the possibility of classifying samples of the population and of identifying training needs. From the identification of these characteristics, intervention plans could be created to promote strategies and motivation, central aspects that are neglected in our educational system.

## REFERENCES

Cadoche, Stegmayer, Burioni and Bernandez (1998). Seminary's paper on Surveys on Education, Argentina, http://www.uni.edu.ar/fave/sei/encuestas/index.htlm

Castañeda, S. (2004). *Educación, aprendizaje y cognición: teoría en la práctica.* México: El Manual Moderno.

Castañeda, S. and Ortega, I. (2004). Evaluación de estrategias de aprendizaje y orientación motivacional al estudio. In S. Castañeda (ed.). *Educación, aprendizaje y cognición: teoría en la práctica*. México: El Manual Moderno, pp. 277-299.

Coolican, H. (1997). *Métodos de investigación y estadística en psicología*. México: El Manual Moderno.

Dembo, M. H., Junge, L.G., and Lynch, R. (2004). Becoming a self regulated learner: implications for web based education. Paper read it at the *Annual Conference of the American Educational Research Association*, San Diego.

Kerlinger, F. (1981). *Investigación del Comportamiento. Técnicas y Metodología*. México: Interamericana.

Kerlinger, F. and Lee, H. B. (2002). *Investigación del comportamiento. Métodos de Investigación en Ciencias Sociales*. México, McGrawHill.

Namakforoosh, M. (2000). *Metodología* de *la Investigación*. México: Limusa.

Pintrich, P.R. (2000) The role of goal orientation in self-regulated learning. In M. Boakerts, P. Pintrich and M. Zeidner (eds.), *Handbook of self-regulation*. San Diego: Academic Press, pp. 451-502.

Pintrich, P. R., Smith, D. A., García, T., and Mckeachie, W. J. (1991). A manual for the use of the Motivational Strategies for Learning Questionnaire (MSLQ). *Educational and Psychological Measurement, 53*, pp. 801-813.

Roces, C., González-Pineda, J. A., Nuñez, J. C., González-Pumariega, S., García, M. S., and Álvarez, L. (1999). Relaciones entre motivación, estrategias de aprendizaje y rendimiento académico en estudiantes universitarios. *Revista Electrónica del Departamento de Psicología. Universidad de Valladolid. 1*, 1, pp. 41-50.

Silva, A. (1992). *Métodos cuantitativos en psicología. Un enfoque metodológico*. México: Trillas.

Vega, Z., Peñalosa, E., and Landa, P. (2006). *Relación entre estrategias de aprendizaje, orientación motivacional al estudio y diversas tareas académicas*. Paper read it at the XXXIII Congreso Nacional del Consejo Nacional para la Enseñanza e Investigación en Psicología. Veracruz, México.

Weinstein, C. E., Powdrill, L., Husman, J., Roska, L. A., and Dierking, D. (1998). Aprendizaje estratégico: un modelo conceptual, instruccional y de evaluación. In S. Castañeda (ed.), *Evaluación y fomento del desarrollo intelectual en la enseñanza de las ciencias, artes y técnicas* (pp. 197-228). México: UNAM-Concayt-Porrúa.

Wine, P. H. and Perry, N. E. (2000). Measuring self-regulated learning. In M. Boekaerts, P. Pintrich, and M. Zeidner (eds.), *Handbook of self-regulation*, pp. 531-566. Orlando, FL: Academic Press.

Zimmerman, B. J. and Martinez-Pons, M. (1986). Developing a structured interview for assessing student use of self-regulated Learning Strategies. *American Educational Research Journal, 23*, 614-628.

Zimmerman, B. and Martínez-Pons, M. (1988). Construct validation of a strategy model of student self-regulated learning, *Journal of Educational Psychology, 80,* 3, pp. 22-63.

In: Hispanic Psychology Yearbook Volume 1
Ed: Cirilo H. García pp. 47-54
ISBN: 978-1-60741-786-6


*Chapter 4*

# HOMES AND FAMILIES: A PRELIMINARY PERSPECTIVE FROM ENVIRONMENTAL PSYCHOLOGY*

***Jose Gomez Herrera***

*I would give all I know for half of what I do not.*
DESCARTES

## ABSTRACT

Studying family-home inter-relationships from the environmental psychology perspective implies tackling several epistemological and methodological aspects. In this paper some preliminary answers concerning the same are provided. In the first place, it is proposed that home-family inter-relationships be approached as a *system* composed of biological, psychological and socio-cultural components. The *family-housing system contemplates objective aspects* (daily activities) and *subjective aspects* (appreciation and affection). Aimed at including the notion of development in the analysis, the reconsideration of life cycles from developmental psychology and the classification of family life cycles from systemic theory are proposed. A proposal is made to reformulate both classifications in the framework of environmental psychology and, consequently a system to analyze dynamic diachronic and synchronic inter-relations in the housing-family system.

**Keywords**: Home, house, residential environments, family life cycles.

---

* A version of this chapter was also published in the *International Hispanic Psychology Journal, Volume 1 Issue 1*, published by Nova Science Publishers, Inc. It was submitted for appropriate modification in an effort to encourage wider dissemination of research.

## INTRODUCTION

In psychological literature, it is generally emphasized and accepted that the environment is transcendental for humankind; however, rarely is special attention given to the manner in which the physical environment affects our behavior. Canter (1975) used the following allegory concerning this aspect: *a fish is the last one to be aware of the fact that he lives in water.*

Undoubtedly, each of our behaviors is performed in a "place" and this place conditions, limits and, eventually, determines our behavior, our attitude, and our life style. In addition, this "place" is located in time and within a culture. In the study of human behavior, psychologists have paid special attention to interpersonal and social transactions. One of the purposes of Environmental Psychology is to rectify this.

Environmental psychology has its roots in social psychology and its objective is to explain transactions between individuals and their environment (Levy-Leboyer, 1980). According to Moser (2003), environmental psychology takes the environment and its socio-physical aspects into account and attempts to analyze people's behavior in all places where daily life occurs, such as: houses, buildings, offices, hospitals, classrooms, streets, transportation systems, etc.

In summary, we can state that environmental psychology studies the reciprocal relationships between individuals' behavior and the natural and the built socio-physical environment.

Environmental psychology offers possible solutions for solving problems. In an attempt to illustrate this point I will cite some examples, such as the work conducted in France by Gabriel Moser, in which he approaches vandalism of urban telephones (1988), or the one in which he investigates urban stress (1992) or in which he analyzes chance and the feeling of the lack of safety in victims mugged on the streets (1998). Another good example is the investigation by Mercado and colleagues regarding the ability to live in "social" housing in Mexico (1994, 1995 and 2002); or papers by Pool and colleagues (2001) concerning environmental and social identity: the case of the Olympic village in Barcelona; or the investigation by Lawrence in Switzerland (1987) concerning the evaluation of inter-relationships between the characteristics of housing and the health of their inhabitants.

With these examples it is possible to observe that Environmental Psychology is a science applied to concrete situations and its methodology is applicable only to *in situ* investigation. In addition, and due to the nature of its object, something which is also shared with architecture, urbanism, geography, ergonomics, and ecology, environmental psychology benefits from the exchange of knowledge with these sciences in an interdisciplinary manner. This reciprocity is equally valuable for those investigations in which the main interest is the interaction between individuals and groups.

The initial premise of Environmental Psychology is that behavior, attitudes and appreciation only have meaning within the context of the environment in which they manifest themselves. Human beings are influenced by the place where they live in and, in a reciprocal manner, individuals influence the place. This leads us to affirm that the environment is not neutral; it is formed by the expression of values from a specific culture. We may state that the environment is characterized by the culture of belonging of the population inhabiting it and, reciprocally, human beings acquire their identity from the interactions with their environment, according to the culture to which they belong.

This paper is particularly interested in presenting a theoretical and methodological proposal to study the interdependence between the behavior of members of a family and their housing. For this reason, I begin by recognizing that the study of the family-housing interaction involves several challenges. The first challenge consists of characterizing the "family-housing" interaction as a system (Wapner, 1998), and of explaining the dynamic interdependence of its elements, instead of describing causal relationships between variables (Werner and Altman, 1998). The second challenge implies considering the notion of development of each family member as and individual and of the family as a whole. Finally, one must also take into account that the "family-housing" system is found immersed in a culture. The tentative response to the first challenge consists of implementing the study of the family-housing inter-relationships as a *system.*

The inter-relationships of the "family-housing" system are structured by biological, psychological and socio-cultural components. The biological component refers to the development and bodily maturity of each individual; the psychological component is concerned with the different levels of development of behavior and subjectivity (including affection) of each family member; the socio-cultural component indicates multiple inter-family relationships as well as interdependency of the family member's cultural group.

The main characteristics of the family-housing inter-relationships as a *system* are:

(1) Individuals, family and housing define each ~~an~~other in a diachronic process that is simultaneous with a synchronic process. The diachronic process refers to the fact that individuals, families and housing evolve historically and in a gradual manner. The synchronic process refers to the simultaneous and interdependent relationship of the development of individuals, families and housing.
(2) The "family-housing" system evolves in a dynamic balance, where change in one of the elements simultaneously modifies the other elements and the system as a whole.
(3) In "family-housing" inter-relationships an interdependence between that established and change coexists.
(4) Daily "family-housing" inter-relationships include subjective aspects (cognition and affection) and objective aspects (activities).

In order to provide a tentative response to the second challenge, which consists of taking into account individual and family development, I feel it is necessary to reconsider each individual's life cycles, which are: childhood, adolescence, adulthood and old age. In the same way, and in a complementary manner, I also feel it is necessary to reconsider and reformulate ~~the~~ family's life cycle, which is: formation of the couple, birth of the first child, breeding and education of children from infancy to adolescence and departure of children from the paternal home.

Reconsideration of both classifications of life cycles has the intention of analyzing the interdependence between individual life cycles and family life cycles in a dynamic diachronic and synchronic interdependence; that is to say, in their historical evolutionary interdependence and their simultaneous interdependence.

Individual or family "daily life cycles" are concepts that I use to identify *"the repetition of usual daily activities over a period of time."* That repetition of daily activities is not static, rigid or permanent; since life cycles are in permanent evolution, and each individual or family daily activity coexists, in an inherent and constant manner, with that established and changed.

In addition, each individual and family activity is found within a macro social structural framework that includes, among other values, customs, economics, religion and politics.

The daily life cycle for each individual and the family cycle of life are spread out in an interdependent manner. This interdependency occurs through a set of dynamic bi-directional and reciprocal inter-relationships between daily individual activities and daily family activities, as a group.

Daily individual activities and daily family activities are distributed in two dimension of time. The first dimension of time refers to the distribution of activities during a 24 hour day; I intentionally avoid referring to the day/night binomial, a differentiation that is only possible with the presence or absence of solar light during a 24 hour period, because, when we are found farther from the equator, the use of time changes and, as a consequence, it would implicitly exclude individuals and families that live in regions found nearer the poles, where dusk and dawn last for months. The second division of refers to macro social assessments, classified in days, weeks, months, years, seasons, etc. With regard to this point, one also has to consider the existence of different criteria, dependent on the cultural group and on geographic location; for example: for Westerners, the year begins in January, for the Chinese it begins in February and for Iraqis it begins in April.

Within the time constraints of a normal day, each individual distributes his/her activities according to his biological, psychological and social development. Daily activities distributed in 24 hour periods provide form, rhythm and content to a daily life cycle and the distribution of activities that are repeated throughout the week give rhythm, form and content to a weekly life cycle, etc.

As a consequence, each individual has a specific behavior and a personal distribution of his daily activities during a 24 hour day; a daily schedule co-exists in a diachronic and synchronic manner with the daily schedules of the other family members.

Each family member lives in biological stages of development, a level of development that defines his/her daily cycle of life and determines her/his inter-connection with the family. The degree of biological development conditions him/her and on occasions determines the distribution of time for her/his activities. For example, a baby sleeps a lot, several times a day, and we can say that he/she sleeps almost anywhere, because she/he is concluding his a period of neurological maturity. An adolescent, sleeps only a little and poorly because he/she is beginning hormonal maturity and her/his interests and social activities are changing. An older person sleeps only a little and poorly and several times a day, and almost anywhere, because he/she needs to rest and recuperate energy frequently, in addition to the fact that she/he usually does not have remunerative employment or a strict schedule.

This example clearly demonstrates how several generations live together side by side under the same roof with each individual indicating her/his needs and organizing his/her daily activities according to his/her levels of biological, psychological and social development. There is an inherent interdependence between daily activities and the cultural framework of the social group an individual belongs to with the life cycles of each individual and those of the family as a group.

As previously stated, this paper proposes to once again instrument the classification of family life cycles, a classification that is based on children's cycles of life. In my opinion, this classification is limited because it does not consider the life cycles of the couple and, evidently, it also lacks the relationship with housing.

Concerning this topic, I propose the following re-formulation of family life cycles:

- Formation of the couple (only couples who have the explicit objective of having children).
- Establishment of marital life.
- First pregnancy
- Birth of the first child and re-structuring of the couple.
- Education of the first-bor child and definition of parenting roles.
- Second pregnancy and re-structuring of the couple and family
- Education of the children (parent and sibling relationships) and re-structuring of the couple and family.
- Education of adolescent children, re-definition of parenting roles, restructuring of the couple and of the family.
- Children leave the family home and restructuring of the couple.

Currently, "family" is undergoing an important social transformation in several countries (including Mexico and France) and today it is also necessary to take into consideration recomposed families (families that are formed by at least one divorced person with or without children), parents that adopt (by desire or due to sterility), and it is equally important to consider single parent families (families formed by the father or mother and at least one child). An important example of this latter classification is data from the INSEE (2007), an institution reporting that 18% of families are single-parent families, most of which are composed by the mother and a child, living in residential areas on the outskirts of Paris (la Banlieue). In order to weigh this data, it must be considered that 48% of the Parisian population lives in the outskirts (Banlieue).

To begin the dissertation on a tentative response to the third challenge, consisting in consider a "family-housing" system immersed in a culture, I will begin with the following environmental psychology precept: individuals are always in a specific situation and in a specific context. I coincide with Gifford (2002), who affirms that when we want to learn about the behavior of an individual, we need to analyze the natural and built context in which he/she lives and the structural interdependencies in her/his environment.

In addition, it is necessary to consider that each individual is initially and primarily socialized in a social group through his family. It is clear that family inter-relations and the behavior of each of its members are immersed in a set of values and customs of the social group to which he/she belongs (Evans, 1994).

In that manner, we can affirm that each individual is the product of family values, habits and customs, which are at the same time the reflection of the values, habits and customs of his/her culture. In conclusion, the behavior of every human being is established, controlled, corrected, adjusted and even, occasionally, imposed, initially and primarily by his family. An example of this situation is the refusal of Muslim students, due to a law that was passed prohibiting them to use "veils" (material covering their hair and neck) in French educational institutions. This refusal was argued under the terms that for an Arab family the veil represents a transcendental cultural value and that they would drop out of school before abandoning its use.

At this point in this paper, it is necessary to add that the predominant context for the development of daily family life is, a house that with daily inter-relations is qualitatively transformed into a home (in English), un hogar (in Spanish), chez-soi (in French), zuhause (in German), minha casa or lor (in Portuguese), a casa mia or da me (in Italian) or uchi no (in Japanese).

As a general precept, human beings are influenced by the place where they live in and individuals influence that place. Authors such as Proshansky, Ittelson and Rivlin (1970) affirm: the environment is not neutral -- it is a vehicle for the expression of the cultural values of its inhabitants. Another investigator adds by stating: and viceversa, human beings construct their identity according to the environment surrounding them (Little, 1987).

Continuing along these lines, we can add that the "natural" environment is permeated with cultural values and activities of its inhabitants. It is sufficient to mention air pollution to illustrate that nature does not exist as an immaculate reality outside of the reaches of human activity. An extreme example is global warming, caused mainly by the production of heat from large industrial centers, which is modifying global temperature (an average of 4 degrees), affecting all of us, even in the most remote areas of the world where people have never even heard of the topic. Another example is news on French television concerning a child from Breton (an inhabitant in the northern region of France) who found a bottle with a message written by a little boy in Florida, in the United States of America. The news would have been trivial and irrelevant in another situation; but, if a bottle thrown into the sea as part of a didactic exercise for a group of school children arrives in as a demonstration of ocean currents, it is evident that all types of objects, trash, industrial waste, etc. also arrives. This reminds us of and confirms what experts call "the butterfly effect".

Returning to our topic, the "family-housing" system has an intrinsic dynamic and bi-directional interdependence. In this system, the decor, furniture and its use depend on the customs, values and needs of each family member. Reciprocally, the characteristics of the house and of each one of its rooms make daily activities possible, difficult or impossible for individuals or for family interaction. For example, the size of the kitchen or the arrangement of furniture makes activities such as cooking, eating or gatherings possible, limited or impossible. As part of my data, I found that in the "banlieue" of Paris, there are apartments with kitchens that have a passage between the cabinets and walls measuring 60 centimeters. Evidently, in this "kitchen" it is impossible for it to be used by two persons at once or for it to be a gathering place. As a consequence, family meals in these apartments are practically impossible.

In addition to the re-formulation of family life cycles, this paper tentatively proposes to study the development of a "family-housing" system as shown by the following table. In this table, synchronic development is found on horizontally, and diachronic development is found vertically.

On the previous table the squares for pregnancies, the birth of children and the redefinition of the couple are repeated depending on the number of children in family. For example: the average family in Mexico has 4 children (INEGI, 1995) and according to official figures from the INSEE (2007), French families have an average of 2 children.

| Family Life Cycles | Development of the Couple and Children as a Family System | Life Cycles for the House |
|---|---|---|
| Formation of the couple | Establishment of daily conjugal activities. | Establishment and appropriation of first conjugal home |
| First pregnancy | Couple is restructured. | |
| Birth of frst child | Couple is restructured. Definition of parenting roles for education of first born. | Modification of house with primary criteria on safety, hygiene and infant decoration. |
| Second pregnancy | Couple is restructured.<br>Restructuring of parenting relationship with first child.<br>Establishment of affective relationship of first child with brother/sister. | Modification of decoration, furniture and utensils in home, in expectation of arrival of second child. |
| Birth of second child | Couple is restructured.<br>Redefinition of parenting roles for educating and raising children during infancy.<br>Establishment of fraternal relationship. | Redefinition of use and spatial reassignment of rooms.<br>Temporary modification of the use of rooms. |
| Adolescent children | Couple is restructured<br>Redefinition of parenting roles<br>Redefinition of daily individual and family activities. | Modification and restructure of use and temporary spatial appropriation of rooms. |
| Children leave family home | Couple is restructured (due to age, health, labor condition, etc.). | Modification and restructure of daily use of house. |

In January of 2007, the INSEE reported that 18% of the families in the Parisian "banlieue" are single-parent families; the same agency reported that divorce is more and more frequent in Paris and that couples last an average of three years; which, for example, implies that a mother's bedroom is used in an individual or family manner and the concept of a master bedroom is disappearing and recomposed families are becoming more frequent.

## REFERENCES

Canter, D. (1975). *Environmental interaction. London*, Surrey University Press.

Evans, G. (1994). Moderating and Mediating Proccess in Environment-Behavior Research. In G. More, and R. Marans (eds.), *Advances in Environment, Behavior and Design*. New York: Plenum

Gifford, R. (2002). Making a difference: Some ways environmental psychology has improved the world. In R. B. Bechtel, and A. Churchman (eds.), *Handbook of Environmental Psychology*. New York: John Wiley and Sons, Inc, pp 255 – 286.

Lawrence, R. (1987). *Housing, Dwelling and Homes. Design theory, research and practice.* London: John Wiley and Sons.

Legendre, A. (ed.). (2005). *Psychologie et société.* Francia, Centre national du livre et de l'Université de Provence.

Levy L. (1980). *Psychologie et environnement.* Paris, PUF.

Little, B. R. (1987). Personality and the environment. In D. Stokols and I. Altman (eds.), *Handbook of Environmental Psychology*. New York: John Wiley and Sons, pp 205 – 244.

Mercado, S., Ortega, P., Luna, G., and Estrada, C. (1994). *Factores psicológicos y ambientales de la habitabilidad de la vivienda*. México, D. F., Facultad de Psicología, UNAM.

Mercado S., Ortega, P., Luna, G. and Estrada, C. (1995). *Habitabilidad de la Vivienda Urbana*. México, D. F.

Mercado, S. (2002). La evaluación de ambientes institucionales: una perspectiva cognoscitiva. *Temas selectos de psicología ambiental.* México, D.F. pp. 179 – 186.

Moser, G. (1988). Vandalism in urban public telephones. In J. C. Jesuino (ed.), *Environmental social psychology,* pp. 66-75. Norwell : Kluwer Academic Publishiers.

Moser, G. (1992). *Le stress urbains*. Paris: Armand Colin Ed.

Moser, G. (1998). Attribution causal et sentiment d'insécurité des victimes. *Les cahiers Internationaux de Psychologie Sociale,* 39, 43-52.

Moser, G. and Weiss, K. (eds.) (2003). *Espaces de vie: Aspect de la relation homme-environnement.* Paris: Armand Colin Ed.

Pol E., Vidal, T., and Romeo, M. (2001). Supuestos cambios de actitud y conducta usados en las campañas de publicidad y los programas de promoción ambiental. El modelo de las cuatro esferas. *Estudios de psicología,* 22 (1), 111-126.

Proshansky, M., Ittelson, W., and Rivlin, L. G. (eds.) (1970). *Environmental Psychology: Man and his physical setting*. New York: Holt, Rinehart and Winston.

Wapner, S. (1998). A holistic, Development, system-oriented perspective: Child, Cities, and Psychological Theories: Developing Relationships. Berlin-New York: de Gruyter, pp. 278-300.

Werner, C. M. and Altman, I. (1998). A dialectical / transactional framework of social relations: implications for children and adolescents. In Gorlitz, J. Valsiner, H. J., and Harlof, G, Mey (eds.), Child, Cities, and Psychological Theories: Developing Relationships. Berlin-New York: de Gruyter, pp. 123-154.

In: Hispanic Psychology Yearbook Volume 1
Ed: Cirilo H. García pp. 55-75
ISBN: 978-1-60741-786-6


*Chapter 5*

# SOCIAL REPRESENTATION OF MATRIMONY IN MARRIED COUPLES IN NUEVO LEÓN (MEXICO)*

***José Moral de la Rubia*** [1]
Universidad Autónoma de Nuevo León, Verónica Carrillo Carrillo and
Claudia I. Griffens Sauceda, Universidad Autónoma de Ciudad Juárez

## ABSTRACT

The objective of the study was to determine the semantic content associated to being married, considering the sample as a social group, as well as to delimit sub-groups of subjects and characterize them by comparing them in psychometric measures related to marital adjustment. A self-reporting questionnaire was administered to a sample of 100 married couples. The questionnaire was formed by a free association test, questions concerning socio-demographic data, sexual relations and nine scales (dyadic adjustment, marital satisfaction, sexual dissatisfaction, alexithymia, state-trait anxiety, depression, positive and negative affect, social desirability and marital aggrandizement). An analysis of thematic content was applied to data from the free association test. Fifteen specific categories were defined as well as a residual category with an initial average inter-rater reliability of .81 and a final one of .93. The central nucleus of social representation is formed by couple and family obligations and functions, positive feelings emphasizing love, fidelity values, a family formed by parents and children, as well as values for living together; that is to say, the image of a united, happy family that struggles for its stability through fidelity, and living together in peace and harmony. The 200 subjects, with basis on a cluster analysis concerning the 15 specific semantic categories, were classified into 4 groups: 1) being married because of children, 2) being married for the company of his/her spouse, 3) being married for conjugal and family duties and 4) being married for love.

---

* A version of this chapter was also published in the *International Hispanic Psychology Journal, Volume 1 Issue 1*, published by Nova Science Publishers, Inc. It was submitted for appropriate modification in an effort to encourage wider dissemination of research.

[1] Address for correspondence: Facultad de Psicología, UANL, Mutualismo 110, Mitras-Centro, C. P. 64460, Monterrey, Nuevo León, México. Phone and Fax: 001-81-83483781. Email: jose_moral@hotmail.com

The group married because of love is closer to the nucleus of social representation and reports better adjustment and marital satisfaction.

**Keywords:** Social representation, matrimony, dyadic adjustment, marital satisfaction, sexual satisfaction.

## RESUMEN

Los objetivos del estudio son determinar el contenido semántico asociado con el estar casados, considerando a la muestra como grupo social, así como delimitar subgrupos de sujetos y caracterizarlos comparándolos en medidas psicométricas relacionadas con ajuste marital. Un cuestionario de auto-reporte se administró a una muestra de 100 parejas casadas. El cuestionario estaba integrado por un test de asociación libre, preguntas sobre datos sociodemográficos, relaciones sexuales y nueve escalas (ajuste diádico, satisfacción marital, insatisfacción sexual, alexitimia, ansiedad rasgo-estado, depresión, afectos positivos y negativos, deseabilidad social y engrandecimiento marital). Sobre los datos del test de asociación libre se aplicó un análisis de contenido temático. Se definieron 15 categorías específicas y una residual con una confiabilidad promedio inicial de .81 y final de .93. El núcleo central de la representación social está constituido por obligaciones y funciones de pareja y familia, sentimientos positivos destacando el amor, valores de fidelidad, la familia formada por padres e hijos, así como valores de convivencia, es decir, la imagen de una familia unida, feliz, que lucha por su estabilidad a través de la fidelidad, armonía y paz en la convivencia. Los 200 sujetos, con base en un análisis de cluster sobre las 15 categorías semánticas específicas, fueron clasificados en 4 grupos: 1) estar casados por los hijos, 2) estar casados por la compañía del cónyuge, 3) estar casados por deberes conyugales y familiares y 4) estar casados por amor. El grupo de casados por amor se aproxima más al núcleo de la representación social y reporta más ajuste y satisfacción maritales.

*Palabras claves:* Representación social, matrimonio, ajuste diádico, satisfacción marital, satisfacción sexual.

## INTRODUCTION

The image of the relationship of the couple has been determined by society and we retain it as a model to be followed. Montecino (1996) states that gender identities are defined as being a mother for women and being as a son or absent father for men in today's world, just as in the past. In spite of a woman's growing participation in the work environment she continues to be viewed essentially as the person who cares for and attends to her children and her husband; and, at the same time men, although they participate more frequently in household tasks and in the education of their children, continue to be considered only as providers.

The couple emerges as an individual dimension, the sole concept alludes to a set of two units that have something in common, a strong attraction that binds them and keeps them together. The words spouse, husband/wife, evoke the notion of a dyad, of a duet composed of two individuals. With this it is understood that the couple must be complementary and this goes beyond sharing a life in common. It is also understood that the couple is constructed with the condition that the two persons implied visualize the same objective (Perrone, 2006).

Marriage is usually viewed as a contract based on social and emotional obligations, since the selection of a couple is based on our ideals of cultural standards and rules more than on our own decisions. Social and family pressure can lead a marriage or a married person to undergo different negative situations, for example to remain married only because of the children in order to avoid conflicts with their environment, to desperately search for a partner to attain social achievement or to remain married throughout his/her lifetime in spite of the fact that life with his/her partner is very unsatisfying (Rodríguez-Salazar, 2001).

All of this entails one of the most important problems in Mexican society today -- the rupture of marriages because of a lack of communication, affection and due to infidelity. It is for this reason that among the meanings associated with "being married" it is probable that values and attitudes of living together may appear, as well as values of fidelity, trust and respect, which have a special emphasis on the importance of understanding, tolerance, patience, support, loyalty and honesty. Thus, being married implies adapting oneself to another rhythm of life, adopting obligations and functions, as well as values that lead the couple to share a good life together. In Mexico, in 2004, 600 thousand marriages were registered and the average age of the bride and groom was 27.5 years for men and 24.7 years for women. In the same year there were 67 thousand divorces; and the average age of divorce was 34.5 years for women and 37.2 years for men. This means that there were 11.3 divorces per 100 marriages. By state, Chihuahua (28.8%), Baja California (26.2%) and Yucatán (23.4%) had much higher divorce rates. 34% of divorces take place during the first 5 years of marriage, 19% during the sixth and ninth year and 47% after 10 or more years of marriage (INEGI, 2005).

One of the ways society determines the behavior of subjects with respect to an object is through constructed and shared meanings. From this perspective, the theory of social representation can be a very useful framework to interpret the meanings associated with marriage.

Social representations are cognitive formations produced socially and they are therefore socially differentiated. They belong to a social group that possess a history and an identity and they are relevant with respect to an object in the social life of that group and are formed in verbal and non-verbal communication between the members of the group (Moscovici, 1961). In their study we can distinguish the following aspects: semantic-informative (meanings and beliefs) aspects, value-attitude (values, attitudes and stereotypes) aspects, and normative (standards and precepts) aspects (Moscovici, 1988). These elements, far from being an amalgam, take on a structure within the representation. In our study the object of representation is marriage.

The representation of an object, understood as a meaning constructed by a group and associated to the object, has some determiners of a superior order such as values, ideology and group identity, as well dimensions that underlie social thought are known as themata. At the same time, the representation determines social attitudes and practices directed towards the object. From this stems the important theoretical value of this construct that articulates and gives coherence to a very wide group of socio-cognitive concepts (Flament and Rouquette, 2003). In the formation and evolution of social representations, two processes play an important role: objectivization (making explicit abstract elements of the social object) and anchorage (the process of familiarization with new aspects or those that have undergone change) (Moscovici, 1961).

One of the functions of social representations consists of being accepted by those involved in the instituted social reality, contributing to the fact that individuals are satisfactorily integrated into the social condition corresponding to their position. This is similar to ideologies, but in a more concrete manner, social representations contribute to the legitimacy of the social order (Herrera, Weisser and Salazar, 2004).

There are several methods for studying the structure of representations and one consists of distinguishing the central nucleus of peripheral elements. The central nucleus has rigid characteristics that make it very resistant to change, with strong social determination, being relatively independent of specific social environment. The peripheral system is flexible, dynamic and more permeable to change, it has a more personalized and contextualized determination, allowing for psychological anchorage in the mediated reality (Abric, 1993, 2003; Casado, 2001). Social representations are a grid for interpreting social reality since they guide the behavior of members of the group and, at the same time, can be modified by changes in social practices (Ortega, 2006). The methodology recommended for the study of social representations is qualitative or mixed and it preferably uses multiple methods, as tests of free word association, semi-structured interviews, projective tests and content or discourse analysis applied to sources such as public documents, speeches, literature and films. Designs of comparisons between groups are also suggested, and longitudinal designs are even used to determine dynamic characteristics (Flament and Rouquette, 2003). Nevertheless, in practice there is a tendency to use transversal designs from only one group to determine the structure of representation, with the limitation of losing dynamic data and lacking differential elements that would enrich the interpretation.

The objective of this paper is to study the semantic content associated to being married. First, by categorizing definitions given to the associated words; second, by considering the sample as a social group in order to distinguish a central nucleus and peripheral elements; third, by delimiting groups of subjects in accordance to their communalities in the associated meanings; and fourth, by contrasting gender differences into semantic categories and schema of representation. In the same manner, to examine the difference or relationship between the groups of subjects defined from the shared meanings associated to word-stimulus "being married" in regard to socio-demographic variables, reasons for getting married, sexual behavior and psychometric scales (dyadic adjustment, marital satisfaction, sexual dissatisfaction, neuroticism, alexithymia, emotional states, marital aggrandizement and social desirability).

## METHOD

This is a descriptive-correlated study with a non-experimental trans-sectional design; a non-probabilistic sample of paid voluntary subjects is used. The random nature of sample, the independence of the pairs of subjects and the quality of data are all guaranteed.

## Subjects

The sample consists of 100 married couples. The mean age is 34 years, with a standard deviation of 10 and a range that varies from 18 to 60 years. The mean and median of education corresponded to preparatory school. 4% studied primary school but did not finish it, 6% finished studying primary school, 24% finished junior high school, 25% finished high school, 15% finished technological studies, 23% finished their college studies and 3% finished graduate studies. The median and mode of the social class one believes he/she belongs to corresponds to the middle-middle social class. 66% consider themselves to be middle-middle, 26% lower middle, 5% upper middle, and 3% lower. The mean amount of time engaged was 3 years with a standard deviation of 2 years, a median of 2 and a range of from 6 months to 9 years. The mean of years of marriage is 11 years with a standard deviation of 9 years, a medium of 8 years and a range of from 1 month to 37 years. 5% of those surveyed have had one divorce before their present marriage. The mean of children is 2 and the standard deviation is 1, the median and mode coincide at 2 children, and the range varies from 0 to 5 children.

## Measurement Instrument

An self-report questionnaire is used, which is integrated by a 5-word free association test that responds to the word-stimulus "to be married", closed questions on socio-demographical data (age, gender, years married and years engaged, studies and social class to which they relieve they belong), reasons for being married, sexual behavior (frequency of sexual relations and masturbation) and nine psychometric scales: Dyadic Adjustment Scale (DAS) by Spanier (1976), Relationship Assessment Scale (RAS) by Hendrick (1988), Index of Sexual Dissatisfaction (ISD) by Hudson (1982), Marital Aggrandizement Scale (MAS) by O-Rourke and Cappeliez (2002), Toronto Alexithymia Scale (TAS) by Bagby, Parker and Taylor (1994), Social Desirability Scale (SDS) by Crowne and Marlowe (1960), State-Trait Anxiety Inventory (STAI) by Spielberger, Gorsuch and Lushene (1970), Beck Depression Inventory (BDI) by Beck and Steer (1987), Positive and Negative Affect Scales (PANAS) by Watson, Clark and Tellegen (1988) (See Table 1).

In the samples of husbands and wives treated as independent subjects (n=200) psychometric properties of the scales used are studied. Since all of them were developed in English speaking countries and since they are in English, they were translated by a Spanish-English/English-Spanish double translation procedure, using two experts, with the exception of the State-Trait Anxiety Inventory (STAI) for which the adaptation for the Mexican population by Spielberger and Díaz-Guerrero (1975) was used. For exploratory and confirmatory factor analysis, the number of questions was selected from each scale. On the scale DAS two items were eliminated (29 and 32), and on the MAS two items were also eliminated (13 and 17), on the SDS thirteen items were eliminated (1, 2, 4, 7, 13, 17, 18, 20, 24, 27, 29, 31 and 33), and for the others, all were included (see Table 1).

In this sample (n=200), the psychometric properties of the measure instruments were good. The internal consistency varied from $\alpha$=.75 for the Social Desirability Scale (SDS) to $\alpha$=.93 for the Dyadic Adjustment Scale (DAS). The distributions of the scales defined by the simple sum of items was adjusted to a normal curve based on the Kolmogorov-Smirnov test, with p>.05, except for the Relationship Assessment Scale (RAS) (p=.004), the Index of Sexual Dissatisfaction (ISD), the Beck Depression Inventory (BDI) and the Negative Affect Scale (NA) from the PANAS (see table 1).

**Table 1. Psychometric properties of instruments of measurement**

| Scales | NII | NSI | Alfa | Nor. | Factors |
|---|---|---|---|---|---|
| Dyadic Adjustment Scale (DAS) | 32 | 30 | .93 | Yes .301 | F1 Consensus<br>F2 Satisfaction<br>F3 Cohesion<br>F4 Affectional expression |
| Relationship Assessment Scale (RAS) | 7 | 7 | .80 | No .004 | Marital satisfaction |
| Index of Sexual Dissatisfaction (ISD) | 25 | 25 | .91 | No .014 | F1 Sexual Dissatisfaction with partner<br>F2 Rejection of conjugal sex<br>F3 Sexual avoidance by the partner |
| Marital Aggrandizement Scale (MAS) | 18 | 16 | .78 | Yes .931 | F1 Being in love<br>F2 Arguments |
| Toronto Alexithymia Scale (TAS) | 20 | 20 | .86 | Yes .304 | F1 Difficulty identifying feeling<br>F2 Difficulty describing feeling<br>F3 Externally oriented thinking |
| Social Desirability Scale (SDS) | 33 | 20 | .75 | Yes .173 | F1 Negation of defects<br>F2 Attribution of qualities |
| Trait-Anxiety Inventory (STAI-T) | 20 | 20 | .90 | Yes .689 | Neuroticism |
| State-Anxiety Inventory (STAI-S) | 20 | 20 | .93 | Yes .144 | F1 Anxiety<br>F2 Control |
| Beck Depression Inventory (BDI) | 21 | 21 | .91 | No .003 | Depression-state |
| Positive and Negative Affect Scales (PANAS) | NA 10<br>PA 10 | NA 10<br>PA 10 | NA .88<br>PA .84 | NA .000<br>PA .864 | F1 Negative affect<br>F2 Positive affect |

NII – Number of initial items in the scale. NSI – Number of selected items. Alfa – Cronbach's alfa with standardized items. Nor – Probability of the Kolmogorov-Smirnov's test for the null hypothesis of normality. Factors – Principal axis factoring, rotation by Varimax and/or Oblimin.

## Procedures

The members of each couple answered their questionnaires in separate rooms to avoid any type of communication. The sample was collected between September 2005 and April 2006 and couples were paid for their voluntary participation (200 pesos per couple). The couples were obtained through announcements on publicity posters and the study was financed by a grant of Universidad Autónoma de Nuevo León (PAICYT2005). All questionnaires were prefaced by an informative sheet, in which the confidentiality and anonymity of the answers was guaranteed, ending with a closed question asking whether the subject wanted to be included in the study or not. The time spent on the questionnaire was approximately 70 minutes. An analysis of thematic content was carried out for the definitions given to words associated to the word-stimulus "being married", by creating 15 specific categories and a residual one. The inter-rater reliability for this system of categories was calculated by the percentages of agreement and Cramer's V coefficients between two independent codifiers (Carrillo and Griffens) in a first phase. To improve reliability, definitions were made more precise. Once again inter-rater reliability was calculated, on one hand the two initial codifiers worked together to reach a 100% agreement and they redefined the categories, and on the other hand, an independent evaluator (Moral) worked with the final definition of the categories. The percentages of agreement and Cramer's V coefficients were calculated between the dyad of codifiers and the new evaluator.

Each category was converted into an ordinal variable by way of the weighted sum of the times it was used in the 5 orders of association for each subject, varying from 0 (not used in any association) to 15 (used in all 5 associations). The mean of these ordinary variables is called range of importance (by category). The number of times each category was used in the 5 associations by the set of subjects is called the frequency of use.

To identify the central nucleus and peripheral elements of the social representation, the Vergès procedure (1994) was used, treating the sample as a social group. This is based on the mean of the importance ranges and median of the use frequencies of the semantic categories treated as ordinal variables. The central nucleus is defined by the semantic categories of high frequency of use (>median of frequencies of use) and high importance range (>mean of average ranges). The first periphery is formed by the categories of high frequency of use and low importance range (≤mean of the average ranges). The second periphery was formed by categories of low frequency of use (≤median of frequencies of use) and high importance range. Finally, the third was formed by frequency of low use and low importance range.

A hierarchical cluster analysis was used to define groups of subjects related to the meanings associated to the word-stimulus "being married". The analysis was applied to semantic categories treated as ordinal variables. The squared Euclidean distance was used as the interval measure of proximity and the Ward method as a procedure for grouping subjects.

Differences of frequencies or central tendency between the groups of subjects defined by cluster analysis in regard to socio-demographic variables, reasons of having gotten married, religious variables and psychometric scales were contrasted by Pearson's Chi-square, Kruskal-Wallis' test, analysis of variance; as well as the relationship by the Cramer´s V coefficient and the eta coefficient.

The level of statistical meaning was set with values of p less or equal to .05 and the tendency to the statistical significance was set at values of 0.51 to .099. Calculations were done with SPSS12.

# Results

## Reliability of Content Analysis

On the association test, a spontaneous association of five words was requested for the word-stimulus "being married", then the associated words were placed in order by degree of representative force and each one of them was defined (De Rosa, 1988). After thoroughly reading the content of the definitions given to the associated words, a system of 15 specific semantic categories was created (adaptation, conflicts and violent behaviors, economics, stereotypes and cultural standards, family, children, ideals of marriage, obligations and functions, couple, family patrimony, negative feelings, positive feelings, sexuality, values and attitudes of living together, values of fidelity, trust and respect) and a residual category, using a content analysis of the thematic type. The initial mean percentage of agreement for the total of words in the five associations to the word-stimulus "being married", considering the 16 semantic categories, was 76%, varying from 84% for the words associated in first place to 69% for the words associated in third place. The correlation between the two codifiers, calculated by Cramer's V coefficient, varied from .836 for the words associated in first place to .789 for the words associated in fourth place, with a mean of .815. By category considering its use in 5 associated words, the mean percentage of agreement was 75%, varying from 100% (sexuality and conflicts and violent behaviors) to 47% (stereotypes and cultural standards).

The definition of nine categories was modified to better delimit the information contained in each of them. Inter-rater reliability was once again calculated between the joint correction of the two initial codifiers and a third evaluator. The mean percentage of agreement to the total of words in the five associations was 89%, varying from 92% for the words associated in second place to 88% for the words associated in fourth place. The correlation between codifiers, calculated by Cramer's V coefficient, varied from .951 for the words associated in second place to .912 for the words associated in fourth place, with a mean of .930. Thus, we have a high level of inter-rater reliability. By category considering its use in 5 associated words, the mean percentage of agreement was 89%, varying from 100% for the categories of "sexuality" and "conflicts and violent behaviors" to 77% for "stereotypes and cultural standards". Four categories had percentages under 80%: "cultural stereotypes and standards" (76.92%), "adaptation" (77.78%), "negative feelings" (78.26%) and "family" (78.38%). With redefinition of the categories reliability improved and reached a high level.

## Representation of "Being Married" in the Sample Set

The central nucleus and the three peripheries were defined using Abric's model (1993) and Vergès's analysis procedure (1994). The mean of the importance ranges was .94 and the median of frequency of use was 35. In the central nucleus we have 5 categories (obligations and functions, positive feelings, values of fidelity, trust and respect, couple, values and attitudes of living together), in the first periphery 3 categories appear (ideals of marriage, children, family), in the second periphery no category appears and in the third there are seven categories (economics, negative feelings, family patrimony, adaptation, sexuality, cultural stereotypes and standards, conflicts and violent behaviors) (See figure 1)

## Gender Difference by Semantic Category and Outline of Representation

When comparing the categories dealt with as ordinal variables by gender, the only significant difference is found in the category of economy ($U$=3001, $Z_U$=-4.357, $p$=.000) in which men associated more content to the desire for stability and economic solvency than women.

| Social representation of "being married" | | Range of importance | |
|---|---|---|---|
| | | *≥.94* | *< .94* |
| Frequency of use | *≥ 35.50* | *Central Nucleus*<br>Obligations and functions<br>Positive feelings.<br>Values of fidelity trust and respect.<br>Couple.<br>Values and attitudes of living together. | *First periphery*<br>Ideals of marriage.<br>Children.<br>Family. |
| | *< 35.50* | *Second periphery* | *Third periphery*<br>Economy.<br>Negative feelings.<br>Family patrimony.<br>Adaptation.<br>Sexuality.<br>Cultural Stereotypes and standards.<br>Conflicts and violent behaviors. |

Median of frequency of use = 35.50 and mean of the importance ranges = .94.

Figure 1. Schema of central nucleus and three peripheries of "being married".

There is a tendency to the statistical significance in cultural stereotypes and standards ($U=3653$, $Z_U=-1.921$, $p=.055$), negative feelings ($U=3610$, $Z_U=-1.853$, $p=.064$), as well as in values and attitudes of living together ($U=3354$, $Z_U=-1.840$, $p=.066$). Women tend to associate more content with cultural standards, such as serving her husband, home and children and, at the same time, there are negative feelings of dissatisfaction, boredom and insecurity. Men tend to associate more content on values and attitudes of living together that include unity, understanding, tolerance and patience. If we calculate the mean of the importance ranges and the median of the frequency of use of the categories by gender for defining the central nucleus and the three peripheries for men and women, only two categories are affected. For women, family appears in the first periphery and for men it is in the third periphery; economy appears in the first periphery for men and in the third periphery for women. There is nothing found in the second periphery for any category.

## Cluster Analysis of the 15 Specific Semantic Categories

The 15 specific categories treated as ordinal numbers (from 0 to 15) was introduced in the cluster analysis. The analysis of grouping is done by cases. From the study of the dendrogram, it appears that 4 groups of subjects are defined at a height of between 10 and 15 units, thus the program is requested to classify all of the subjects into 4 groups. These 4 groups are not equivalent to the number of subjects ($\chi2=16.695$, g.l.=3, $p=.001$). The first group has the most subjects and the second group has the fewest subjects.

The groups were then characterized by differences in the average of the 15 specific categories. The groups are named with basis on differential high and low averages. There is significant difference in 8 variables: adaptation (p=.004), economics (p=.026), children (p=.012), ideals of matrimony (p=.040), obligations and functions (p=.000), couple (p=.000), positive feelings (p=.000), values of fidelity (p=.000), as well as values and attitudes of living together (p=.000); and in the same manner the tendency to the statistical significance in one, family patrimony (p=.090) (See Table 2).

**Table 2. Comparison of the central tendency of categories by semantic groups**

| Semantic categories | Group | N | Mean Range | Kruskal-Wallis $\chi 2$ | df | P |
|---|---|---|---|---|---|---|
| Adaptation | 1 | 65 | 97.77 | 13.410 | 3 | .004 |
| | 2 | 29 | 84.71 | | | |
| | 3 | 47 | 85.27 | | | |
| | 4 | 36 | 81.50 | | | |
| Conflicts and violent behavior | 1 | 65 | 91.02 | 2.386 | 3 | .496 |
| | 2 | 29 | 88.50 | | | |
| | 3 | 47 | 89.20 | | | |
| | 4 | 36 | 85.50 | | | |
| Economics | 1 | 65 | 98.29 | 9.287 | 3 | .026 |
| | 2 | 29 | 84.95 | | | |
| | 3 | 47 | 84.80 | | | |
| | 4 | 36 | 80.97 | | | |
| Stereotypes and cultural standards | 1 | 65 | 89.59 | 1.718 | 3 | .633 |
| | 2 | 29 | 89.97 | | | |
| | 3 | 47 | 85.81 | | | |
| | 4 | 36 | 91.32 | | | |
| Family | 1 | 65 | 87.65 | 4.956 | 3 | .175 |
| | 2 | 29 | 94.50 | | | |
| | 3 | 47 | 81.19 | | | |
| | 4 | 36 | 97.21 | | | |
| Children | 1 | 65 | 101.20 | 11.037 | 3 | .012 |
| | 2 | 29 | 78.17 | | | |
| | 3 | 47 | 81.69 | | | |
| | 4 | 36 | 85.24 | | | |
| Ideals of marriage | 1 | 65 | 98.28 | 8.308 | 3 | .040 |
| | 2 | 29 | 79.83 | | | |
| | 3 | 47 | 88.16 | | | |
| | 4 | 36 | 80.72 | | | |
| Obligations and functions | 1 | 65 | 90.53 | 71.624 | 3 | .000 |
| | 2 | 29 | 57.28 | | | |
| | 3 | 47 | 135.14 | | | |
| | 4 | 36 | 51.56 | | | |
| Couple | 1 | 65 | 87.52 | 85.587 | 3 | .000 |
| | 2 | 29 | 155.97 | | | |
| | 3 | 47 | 69.29 | | | |
| | 4 | 36 | 63.47 | | | |

| Semantic categories | Group | N | Mean Range | Kruskal-Wallis | | |
|---|---|---|---|---|---|---|
| | | | | χ2 | df | P |
| *Family patrimony* | 1 | 65 | 88.48 | 6.499 | 3 | .090 |
| | 2 | 29 | 100.59 | | | |
| | 3 | 47 | 86.51 | | | |
| | 4 | 36 | 83.86 | | | |
| Positive feelings | 1 | 65 | 51.87 | 64.320 | 3 | .000 |
| | 2 | 29 | 96.07 | | | |
| | 3 | 47 | 109.54 | | | |
| | 4 | 36 | 123.53 | | | |
| Negative feelings | 1 | 65 | 92.76 | 3.212 | 3 | .360 |
| | 2 | 29 | 87.29 | | | |
| | 3 | 47 | 88.81 | | | |
| | 4 | 36 | 83.83 | | | |
| Sexuality | 1 | 65 | 88.66 | 4.978 | 3 | .173 |
| | 2 | 29 | 94.09 | | | |
| | 3 | 47 | 91.69 | | | |
| | 4 | 36 | 82.00 | | | |
| Values and attitudes of living together | 1 | 65 | 98.78 | 18.790 | 3 | .000 |
| | 2 | 29 | 63.28 | | | |
| | 3 | 47 | 79.00 | | | |
| | 4 | 36 | 105.13 | | | |
| Values of fidelity, trust and respect | 1 | 65 | 81.56 | 65.485 | 3 | .000 |
| | 2 | 29 | 70.26 | | | |
| | 3 | 47 | 68.54 | | | |
| | 4 | 36 | 144.24 | | | |

Groups: 1 – being married because of children, 2 – being married for the company of his/her spouse, 3 – being married for conjugal and family duties, 4 – being married for love.

Group 1. This group includes the greatest number of persons surveyed (65). It has a high average for the categories of children, marriage ideals, economics and adaptation,; low for positive sentiments. It is considered that the basis of marriage is children, the search for balance in the couple, economic solvency, the struggle for an ideal future with stability and harmony, sacrificing or not appreciating positive feelings such as love, affection, and understanding. We can call this "being married because of children".

Group 2. This is the group with the lowest number of subjects (29). It has a high average for the couple and family patrimony; a low average for children, ideals of marriage, obligations and functions, values and attitudes of living together, as well as the values of fidelity, trust and respect. It especially values having a partner and having his/her support, not having economic problems, giving little importance to the role of children, obligations and values of fidelity. We can call this "being married for the company of his/her spouse".

Group 3. This is the second group in order of the number of subjects (47). It has a high average for obligations and functions; a low average for the couple and values of fidelity, trust and respect. The group associates being married to obligations and functions, it gives little importance to the partner's company and to the values of fidelity. We can call this group "being married for conjugal and family duties".

Group 4. This is the third group in the number of subjects (36). It has a high average for positive feelings (love), values and attitudes of living together, as well as the values of fidelity, trust and respect; it has a low average for the couple, obligations and functions, economics and adaptation. It associates being married with positive feelings such as love, fidelity and affection, as well as the values of fidelity, trust, understanding, family company and giving. We can call this "being married for love".

Groups 1 and 4 seem to be the most opposite as far as meaning associated to being married (children, ideals versus positive feelings). At the same time, groups 2 and 3 appear rather opposite (partner versus obligations), although these last two coincide in associating low values to fidelity, trust and respect.

There is a significant difference in the level of studies ($F=6.575$, $p=.000$) (K-W: $\chi2=17.458$, $df=3$, $p=.001$). The difference occurs between the fourth group and the first and third. The highest level of studies appears in the fourth group (being married for love) and the lowest in group 3 (being married for conjugal and family duties), followed by the first group (being married because of children). The association between the level of studies and the four semantic groups estimated by the eta coefficient is .321, thus sharing 10% of the variance.

## Comparisons of Four Semantic Groups in Reasons for Being Married, Sexual Behavior and Psychometric Scales

As the main reason for marriage, 85.5% of the sample indicates love, 5% an unwanted pregnancy, 2% family pressure, 2% physical beauty, 1% loneliness, .5% because they had already given their word and didn't know how to back out, .5% because they wanted to get married and didn't have a better option, .5% because they were embarrassed by his/her insistence and the other 3% gave a different motive from the 9 reasons specified. 6% add that the additional reason was physical beauty, 4.5% because of an unwanted pregnancy, 3.5% because of loneliness, 1% because of family pressure, 1% because he/she had already given his/her word and couldn't back out, 1% another reason different from the 9 reasons specified and .5% because he/she was embarrassed because of the other person's insistence. There is no contingency between the main reason for marriage indicated by the subject and the 4 semantic groups ($\chi2=24.864$, $df=24$, $p=.413$), or any other reason ($\chi2=18.250$, $df=18$, $p=.439$).

The joint sample reported the mean for sexual relations with the spouse on an ordinal scale that ranges from 1 (once a month) to 4 (several times a week) is 3.24, in other words, between at least once a week and several times a week, with a standard deviation of .887. The median for sexual relations is 3 (at least once a week) and the mode is 4 (several times a week) (47% of the sample). 7% of the sample reports having sexual relations with their spouse at least once a month, 9% less than once a month, 37% at least once a week and 47% several times a week. 48% of those surveyed have never masturbated after getting married, 9% once, 22% a few times, 15% several times, 3% quite a few times and 3% many times. The median falls at once, that is to say that the frequency of masturbation is very low. There is no difference in the central tendency of frequency of sexual relations ($\chi2=.526$, $df=3$, $p=.913$) or of masturbation ($\chi2=5.876$, $df=3$, $p=.118$) between the four semantic groups.

Significant differences of means were found in 5 variables (DAS, RAS, IIS, MAS and BDI) and a tendency to the statistical significance was observed in two scales (SDS and STAI-T). Based on the test of Least Significant Difference (LSD), on the Dyadic Adjustment

Scale (DAS), the fourth group has a higher average than the first and second groups; on the Relationship Assessment Scale (RAS), the fourth group has a higher average than the other three groups; on the Index of Sexual Dissatisfaction (ISD) the first group averages higher than the fourth; on the Marital Aggrandizement Scale (MAS), the fourth group averages higher than the other three groups; on the Beck Depression Inventory (BDI), the first group averages higher than the fourth and third groups and the second group averaged higher than the fourth, with the fourth group having the lowest average; on the Scale for Trait-Anxiety (STAI-R), the first groups averages higher than the fourth. The associations estimated by the eta coefficient between the five psychometric variables (DAS, RAS, ISD, MAS and BDI) and the 4 semantic groups are weak and they varied from .307 to .216; that is to say, the percentage of variance shared varied from 9 to 5% (see Table 3).

The fourth group (being married for love) has the highest average for dyadic adjustment, marital satisfaction, marital aggrandizement and social desirability and the lowest average for sexual dissatisfaction, depression and trait-anxiety. The first group (being married because of children) has the lowest average on dyadic adjustment, marital satisfaction and marital aggrandizement, but the highest average for sexual dissatisfaction, trait-anxiety and depression. The second group (being married for the company of his/her spouse) and the third group (being married for conjugal and family duties) are those with the lowest average on social desirability; that is to say, they are more sincere. In trait-anxiety, depression and sexual dissatisfaction, the second is closer to the first; for dyadic adjustment and marital satisfaction, the second group is closest to the fourth (see table 3).

**Table 3. Comparison of the mean on psychometric scales for the 4 semantic groups**

| Psychometric scales | Group | N | Descriptives | | ANOVA | | Eta |
|---|---|---|---|---|---|---|---|
| | | | Mean | S. D. | F | P | |
| DAS | 1 | 65 | 104.64 | 18.720 | 4.950 | .003 | .281 |
| | 2 | 29 | 111.28 | 19.714 | | | |
| | 3 | 47 | 108.41 | 18.644 | | | |
| | 4 | 36 | 119.14 | 16.218 | | | |
| RAS | 1 | 65 | 28.17 | 4.533 | 6.018 | .001 | .307 |
| | 2 | 29 | 29.79 | 4.378 | | | |
| | 3 | 47 | 29.13 | 4.514 | | | |
| | 4 | 36 | 31.92 | 3.434 | | | |
| ISD | 1 | 65 | 66.17 | 23.385 | 2.810 | .041 | .216 |
| | 2 | 29 | 59.41 | 21.437 | | | |
| | 3 | 47 | 58.47 | 19.787 | | | |
| | 4 | 36 | 53.61 | 21.866 | | | |
| MAS | 1 | 65 | 66.06 | 15.066 | 5.499 | .001 | .295 |
| | 2 | 29 | 67.97 | 12.022 | | | |
| | 3 | 47 | 68.19 | 15.040 | | | |
| | 4 | 36 | 77.66 | 12.778 | | | |
| TAS | 1 | 65 | 58.77 | 14.780 | 1.544 | .205 | .161 |
| | 2 | 29 | 53.00 | 16.109 | | | |
| | 3 | 47 | 58.47 | 16.004 | | | |
| | 4 | 36 | 53.06 | 21.044 | | | |

**Table 3. (Continued)**

| Psychometric scales | Group | N | Descriptives | | ANOVA | | Eta |
|---|---|---|---|---|---|---|---|
| | | | Mean | S. D. | F | P | |
| SDS | 1 | 65 | 10.02 | 3.370 | 2.574 | .056 | .207 |
| | 2 | 29 | 9.38 | 4.032 | | | |
| | 3 | 47 | 9.35 | 4.138 | | | |
| | 4 | 36 | 11.58 | 4.588 | | | |
| STAI-S | 1 | 65 | 40.74 | 12.063 | 1.448 | .231 | .156 |
| | 2 | 29 | 40.14 | 14.022 | | | |
| | 3 | 47 | 37.23 | 9.349 | | | |
| | 4 | 36 | 36.47 | 12.314 | | | |
| STAI-T | 1 | 65 | 42.03 | 9.977 | 2.296 | .079 | .196 |
| | 2 | 29 | 39.86 | 11.167 | | | |
| | 3 | 47 | 38.40 | 9.280 | | | |
| | 4 | 36 | 36.64 | 12.502 | | | |
| BDI | 1 | 65 | 13.74 | 10.451 | 3.955 | .009 | .253 |
| | 2 | 29 | 12.31 | 10.991 | | | |
| | 3 | 47 | 9.91 | 7.445 | | | |
| | 4 | 36 | 7.14 | 9.978 | | | |
| PA | 1 | 65 | 31.45 | 8.051 | .443 | .723 | .087 |
| | 2 | 29 | 30.79 | 9.178 | | | |
| | 3 | 47 | 30.79 | 6.975 | | | |
| | 4 | 36 | 32.58 | 6.600 | | | |
| NA | 1 | 65 | 17.25 | 6.459 | .662 | .576 | .107 |
| | 2 | 29 | 16.64 | 7.472 | | | |
| | 3 | 47 | 15.40 | 5.988 | | | |
| | 4 | 36 | 16.50 | 7.980 | | | |

Group: 1 – being married because of children, 2 – being married for the company of his/her spouse, 3 – being married for conjugal and family duties 4 – being married for love.

## DISCUSSION

If we consider that the 100 couples have received socialization in certain similar aspects, because they form part of a culture, are under the influence of the same educational system and mass communication that that frequently talks about a socially relevant topic such as matrimony and what it means to be married, we can talk about a social representation and characterize the same. The central nucleus is represented by meanings such as obligations and functions of the couple and family, positive feelings, values of fidelity, trust and respect, the idea of a primary social structure formed by parents and children, as well as values and attitudes of living together. The most resistant to change and the most defining is the image of a united, happy family struggling for its stability through the values of fidelity, living together in harmony and peace. This representation lacks elements of high frequency of use and low valuation (importance range). For that reason, that which is most present in social communication about being married is given much importance and is considered to be representative.

Peripheral elements of low frequency in use, but which are valued as being representative are long term objectives such as plenitude, well-being and stability, considering children as the basis of marriage, as well as mentioning the rest of the family, such as in-laws or grandparents. The first two elements are clearly implicit in the central nucleus. The last element of first periphery deals with an extended family which is very common within the life of married Mexican couples.

Economy, negative feelings, family patrimony, adaptation, sexuality, stereotypes and cultural standards as well as conflicts and violent behavior are the most peripheral, least mentioned and least representative elements, constituting the third periphery. Thus the most concrete material aspects, negative feelings, violence and sexuality are linked to the couple, but not in a very representative manner and they can be very easily varied.

Specifically, schools, the parishes and mass media transmit this central nucleus of being married, not as the material pleasure of two, but as a social function that must be kept separate from problems and difficulties. It must have good feelings and children play a very important role.

Upon considering the gender comparison in the four semantic groups as well as the 15 specific categories of the meanings associated with "being married", a significant difference was found in the category of economics, since men associate more content to the desire of stability and economic solvency than women. Pacheco (2001), when talking about the myth of secretaries in Mexican culture mentions that women inevitably renounce their personal projects and submit themselves to their husbands and children, to dedicate themselves solely to domestic tasks. Fernández-Perera (2001), upon confronting the "macho" myth and male chauvinism in Mexican culture, indicates that the role of men is based on authoritarianism, physical and moral violence, labor superiority, power in the family and on many other areas; it continues to be the man who exercises his authority according to models imposed by machismo. The role of men and women is determined by society and for this reason, as time has passed, men are seen as the only ones in charge of the household economy and women are envisioned as those who serve the home; as someone who subjects herself to the interest of those who surround her in the role of domestic service and maternal care, and it is not her responsibility to guarantee the economic solvency of the family. Díaz-Guerrero (2003) speaks of the socio-cultural premises of the roles assigned to men and women in our society; among the premises it is mentioned that men are by nature superior to women, that men must always wear the pants in the family, that a woman's place is in the home, and that men must possess all of the power and women all of the love. However, between the associations and their definitions no markedly male chauvinist discourse is observed. The way the subjects surveyed express themselves is more subtle and perhaps implies the usual content of that discourse.

A tendency to the statistical significance was found in the categories of cultural stereotypes and standards, negative feelings, as well as for values and attitudes of living together. Alegría (2005) mentions that since childhood women learn all of the activities that are assigned to their gender and they know that they must assimilate them so that as they grow they conform to accepted feminine ideals and, in this manner, the role given women is consolidated.

Women tend to more greatly associate the content of cultural standards, such as being at their husband's service, the house and children, as well as negative feelings of dissatisfaction, boredom and insecurity to marriage, while men tend to associate the content of values and attitudes of living together as union, understanding, tolerance and patience. Some anthropologists, such as Anastassiou and Pantoja (1998), indicate that the transmission of cultural standards is a role traditionally linked to breeding and women, and from this her key role in conserving the culture of the group is derived; this role is even reflected in the tendency for women to associate more traditional standards to marriage, as well as to the topics of the home and children than men. On the other hand, the tendency in differences concerning negative feelings that are more important for women and values of living together that are more important for men may be attributed to the dynamics of some married couples, reflected in literature and in popular humor such as "el mandilón" (the male weakling), in which complaints and dissatisfaction are found to form a part of the role of the woman, linked to the house, and the request of living together in peace in the man who is usually the object of these complaints and reproaches. Although there is no difference in the composition of the 4 groups by gender, if we observe percentages, there are more men in group 1 (being married because of children), 40% men in comparison to 33% women; and there are more women in the third group (being married for conjugal and family duties), 31% women in comparison to 22% of men. The lack of the sentiments of love and the justification of being married because of children seems to be more common among men and the duties as a spouse and as caretaker of the house are more common among women. This could give us some idea of the underlying the dynamic previously indicated concerning complaining wife and requesting husband.

When comparing the reason for being married, the majority of subjects place love in the first place, and there is no difference in this between the 4 semantic groups; however, there is a difference in educational level. This is highest in the fourth group (married because of love) and lowest in the third (being married for conjugal and family duties). This can indicate that the reason for being married is similar in all groups, love, but the dynamics of living together generates a differential valuation. People with more education continue to place weight on love above all and the persons with a lower level of education place more social value on spousal and family duties. It seems that people with a lower level of education assume more social values and customary duties and people with a higher level of education are more critical and they have a more individualistic orientation, favoring the personal dimension of love and not placing as much importance on the social dimension of children and the family. Precisely, the group that did not finish primary school has a significantly larger average number of children (between 3 and 4 children ($F=3.724$, $p=.000$) than subjects with high school, technical studies and college studies (between 1 and 2 children).

The frequency of sexual relations is high, 84% have sexual relations once a week; in addition, this is the same for the four groups. Thus, having sex with their spouse is important for Mexican couples and the meanings attributed to marriage are not of importance in this area. We must consider that the sexual act is the nearest form of bodily intimacy and it is very difficult to tolerate this when there is rejection and indifference. Based on the scores on the Index of Sexual Dissatisfaction, 70% of those surveyed stated that they were sexually satisfied and in the sample there was no case of sexual abuse (Moral, in the press). Thus it appears that there is intimate and satisfying sex. Those who state that they are married for love (group 4) report the greatest sexual satisfaction and those who state that they are married because of children (group 1) have the least sexual satisfaction, thus feelings of love and positive feelings in general play a key role in enjoying sexual relations. At the same time, marital adjustment and satisfaction follow the same relationship. These results confirm that found in neurobiological studies on the bond and sexuality (Gonzaga, Turner, Keltner, Campos and Altemus, 2006).

When comparing the 4 semantic groups, a significant difference was found in the mean for the following variables: Dyadic Adjustment Scale (DAS), Relationship Assessment Scale (RAS), Marital Aggrandizement Scale (MAS), Beck Depression Inventory (BDI), Index of Sexual Dissatisfaction (ISD) and a tendency to the statistical significance for the Social Desirability Scale (SDS) and in the State-Trait Anxiety Inventory (STAI). These differences allow us to better describe the semantic groups and complement the information supplied by differences in semantic categories, which were developed from definitions given to the words associated to the word-stimulus "being married".

Group 1 "being married because of children" is the largest group surveyed and this may best represent the majority of marriages in Nuevo León. From the semantic categories, the subjects in this group are characterized by considering that the basis of marriage is children, by searching for balance in the couple and economic solvency, by struggling for an ideal future with stability and harmony, by sacrificing positive feelings. These subjects place less value on the relationship (RAS), show dissatisfaction with the couple (DAS) and report less sexual enjoyment or satisfaction (ISD). They have the highest level of trait-anxiety with characteristics such as nervousness, tension, preoccupation and restlessness. They have the highest average on the depression scale, showing pessimism, low self-esteem, lack of motivation and somatic problems. They tend to attribute socially desirable characteristics to themselves and deny those that are not approved by society; however, this is the group that reports the lowest level of marital aggrandizement. Thus, their distortion in their self-report is a personal evaluation, not an evaluation as a couple.

Group 2 "being married for the company of his/her spouse" is the group with the lowest number of subjects. From the semantic categories, the subjects in this group are characterized as placing importance on having a spouse and counting on his/her support, as lacking economic problems, and placing little value on the role of the children, obligations and fidelity. From the differences in the scales, the group shows marital adjustment, that is, the best process of adaptation to living together as a couple, in which consensus, satisfaction, cohesion and affectional expression are the predominant characteristics. Even with the second highest average for marital adjustment, the group also presents traits of anxiety and depression, such as pessimism, somatic preoccupation, nervousness, tension, restlessness, melancholy, despair and feelings of incapacity. The group has a low score on marital aggrandizement and social desirability, which indicates that they do not try to aggrandize the image of the couple, or give false information or deny their socially disapproved characteristics.

Group 3, "being married for conjugal and family duties" is characterized by associating marriage to obligations and functions, placing little importance on the company of the spouse and on values of fidelity. The subjects in this group show a slight tendency to falsify information in a socially desirable sense and to deny characteristics that are socially disapproved; however, they are characterized by aggrandizing the image of the couple. Even when it is a group with little marital adjustment and satisfaction, it is the group that enjoys sex the most and they are free from anxiety and depression.

Group 4 "being married for love" associates being married with positive feelings such as the values of fidelity, trust, respect, understanding, family companionship and giving. This group shows the best marital adjustment, in other words, the best adaptation process for living together as a couple where consensus, satisfaction, cohesion and affectional expression are predominant characteristics as well as sexual enjoyment and satisfaction. There is a lower rate of depressive symptoms and anxiety. They tend to aggrandize the image of the couple and give their own information in a socially desirable sense.

When comparing the 4 groups with the social representation of being married, we find interesting differences. The fourth group, the one reporting more happiness and satisfaction, is the one that is most similar to the social representation. This group stands out because of its positive feelings, especially, love, values of fidelity and living together, as well as low levels of negative emotions. The next group closest to the central nucleus of representation is the third group that gives most weight to family duties and functions. It is a group with sexual satisfaction but not as much marital satisfaction. The second group, the least numerous one, is the one furthest from the central nucleus; it values the spouse as company, seeks economic stability and it is the one that least associates contents related to children, to the values of fidelity and obligations; it is second in the quality of adjustment. The first is the most numerous; it is most defined by elements of low frequency of use, but the central weight (first periphery), such as considering children to be the basis of marriage, associating future objectives to be carried out and stability; giving importance to economic stability and giving less importance to positive feelings; it shows low satisfaction and high levels of negative emotional states (anxiety and depression). When a group is closer to the central nucleus of the representation, there is more adjustment, satisfaction, happiness and fewer negative feelings. However, when a group is further away from the central nucleus, this does not imply less adjustment and more negative feelings. It is the accentuation of the role of children taking importance away from positive feelings that generates worse adjustment and more negative feelings and this is the position of the biggest group, which represents to one third of the sample.

The most important predictor of dyadic adjustment in this sample is marital aggrandizement, which can be understood more as a bias in self-reports (O'Rourke and Cappeliez 2002), as a way of facing marital difficulties, close to the feeling of being in love with characteristics of idealizing qualities and denying problems (Moral, in the press). Precisely, group 4 (being married for love), the group most adjusted and satisfied with the relationship, is the one with the highest average in marital aggrandizement and social desirability. On the contrary, group 1 (being married because of children) is the least adjusted and satisfied with the spouse and it is the group with the lowest average in marital aggrandizement, but this is not so for social desirability, where it has the second highest average. Thus marital aggrandizement and social desirability are two different constructs; their correlation is .39, sharing only 15% of the variance.

The trans-sectional nature of the design, the lack of comparison groups and complementary methods for collecting data different from the test of free association in relation to the word-stimulus "being married" are limitations in this study that must be noted. All of this data (longitudinal, comparative and multi-method) would enrich the interpretation and allow going deeply into the representation of marriage.

In conclusion, the central nucleus of the social representation of being married is comprised of obligations and functions of the couple and family, positive feelings with an emphasis on love, the values of fidelity, trust and respect, the idea of a primary social structure formed by parents and children, as well as values and attitudes of living together, in other words, the image of a united, happy family that struggles for its stability through the values of fidelity and living together in harmony and peace. Four groups can be defined by cluster analysis. The most numerous group is the one that justifies being married because of children. This is contrasted to the group that attributes being married because of love. A third group emphasizes the company of the spouse and a fourth group associates being married with conjugal and domestic duties. The group characterized as being married for love is closest to the nucleus of the social representation and it reports the most dyadic adjustment and marital satisfaction. The group furthest from the central nucleus of representation is the one that indicates that they are married because of the company of the spouse, but the group that is most dissatisfied and most poorly adjusted is the one that is married because of children. The 4 groups differ in their levels of education. The highest educational level appears in the group that states that it is married because of love and the lowest level of education is found in the group that emphasized that they are married for conjugal and family duties. It appears that people with more studies accentuate the personal dimension of affect and the people with fewer studies stand out the social dimension as family duties. So people with fewer studies have more children. In regard to gender differences men associate the guarantee of economic solvency more than women, which emphasizes that the traditional role of the male as the provider is still present in Mexican social thought.

From these results it would be interesting for future investigations to analyze speeches on marriage and about being married in schools, parishes and in mass communication to compare similarities and differences, as well as to complete data with an open question survey concerning life as a couple in order to further explore diverse elements of the representation. It would also be interesting to compare the results with other populations as Mexican indigenous people and with the children of Mexican immigrants residing in foreign countries as the United State of America.

## REFERENCES

Abric, J. C. (1993). Central system, peripheral system: Their functions and roles in the dynamics of social representations. *Papers on social representation*, *2*, 267-275.

Abric, J. C. (2003). La recherche du noyau central et de la zone muette des représentations sociales. In J. C. Abric (ed.), *Méthodes d'étude des représentations sociales* (pp. 59-80). Ramonville Saint Agne, Francia: Editions érès.

Alegría, J. (2005). La sexualidad de la mexicana. In R. Bartra (ed.), *Anatomía del mexicano* (pp. 273-280). México: Debolsillo.

Anastassiou, I. and Pantoja, C. (1998). Rol de la mujer del Siglo XXI. *Corriente de opinión*, *1*, 1-6.

Bagby, R. M., Parker, J. D. A. and Taylor, G. J. (1994). The twenty-item Toronto alexithymia scale-I. Item selection and cross-validation of the factor structure. *Journal of Psychosomatic Research*, *38*(1), 23-32.

Beck, A. T. and Steer, R. A. (1987). *Beck Depression Inventory manual.* San Antonio, TX: The Psychological Corporation, Harcourt Brace Jovanovich.

Casado, E. (2001). La teoría de las representaciones sociales. In E. Casado and S. Calonge, *Conocimiento social y sentido común* (pp. 55-105). Caracas: Fondo editorial de humanidades y educación, Universidad Central de Venezuela.

Crowne, D. P. and Marlowe, D. (1960). A new scale of social desirability independent of psychopathology. *Journal of Consulting Psychology*, *24*, 349-354.

De Rosa, A. M. (1988). Sur l'usage des associations libres dans l'étude des représentations sociales de la maladie mentale. *Connexions*, *51*(1), 27-50.

Díaz-Guerrero, R. (2003). *Bajo las garras de la cultura: Psicología del mexicano 2.* México: Trillas.

Fernández-Perera, M. (2001). El macho y el machismo. In E. Florescano (ed.), *Los mitos mexicanos* (pp. 231-238). México: Taurus.

Flament, C. and Rouquette, M. L. (2003). *Anatomie des idées ordinaires. Comment étudier les représentations sociales*. París, Francia: Armand Colin.

Gonzaga, G. C., Turner, R. A., Keltner, D., Campos, B. and Altemus, M. (2006). Romantic love and sexual desire in close relationships. *Emotion*, 6, 163-179.

Hendrick, S. S. (1988). A generic measure of relationship satisfaction. *Journal of Marriage and the Family*, *50*, 93-98.

Herrera, B., Weisser, B. and Salazar, D. (2004). Imágenes y conceptos de familia expresados en las representaciones sociales de mujeres de sectores urbano- populares de la ciudad de Temuco, Chile. *Limite (Arica).* Retrieved on July 26, 2007 en http://aridaterra.uta.cl/scielo.php?script=sci_arttextandpid=S0718-13612004001100001andlng=esandnrm=iso.

Hudson, W. W. (1982). *The clinical measurement package: A field manual.* Chicago: Dorsey.

Instituto Nacional de Estadística, Geografía e Informática (INEGI) (2005). *Estadísticas Vitales del Estado de Nuevo León*. México: INEGI.

Montecino, S. (1996). Identidades de género en América Latina: Mestizajes, sacrificios y simultaneidades. *Persona y Sociedad. Identidad, modernidad, posmodernidad en América Latina, 10*(1), 162-173.

Moral, J. (in the press). Predicción del ajuste diádico en una muestra Nuevoleonesa. *Revista Interamericana de Psicología*.

Moscovici, S. (1961). *La psychanalyse, son image et son public*. París: Presses Universitaires de France.

Moscovici, S. (1988). Notes towards a description of social representations. *European Journal of Social Psychology, 18,* 211-250.

O'Rourke, N. and Cappeliez, P. (2002). Development and validation of a couples measure of biased responding: The Marital Aggrandizement Scale. *Journal of Personality Assessment*, *78*, 301-320.

Ortega, M. E. (2006). La complejidad de un rostro. Representación social de la pobreza: un estudio comparativo intercultural. *Trayectorias*, *8*(20-21), 152-162.

Pacheco, C. (2001). Las secretarias. In E. Florescano (ed.), *Los mitos mexicanos* (pp. 387-391). México: Taurus.

Perrone, R (2006). Gloria y miseria de la pareja. *Perspectivas sistémicas*, *93*, 10-20.

Rodríguez-Salazar, T. (2001). *Las razones del matrimonio, representaciones, relatos de vida y sociedad.* Guadalajara: Editorial de la Universidad de Guadalajara.

Spanier, G. B. (1976). Measuring dyadic adjustment: New scales for assessing the quality of marriage and similar dyads. *Journal of Marriage and the Family*, *38*, 15-28.

Spielberger, C. D. and Díaz-Guerrero, R. (1975). *IDARE. Inventario de Ansiedad: Rasgo-Estado*. México: El Manual Moderno.

Spielberger, C. D., Gorsuch, R. L. and Lushene, R. E. (1970). *STAI. Manual for the State-Trait Anxiety Inventory (Self-evaluation questionnaire)*. Palo Alto: Consulting Psychologists Press.

Vergès, P. (1994). Approche du noyau central: propriétés quantitatives et structurales. In Ch. Guimelli (ed.), *Structures et transformations des représentations sociales* (pp. 233-253). Ginebra: Délacheux et Niestlé.

Watson, D., Clark, L. and Tellegen, A. (1988). Development and validation of brief measures of positive and negative affect: The PANAS scales, *Journal of Personality and Social Psychology*, *54*, 1063-1070.

In: Hispanic Psychology Yearbook Volume 1
Ed: Cirilo H. García pp. 77-85
ISBN: 978-1-60741-786-6


*Chapter 6*

# STRESS-RELATED SITUATIONS AS PREDICTORS OF ADHERENCE-TO-MEDICATION BEHAVIOR AMONG WOMEN WITH TYPE 2 DIABETES*

***Julio Alfonso Piña López*[1] *and***
***Angélica Magali Torres Plancarte*[2]**
[1]Hermosillo, México
[2]Universidad de Sonora, México

## ABSTRACT

This cross-sectional study was carried out with the main objective to assess the specific role of stress-related situations as predictors of adherence-to-medication behavior in 225 women with type 2 diabetes living in Hermosillo, Mexico, whom responded to a self-administered questionnaire evaluating stress-related situations in three modalities: making decision, tolerance to ambiguity, and tolerance to frustration. A multiple regression analysis (stepwise method) was performed to identify which of those situations predicted the adherence-to-medication behavior. This analysis showed that the stress-related situation in the modality of making decision was a predictor for adherence-to-medication behavior ($F$ [1, 207] = 6.041; $p$ = 0.015). The results point out that experiencing low levels of stress related to making decision facilitate the practice of adherence-to-medication behavior in women with type 2 diabetes and also support the recommendation to monitor psychological well-being related to experiencing stress in patients with type 2 diabetes.

**Keywords:** Stress, adherence, diabetes, psychological well-being.

---

* A version of this chapter was also published in the *International Hispanic Psychology Journal, Volume 1 Issue 1*, published by Nova Science Publishers, Inc. It was submitted for appropriate modification in an effort to encourage wider dissemination of research.

[1]Address for correspondence: Guillermo Prieto 18. Col. Constitución. Hermosillo, Sonora. C. P. 83150 (México). Tel: (+52+662) 215-6850. E-mail: ja_pina@hotmail.com.

## RESUMEN

Este estudio transversal se llevó acabo con el objetivo principal de evaluar el papel específico de las situaciones relacionadas con el estrés como predictoras de la conducta de la adherencia al medicamento en 225 mujeres con diabetes tipo 2, las cuales vivían en Hermosillo, México, y que respondieron un cuestionario auto-administrado, el cual evaluaba las situaciones relacionadas con el estrés en tres modalidades: toma de decisiones, tolerancia a la ambigüedad y tolerancia a la frustración. Se usó el análisis de regresión múltiple (método stepwise) para identificar cuál de estas situaciones predecía el comportamiento de adherencia al medicamento. Este análisis mostró que la situación relacionada con el estrés en la modalidad de toma de decisiones fue un predictor de la conducta de adherencia al medicamento ($F [1, 207] = 6.041$; $p = 0.015$). Los resultados indican que experimentar bajo niveles de estrés relacionado con la toma de decisiones facilita el comportamiento de la práctica de la adherencia al medicamento en mujeres con diabetes tipo 2 y también apoyan la recomendación de monitorear el bienestar psicológico relacionado con la experimentación del estrés en pacientes con diabetes tipo 2.

*Palabras clave:* Estrés, adherencia, diabetes, bienestar psicológico.


## INTRODUCTION

In Mexico, Type 2 diabetes is a chronic disease that has been reached epidemic proportions (Landeros, 2000). For its effective control and in order to avoid health complications, it is necessary to promote that patients with diabetes get involved in a set of adherence behaviors in accordance with the instructions provided by the health team, that includes doing exercise, a balanced diet, self-monitoring of blood glucose, and taking medication as prescribed (Ortiz and Ortiz, 2005; Snowling and Hopkins, 2006; Wen, Sheperd and Porchman, 2004).

Based in the evidence available, patients with diabetes are not practicing those behaviors as expected (Cramer, 2004; DiMatteo, 2004; Hill-Briggs, Gary, Bone, Hill, Levine and Brancarti, 2005; Maddigan, Feeny, Majundar, Farris and Johnson, 2006). Particularly in Mexico it was found that in a study conducted in a Major Hospital of Mexico City with 150 patients with type 2 diabetes, the percentage of adherence to the pharmacologic treatment was 54.2% (Hernández-Ronquillo, Téllez-Zenteno, Garduño-Espinosa and González-Aceves, 2003), whereas in another two studies conducted in a University Hospital of Monterrey City with 94 patients (Samaniego and Álvarez, 2006) and in a Family Medicine Unit of Chihuahua City with 79 patients (Durán-Varela, Rivera-Chavira and Franco-Gallego, 2001), the percentage of taking medication as prescribes was 55% y 63%, respectively.

In a attempt to account for the adherence-to-treatment behaviors in people diabetes mellitus, some authors has been found that experiencing stress is a variable which adversely affect the instrumental exercise of these behaviors (Garay-Sevilla, Malacara, González-Contreras, Wróbel-Zasada, Wróbel-Kaczmarczyk and Gutiérrez-Roa, 2000; Lloyd, Smith and Weinger, 2005). Stress is a variable traditionally defined as reaction or momentary state (Surwit, Feinglos and Schneider, 1992), as well as relationship or transaction (Lazarus and Folkman, 1984; Ortiz, 2006), but in any case appealing to a private processes of cognitive nature —e.g., beliefs, thinking, evaluations, and so on— that suppose later influence how people behaving.

With base in the experimental tradition (Kelley, 1985; Levine, 1985; Moberg 1985), in this paper stress is defined as a biological condition that people experiencing in a interactive situation in which it is key the duration and influence of uncertainly, unpredictability, and ambiguity associated to signal events and consequences produced by behaviors (Ribes, 1990). Such situations, in agreement with a psychological model for the research of the adherence behaviors (Piña and Sánchez-Sosa, 2007), keep a narrow conceptual relation with which in traditional literature it is known like personality (Ribes and Sanchez, 1990), defined as consistent ways of interaction; this is, constitute the unique, singular and idiosyncratic way which a person faces a situation which it makes contact for the first time with this one. It is role is modulating the opportunity, speed and precision of the behaviors as opposed to a situation in which criteria are not prescribed on how there is to respond. Like such, the stress-related situations do not identify with actions or particular behaviors, but with sets or collections of behaviors that affect the operation of the different biological subsystems, which they include the endocrine, immune, cardiovascular systems, among others.

In order to understand the psychological mechanism underlying adherence-to-treatment behaviors (Sánchez-Sosa, 2002), this cross-sectional study carried out with the main objective of evaluating the effects of stress-related situations on adherence-to-medication behavior of taking an oral hypoglycemic agent or injecting insulin.

# METHOD

## Participants

Previous authorization of the Research and Ethics Committees of the Regional Hospital No. 2 (Mexican Institute of Social Security in Hermosillo, México), this cross-sectional study was conducted between September 2006 and February 2007. All patients in this study were diagnosed with type 2 diabetes by the endocrinology specialist, who later sends them to a different Family Medicine Units of the same institution for attention and following. The study sample was limited to a disponibility of the participants in each one of two Family Medicine Units.

The inclusion criteria considered for this study were: a) being female with diagnosis of type 2 diabetes; b) being more than 18 years of age; and c) showing adequate physical and psychological capacity to answer questions. The definitive sample included 225 patients women, with an average age of 56.5 years (SD = 11.41), most of which were married (68.9%), and (71.5%) were six to ten years of education; the rest of socio-demographic and clinical characteristics of the sample as can seen in Table 1.

Then, each participant was asked for informed consent using a brief document where the aims of this study were described. Immediately after this participants were asked to respond a self-administered scale and additionally instructions were offered to them about how to respond to it.

**Table 1. Socio-demographic characteristics of the sample**

| Variables | X | SD | Range | N | % |
|---|---|---|---|---|---|
| Age | 56.56 | 11.41 | 28-84 | | |
| Evolution time of diagnosis | 107.30 | 79.41 | 2-468 | | |
| Glucose level | 174.54 | 78.97 | 10-568 | | |
| Single | | | | 8 | 3.6 |
| Married | | | | 155 | 68.9 |
| Living as Married | | | | 5 | 2.2 |
| Separated | | | | 19 | 8.4 |
| Widowed | | | | 34 | 15.1 |
| Non response | | | | 4 | 1.8 |
| Education | | | | | |
| Non education | | | | 12 | 5.3 |
| Primary uncomplete | | | | 57 | 25.3 |
| Primary complete | | | | 104 | 46.2 |
| Secondary uncomplete | | | | 1 | 0.4 |
| Secondary complete | | | | 44 | 19.6 |
| Non response | | | | 7 | 3.1 |
| Activities | | | | | |
| Home | | | | 96 | 42.7 |
| Retired/Pensioned | | | | 51 | 22.7 |
| Working for Government | | | | 27 | 12.0 |
| Working for Private Company | | | | 22 | 9.8 |
| Own business | | | | 22 | 9.8 |
| Unemployed | | | | 2 | 0.9 |
| Non response | | | | 5 | 2.2 |

## Variables and Self-Administered Questionnaire

As dependent variable a question related to medication behavior of taking an oral hypoglycemic agent or injecting insulin was used. The question is in a Likert type format with four answer options, from 1 (no day of the week) to 4 (every day of the week). As independent variable the *Stress-Related Situations Scale (SRSS-12)* was used (Piña, Corrales, Valencia and Mungaray, 2006). Originally the scale was developed and validated in people diagnosed with HIV from a similar geographic and cultural background as the participants in the sample for this study. In order to be used with type 2 diabetes patients, the scale was adaptated to reflect situations relevant to these patients. Estimation of the coefficient Cronbach's alpha showed a value of 0.833 for the adaptated form. The scale consists of twelve questions grouped in three stress-related situations. Each question was evaluated in a ten-point scale, where 1 (it is not a threatening situation) to 10 (it is a threatening situation):

*Making decision* is a situation in which a person is facing two or more situations, or the same situation with two or more simultaneous conditions than: a) they demand an option and the person perceives the demand; b) who demands an option and the person does not perceive the demand, and c) the person perceives a nonexistent demand; a question example was the following one: "In this moment you are receiving medical treatment and your physician give to you several instructions that you must to complete, but other close persons recommend to you an alternative treatment (e.g., naturist medicine). Then, this is for you...".

*Tolerance to ambiguity*, is a situation in which exists a demand to which the person responds, but there is not correspondence between the demand and the consequences of their behavior, because: a) these are independent; b) there are changes in the demand, and c) they become antagonistic or they become unforeseeable; a question example was the following one: "Your are under medical treatment but you don't know if this will be effective to control the disease. Then, this if for you...".

*Tolerance to the frustration*, is a situation characterized because a person develops some activity and the consequences associated to the behavior: a) are minors; b) are delayed; c) are not granted; d) are retires without reason, and e) a greater execution is demanded to the person; a question example was the following one: "Your are under medical treatment and you practicing all behaviors as prescribed by your physician, but you do not receive positive consequences or support. Then, this is for you..."

## Statistical Analysis

For statistical analysis the SPSS package for Windows, version 12.0, was used. To data analysis descriptive statistic were obtained; a $x^2$ test was used to prove differences between adherent and nonadherents; an index for each factor was calculated; finally a multiple regression analysis (stepwise method) was used to identify which of the stress-related situations predicted adherence-to-medication behavior.

# RESULTS

201 (89.3%) participants responded that they consumed the medication all days of the week —100% adherents—, and 23 (10.7%) some or none day of the week —nonadherents in some level— ($x^2$ = 141,446, 1 FD; p = 0.000). Table 2 reports the global indexes for the three factors: making decision (X = 4.07; range 3-30), tolerance to ambiguity (X = 4.88; range 3-28), and tolerance to frustration (X = 11.4; range 6-50). The mean values for each factor was low, close to the waited values in making decision, as well as tolerance to ambiguity, but not in tolerance to frustration, in which the mean value was slightly high.

**Table 2. Mean values of stress-related situations**

| Variables | X | SD | Observed rank | Possible rank |
|---|---|---|---|---|
| Making decision | 4.07 | 3.66 | 3-30 | 3-30 |
| Tolerance to ambiguity | 4.88 | 4.61 | 3-28 | 3-30 |
| Tolerance to frustration | 11.40 | 7.98 | 6-50 | 6-60 |

Finally, as can seen in Table 3, the regression analysis (stepwise method) showed that only one type of stress-related situation in the modality of making decision predicted the adherence-to-medication behavior, with the ANOVA test being significant (F [1, 209] = 6.150; p = 0.014). The explained variance for the joint model was 0.269, meaning that that variable explaining alone 26.9% of the total variance.

**Table 3. Multiple regression analysis (stepwise method) of the adherence-to-medication behavior in women with type 2 diabetes (n = 225)**

| Step 1: | | *t* | P |
|---|---|---|---|
| Constant | | 59.914 | 0.000 |
| Making decision | -0.150 | -1.931 | 0.055 |
| Tolerance to ambiguity | -0.022 | -0.253 | 0.800 |
| Tolerance to frustration | -0.025 | -0.305 | 0.761 |
| **Step 2:** | | | |
| Constant | | 60.274 | 0.000 |
| Making decision | -0.156 | -2.124 | 0.035 |
| Tolerance to ambiguity | -0.034 | -0.463 | 0.644 |
| **Step 3:** | | | |
| Constant | | 76.012 | 0.000 |
| Making decision | -0.169 | -2.480 | 0.014 |

# Discussion

The practice of adherence behaviors in patients with type 2 diabetes can be modulate by psychological and social variables that includes stress, depression and lack of perceived social support (Fisher, Skaff, Mullan, Arean, Mohr, Masharani, Glasgow and Laurencin, 2007; Glasgow and Toobert, 1988; Lin, Olvera, Katon, Ciechanowsli, Von Korff, Ludman et al., 2004; Polonsly, Anderson, Lohrer, Welch, Jacobson, Aponte and Schwartz, 1995). In this study, most of the patients mentioned that they practiced the medication-to-adherence behavior in a consistent way, which what was predicted by one stress-related situation in it is making decision modality.

To speak of making decision supposes to face situations, as much of daily life as other specific related to the disease and the treatment in himself, which the patients evaluate like potentially disturbing. Whereas making decision is a psychological process, when a patient chooses to consume or not the medication, not only depend of the information available, as well as of it is own competential resources to actually translate this information in competent adherence behaviors (Piña and Sánchez-Sosa, 2007). If it is considered that the mean score obtained by the patients of this sample in the index was of 4.07, a possible rank of 3 to 30 points, in general terms can be assured that this group of patients does not perceive experiencing stress at the time of making decisions with relation to the medication-consumption behavior. Thus, if patients do not perceive or experiencing stress, there is a high probability to the patients adjusts to the requirements imposed by the situation, practicing the medication-consumption behavior in a consistent as well as efficient way.

Although in this study did not evaluate the information level on the disease and treatment, we can suppose that the patients of this study have the necessary and sufficient information on both aspects, which to seem facilitate the correct making decision process and to practice the adherence behaviors in a competent way (Miller and Drotar, 2003, 2005). However, this must be taking with caution because it would be necessary to point out that of the total of patients, only 71 (31.6%) maintenance his glucose level in blood below 200 Mmol/L, which constitutes, along with glycated hemoglobin, two of the health measures for validate the adherence behaviors (Gómez, Zuñiga, García de León and Couttolenc, 2002; Lerman-Garber, Barrón-Uribe, Calzada-León, Mercado-Atri, Vidal-Tamayo, Quintana et al., 2003). In effect, in other studies have been commented on how, even though patients with type 2 diabetes of both sexes reported that they are 100% adherent-to-treatment, in many occasions the results provided by the traditional clinical measures do not seem to correspond directly with the practice of adherence behaviors (Hill-Briggs et al, 2005; Pladevall, Williams, Potts, Divine, Xi and Lafata, 2004; Stys and Kulkarni, 2007).

Despite of the results presented here and of the previous considerations, it is necessary to mention several limitations in our study. First, because one worked with a sample by availability of two family medicine units of an institution of social security, it is possible that by the own characteristics of the participants there has been a slant in the selection of the sample. Second, before the absence of two of the other clinical measures —glycated haemoglobin and blood pressure, mainly—, we cannot to go beyond which the data say by single himself; that is to say, that in terms of self-report most of the participants are adherents to the medical treatment. Finally and in relation to the previous point, the possibility than an over report actually of the evaluated behavior here was occurred.

Because the studies on stress and it is relation with the adherence behaviors in patients with diabetes diagnosis mellitus type 2 have been demonstrated contradictory results, as much in which it does to the "sort" of stress which they consider like a his measurement and the evaluation of his effects on the adherence behaviors and the operation of the endocrine system in individual (Lloyd et al., 2005), it will be necessary to conduct other studies in which along with the instruments use we evaluate other measures —pill count or self-record—, with the additional objective to eliminate the sources of error attributable to the instruments (Asimakopoulou and Hampson, 2005).

Additionally it will be necessary to fulfill two more tasks, one of which include working with a one more representative sample, incorporating for this intention to people with diabetes of both sexes of other two institutions of social security, and to consider the inclusion of other clinical measures, specifically glycated hemoglobin and blood pressure, with the main objective to demonstrate if in the continuous of interaction the consistent and efficient practice of the adherence behaviors influence on decisive way those clinical measures, and consequently, on the operation of the endocrine system (e.g., Baum and Posluszny, 1999; Gonder-Frederick, Cox and Ritterband, 2002).

## REFERENCES

Asimakopoulou, K. G., and Hampson, S. E. (2005). Biases in self-reports of self-care behaviours in type 2 diabetes. *Psychology, Health and Medicine, 10,* 305-315.

Baum, A. and Posluszny, D.M. (1999). Health psychology: Mapping biobehavioral contributions to health and illness. *Annual Review of Psychology, 50,* 137-163.

Cramer, J. A. (2004). A systematic review of adherence with medications for diabetes. *Diabetes Care, 27,* 1218-1224.

DiMatteo, M. R. P. (2004). Variations in patients' adherence to medical recommendations: a quantitative review of 50 years of research. *Medicine Care, 42,* 200-209.

Durán-Varela, B. R., Rivera-Chavira, B., and Franco-Gallego, E. (2001). Pharmacological therapy compliance in diabetes [In Spanish]. *Salud Pública de México, 43,* 233-236.

Fisher, L., Skaff, M. M., Mullan, J. T., Arean, P., Mohr, D., Masharani, U., Glasgow, R., and Laurencin, G. (2007). Clinical depression versus distress among patients with type 2 diabetes. Not just a question of semantics. *Diabetes Care, 30,* 542-548.

Garay-Sevilla, M. E., Malacara, J. M., González-Contreras, E., Wróbel-Zasada, K., Wróbel-Kaczmarczyk, K., and Gutiérrez-Roa, A. (2000). Perceived psychological stress in diabetes mellitus type 2. *Revista de Investigación Clínica, 52,* 241-245.

Gómez, V., Zúñiga, S., García de León, E., and Couttolenc, M. I. (2002). Control of type 2 diabetes. The glucose index as indicator [In Spanish]. *Revista Médica del IMSS, 40,* 281-284.

Gonder-Frederick, L. A., Cox, D. J., and Ritterband, L. M. (2002). Diabetes and behavioral medicine: The second decade. *Journal of Consulting and Clinical Psychology, 70,* 611-625.

Glascow, R. E. and Toobert, D. J. (1988). Social environment and regimen adherence among type II diabetic patients. *Diabetes Care, 11,* 377-386.

Hernández-Ronquillo, L., Téllez-Zenteno, J. F., Garduño-Espinosa, J., and González-Acevez, E. (2003). Factors associated with therapy noncompliance in type-2 diabetes patients. *Salud Pública de México, 45,* 191-197.

Hill-Briggs, F., Gary, T. L., Bone, L. R., Hill, M. N., Levine, D. M., and Brancarti, F. L. (2005). Medication adherence and diabetes control in urban African Americans with type 2 diabetes. *Health Psychology, 24,* 349-357.

Kelley, K.W. (1985). Immunological consequences of changing environmental stimuli. In G.P. Moberg (ed.), *Animal Stress* (pp. 193-223). Bethesda, MD: American Physiological Association.

Landeros, E. A. (2000). Epidemiological review of diabetes mellitus [In Spanish]. *Revista Mexicana de Enfermería Cardiológica, 8,* 56-69.

Lazarus, R. and Folkman, S (1984). *Stress, appraisal and coping.* New York: Springer Publishing Company.

Lerman-Garber, I., Barrón-Uribe, C., Calzada-León, R., Mercado-Atri, M., Vidal-Tamayo, R., Quintana, S. et al. (2003). Emotional dysfunction associated with diabetes in Mexican adolescents and young adults with type-1 diabetes. *Salud Pública de México, 45,* 13-18.

Levine, S. (1985). A definition of stress. In G.P. Moberg (ed.), *Animal Stress* (pp. 51-69). Bethesda, MD: American Physiological Association.

Lin, E. H. B., Olvera, M., Katon, W., Ciechanowski, P., Von Korff, M., Ludman, E. J. et al. (2004). Relationship of depression and diabetes self-care, medication adherence, and preventive care. *Diabetes Care, 27,* 2154-2160.

Lloyd, C., Smith, J., and Weinger, K. (2005). Stress and diabetes: A review of links. *Diabetes Spectrum, 18,* 121-127.

Miller, V. A. and Drotar, D. (2003). Discrepancies between mother and adolescent perception of diabetes related decision-making autonomy and their relationship to diabetes-related conflict and adherence treatment. *Journal of Pediatric Psychology, 28,* 265-274.

Miller, V. A. and Drotar, D. (2005). Decision-making competence and adherence to treatment in adolescents with diabetes. *Journal of Pediatric Psychology* (doi: 19.1093/ jpepsy/jsj122).

Maddigan, S. L., Feeny, D.H., Majundar, S. R., Farris, K. B., and Johnson, J. A. (2006). Understanding the determinants of health for people with type 2 diabetes. *American Journal of Public Health, 96,* 1649-1655.

Moberg, G. P. (1985). Influence of stress on reproduction measure of well-being. In G. P. Moberg (ed.), *Animal Stress* (pp. 245-167). Bethesda, MD: American Physiological Association.

Ortiz, M. (2006). Stress, coping style, and treatment adherence suffering from type I diabetes [In Spanish]. *Terapia Psicológica, 24,* 139-148.

Ortiz, M. and Ortiz, E. (2005). Psychological factors associated to patient's treatment compliance in children diabetic teenagers [In Spanish]. *Revista Médica de Chile, 133,* 307-313.

Piña, J. A., Corrales, A.E., Valencia, M. A., and Mungaray, K. (2006). Validation of a short scale that measure stress related events in HIV positive patients [In Spanish]. *Terapia Psicológica, 24,* 15-21.

Piña, J..A and Sánchez-Sosa, J. J. (2007). A psychological model for the research of treatment adherence behaviors in persons with HIV [In Spanish]. *Universitas Psychologica, 6,* 397-405.

Pladevall, M., Williams, L. K., Potts, L. A., Divine, G., Xi, G., and Lafata, J. E. (2004). Clinical outcomes and adherence to medications measured by claims data in patients with diabetes. *Diabetes Care, 27,* 2800-2805.

Polonsky, W. H., Anderson, B. J., Lohrer, P. A., Welch, G., Jacobson, A. M., Aponte. J. E., and Schwartz, C. E. (1995). Assessment of diabetes-related distress. *Diabetes Care, 18,* 754-760.

Ribes, E. (1990). *Health Psychology: A conceptual analysis* [In Spanish]. Barcelona: Editorial Martínez Roca.

Samaniego, R. A. and Álvarez, J. (2006). Illness's control in patient suffering mellitus type 2 diabetes: A Monterrey's sample [In Spanish]. *Psicología y Salud, 16,* 63-70.

Sánchez-Sosa, J. J. (2002). Treatment adherence: The role of behavioral mechanism and some implications for health care interventions. *Revista Mexicana de Psicología, 19,* 85-92.

Snowling, N. J. and Hopkins, W.G. (2006). Effects of different models of exercise training on glucose control and risk factors complication in type 2 diabetic patients. *Diabetes Care, 29,* 2518-2527.

Stys, A. M. and Kulkarni, K. (2007). Identification of self-care behaviors and adoption of lifestyle changes results in sustained glucose control and reduction of comorbities in type 2 diabetes. *Diabetes Spectrum, 20,* 55-58.

Surwit, R. S., Feinglos. M. N., and Schneider, M. S. (1992). Stress and diabetes mellitus. *Diabetes Care, 10,* 1413-1422.

Wen, L. K., Sheperd, M. D., and Porchman, M. L. (2004). Family support, diet, and excercise among older Mexican Americans with type 2 diabetes. *Diabetes Educator, 30,* 980-993.

In: Hispanic Psychology Yearbook Volume 1
Ed: Cirilo H. García pp. 87-99
ISBN: 978-1-60741-786-6


*Chapter 7*

# PRELIMINARY CONSTRUCT VALIDATION STUDY OF THE REASONS FOR DISCIPLINE AND STRATEGIES TO SUSTAIN DISCIPLINE SCALES IN SPANISH PHYSICAL EDUCATION*

***Juan Antonio Moreno Murcia[1], Eduardo Cervelló Gimeno[2], Celestina Martínez Galindo[3] and Luis Miguel Ruiz Pérez[4]***
[1]University of Murcia
[2]Miguel Hernández University of Elche
[3]Research Department of Physical Education and Sports
[4]University of Castilla La Mancha

## ABSTRACT

The purpose of this study was to adapt two discipline scales (Papaioannou, 1998) to the Spanish educational context. We investigated construct validity and reliability of the instruments designed to measure pupils' reasons to be disciplined in the classroom and perceptions of strategies used by the teacher to maintain discipline in the physical education class. Participants were 356 Spanish pupils aged between 14 and 16. Results obtained from principal components analysis with varimax rotation revealed the existence of (a) five factors for the Reasons for Discipline Scale (RDS), that is: identified reasons, intrinsic reasons, introjected reasons, amotivation and caring reasons for behaving, and (b) four factors for the Strategies to Sustain Discipline Scale (SSDS), that is: caring and responsibility reasons, intrinsic reasons, introjected and external reasons and teacher's indifference to maintaining discipline. The alphas varied between .86 and .58 for the first

---

* A version of this chapter was also published in the *International Hispanic Psychology Journal, Volume 1 Issue 1*, published by Nova Science Publishers, Inc. It was submitted for appropriate modification in an effort to encourage wider dissemination of research.

[1] Address for correspondence: Juan Antonio Moreno Murcia, Facultad de Ciencias del Deporte, Universidad de Murcia, Parque Almansa 30730 San Javier, Murcia, España. E-mail: morenomu@um.es , Phone: 968 39 86 78, Fax: 968 31 86 72.

scale and between .88 and .70 for the second. In addition, the results showed suitable predictive validity. More studies are necessary to corroborate the results found with different populations and cultures.

**Keywords:** discipline, physical education, motivation, self-determination.

## Resumen

El objetivo de este estudio fue adaptar dos escalas de disciplina (Papaioannou, 1998) al contexto educativo español. Calculamos la validez de constructo y la fiabilidad de los instrumentos diseñados para medir las razones del alumno para ser disciplinado en el aula y la percepción de las estrategias usadas por el profesor para mantener la disciplina en clase de educación física. La muestra estuvo compuesta por 356 alumnos españoles de edades comprendidas entre los 14 y 16 años. Los resultados obtenidos mediante el análisis factorial de componentes principales con rotación varimax revelaron la existencia de (a) cinco factores en la Escala de Razones para la Disciplina (RDS): razones identificadas, razones intrínsecas, razones introjectadas, amotivación y razones de interés para ser disciplinado, así como la existencia de (b) cuatro factores en la Escala de Estrategias para Mantener la Disciplina (SSDS): razones de preocupación y responsabilidad, razones intrínsecas, razones introjectadas y externas e indiferencia del profesor para mantener la disciplina. Los alphas obtenidos oscilaron entre .86 y .58 para la primera escala y entre .88 y .70 para la segunda. Además, los resultados mostraron una adecuada validez predictiva. Más estudios son necesarios para corroborar los resultados encontrados con diferentes poblaciones y culturas.

*Palabras Clave:* disciplina, educación física, motivación, auto-determinación.

## Introduction

One of the aspects that has most concerned professionals and researchers in the area of physical education is understanding the cognitive mechanisms related to disciplined and undisciplined behavior in class (Lewis, 1997, 2001; Siedentop, 1991), given that inducing prosocial behavior in children and young people is one of the objectives the educational setting should attain (Anderson, Avery, Pederson, Smith, and Sullivan, 1997). That is why discipline is considered to be one of the most important and difficult educational aspects to deal with in academic environments (Harrinson, Blakemore, Buck, and Pellet, 1996; Mieszalski, 1997; Robertson, 1998). Without discipline teaching would be ineffective (Dreikurs, Grunwald, and Pepper, 1982).

According to Edwards (1993), misbehavior in the classroom, and, more specifically, in physical education lessons, prevents class from functioning properly as it causes serious problems (Tinning, 1987), mainly for novice teachers (Del Villar, 2001; Veenman, 1984). As a result, teaching skill in handling pupils' behavior in the classroom is one of the most important characteristics that make a teacher either effective or ineffective (Siedentop and Tannechill, 1999). However, many people nowadays have a distorted view of what discipline actually is, as well as a misleading concept of why we lack discipline in an educational environment (Dreikurs et al., 1982). This aspect has led to a recent increase in studies in the educational sector examining the determinants of this behavior. Many researchers singled out motivation as one of the key factors behind it.

Self-determination theory (Deci and Ryan, 1985, 1991) is a general theory on motivation and personality. In this theory human behavior is triggered by three primary and universal psychological needs: autonomy, competence and relatedness. One's motivation is dependent on whether these needs are satisfied. The theory also suggests different types of motivation along a continuum varying in levels of self-determination. From less to more self-determination are situated amotivation, extrinsic motivation and intrinsic motivation. Amotivated is an individual that has no intention of doing anything, characterized by having no motivation. Extrinsic motivation is broken down into different forms of regulation. The least self-determined is external regulation, which reflects action motivated by external contingencies. Next is introjected regulation, characterising actions motivated by internal pressures such as when an individual is doing something to avoid feelings of guilt. The following form of regulation is identified regulation, which evolves when the individual thinks that the adopted activity is important, and, lastly, integrated regulation, in which several identifications are assimilated and organized into one structure that triggers action. Intrinsic motivation takes place when one's action is triggered by the pleasure and enjoyment generated by the activity itself.

In this respect, when the most self-determined forms are adopted pupils adopt an activity for their own good and due to the satisfaction the activity generates. The rules of the game are internalised because they are considered necessary to generate challenge and optimum performance and, consequently, pupils behave in the classroom. On the contrary, the least self-determined forms make pupils participate in activities due to external reasons. This is linked with a lack of understanding of the usefulness of guidelines and rules, which are generally seen as imposed. These feelings can lead pupils to abandon an activity and exhibit disruptive behaviors.

To understand disruptive behavior it is necessary to develop instruments that can help us understand what is causing it in the classroom. Currently there are very few instruments created to measure pupil's disciplinary behavior either in primary or secondary education. Hellison (1995) was one of the pioneers in developing strategies promoting responsibility of pupils. Hellison's responsibility model (Hellison, 1995) contains five levels of pupils' responsibility, called: irresponsibility, implying lack of control and discipline; self-control, implying the adoption of external and internal contingencies to control behavior; involvement, which includes identified and intrinsic reasons for undertaking an activity and behaving well; responsibility suggesting that pupils choose to behave responsibly in order to develop an integrated personal identity; and caring indicating supportive and helping behaviors towards classmates.

Based on self-determination theory and Hellison's model, Papaioannou (1998) created two scales connected with disciplined behavior in Physical Education. The first of these scales was called "Reasons for Discipline Scale" (RDS), capturing pupils' reasons for behaving well in Physical Education. This contained 26 items associated with six factors: intrinsic, responsibility, caring, introjected, and external reasons for behaving, as well as reasons for not behaving.

The second scale created by Papaioannou (1998) was called "Strategies to Sustain Discipline Scale" (SSDS). This instrument included 27 items measuring pupils' perception of the strategies used by their teacher to maintain discipline in class. These items loaded to four factors named teaching stategies promoting self-determined, introjected and external reasons of discipline, as well as indifference to sustain discipline.

Later, Spray and Wang (2001) adapted the RDS created by Papaioannou (1998), to the English context. The English version by Spray and Wang (2001) is formed by 18 items grouped into five factors: amotivation (or lack of reasons), external reasons, introjected reasons, identified reasons and intrinsic reasons for behaving. The alpha reliabilities for these subscales varied between .93 and .64.

In a following study, Spray (2002) adapted the SSDS (Papaioannou, 1998), applying it to the English context. This adaptation was formed by 19 items grouped into four factors: teacher's emphasis on intrinsic and identified reasons, teacher's emphasis on introjected reasons, teacher's indifference and teacher's emphasis on caring and responsibility reasons. The alpha reliabilities for these subscales varied between .85 and .72.

In this respect, motivated by the recent increase in misbehavior in educational settings, and in view of the need to develop valid and reliable scales to help us to understand pupils' behavior and, therefore, to be able to establish action guidelines, we decided to conduct a preliminary construct validation study of the RDS and SSDS scales in a sample of Spanish adolescents participating in physical education classes. At this point an exploratory approach was adopted to investigate factor validity of the scales. In order to check the convergent and discriminant validity of both instruments, we related pupils' reasons for behaving in the classroom and the perceived strategies adopted by the teacher to maintain discipline in the physical education class. Based on the contributions made by Gutiérrez (2000), indicating that there is a significant positive correlation between pupils' reasons and the perception they have of their physical education teachers' reasons, we hypothesised that pupils' intrinsic, responsibility and caring reasons for behaving well would be positively connected with perceptions of teaching strategies emphasising intrinsic and responsibility reasons to sustain discipline. On the other hand, pupils' amotivation to behave would be positively associated with perceptions of teacher's indifference to maintain discipline in the physical education class.

# METHOD

## Participants

Participants were 356 Spanish pupils aged between 14 and 16 (*M* = 14.99, *SD* = .72). Of the total sample, 189 pupils were male and 167 female. The sample is formed by pupils belonging to different public and private compulsory secondary education schools in the region of Murcia.

## Measurement Instruments

*Reasons for Discipline Scale (RDS).* This instrument measures pupils' reasons for behaving well in the Physical Education class (Papaioannou, 1998). The majority of the items in the original instrument were adapted from Ryan and Connell's (1989) scale to measure intrinsic, identified, introjected and external reasons for acting, while the responsibility and caring items were developed by Papaioannou (1998) based on Hellison's (1995) model. The original instrument created by Papaioannou (1998) was formed by 26 items grouped into 6 factors: intrinsic reasons for behaving, external reasons for behaving, reasons for not behaving, introjected reasons for behaving, responsibility reasons for behaving and caring reasons for behaving. Our version has been called "Escala de Razones para la Disciplina (ERD)". The items forming the questionnaire were preceded by the phrase: "In the Physical Education class...".

*Strategies to Sustain Discipline Scale (SSDS).* The original instrument was created by Papaioannou (1998) based on the theory and research of Hellison (1995), Ryan and Connell (1989) and Vallerand et al. (1992, 1993) in order to evaluate pupils' perception of the strategies used by their teacher to maintain discipline in the Physical Education class. Our version of the original instrument adapted to the Spanish context was formed by 27 items. This version has been called "Escala de Estrategias para Mantener la Disciplina (EEMD)". The 27 items that form the questionnaire were preceded by the phrase "The Physical Education teacher..."

Due to the fact that in the Spanish academic context, all qualifications of pupils' academic performance range from 0 to 100, all responses were indicated on an 11-point Likert scale anchored to strongly disagree (0) and strongly agree (100) to make it easier for the students' to respond in the usual way.

## Procedure

Following Hambleton's back translation strategy (1996), first the items were translated into Spanish and then a group of translators translated them back into English to find out whether they coincided with the items of the original version. Next, the set of items were assessed by three experts in Sport Psychologists the subject (Lynn, 1986). All of them reckoned that the items were relevant for the measurement of the constructs under investigation and they were correctly worded. Next the complete set was given to 45 pupils of physical education from 14 to 16 years, who were asked to evaluate whether the items were comprehensible. No item was found to be either confusing or ambiguous. Finally, after obtaining the relevant authorisation from the parents/tutors of the fastened minors who were taking part in the study, the administration period was specified. Pupils were reminded that the questionnaires were anonymous and were encouraged to fill in the questionnaires as sincerely as possible. The time needed to fill out the questionnaires was 15-20 minutes.

## Data Analysis

First, the psychometric properties of the RDS and SSDS were analysed, including exploratory factor analyses (EFA) to obtain the factor structure of the scales and internal consistency analyses using Cronbach's alpha statistic. Secondly, in order to find evidence of external validity, we performed a correlation analysis between the two scales, due to previous evidence of a connection between pupils' reasons for behaving and strategies adopted by their teacher to maintain discipline in class.

# Results

## Psychometric Properties of the Reasons for Discipline Scale (RDS)

### *Principal Components Analysis*

We conducted a principal components analysis (Table 1) in order to examine the factor structure of the instrument capturing pupils' reasons for behaving well in the physical education class. Only items loading .40 or above were considered in the analysis (Comrey and Lee, 1992).

**Table 1. Psychometric properties of the RDS**

| Factors | *F1* | *F2* | F3 | F4 | F5 |
|---|---|---|---|---|---|
| Identified reasons | | | | | |
| It is important for me to pay attention | .45 | | | | |
| I try to be a responsible person | .65 | | | | |
| It is important for me to understand where I have got it right or wrong | .67 | | | | |
| I feel responsible when I am learning | .51 | | | | |
| It is important for me to do well in class | .65 | | | | |
| I like to make progress in all the lessons | .75 | | | | |
| It is important for me to improve my skills | .63 | | | | |
| I try to be consistent with myself and others | .64 | | | | |
| It is important for me to be consistent in what I say and do | .59 | | | | |
| Intrinsic reasons | | | | | |
| I enjoy the classes | | .81 | | | |
| It is important for me to learn new skills and games | | .50 | | | |
| The classes are fun | | .76 | | | |
| The classes are stimulating | | .71 | | | |
| Introjected reasons | | | | | |
| I will feel bad if I misbehave | | | .73 | | |
| I will feel ashamed if I misbehave | | | .72 | | |
| It bothers me when I misbehave | | | .71 | | |
| Amotivation | | | | | |
| I do not know why I am disciplined | | | | .67 | |
| I do not understand why I have to be disciplined | | | | .79 | |
| I really feel that it is a waste of my time being disciplined | | | | .70 | |
| Caring reasons | | | | | |
| It is important to me that my classmates understand what is right and wrong | | | | | .63 |
| I like helping my classmates | | | | | .52 |
| It is important to me that my classmates improve in class | | | | | .75 |
| Reliability | .86 | .76 | .71 | .58 | .66 |
| Explained variance | 19.57% | 11.64% | 10.05% | 8.05% | 7.66% |
| Total variance | | | | | 56.99% |

In this respect, items 2, 15, 20 and 22 were excluded from the original instrument because the factor loading was below the established .40 criterion. Then we computed another principal components analysis with varimax rotation without these items. Twenty-two items resulted from the analysis grouped into five factors called; identified reasons, intrinsic reasons, introjected reasons, amotivation, and caring reasons for behaving, with eigenvalues above 1.00 (4.30, 2.56, 2.21, 1.77 and 1.68 respectively) with a total variance explained of 56.9% (19.57%, 11.64%, 10.05%, 8.05% and 7.66% respectively).

### *Analysis of Internal Consistency or Reliability*

The internal consistencies of the RDS subscales were obtained by calculating Cronbach's alpha coefficient. Accordingly, alphas were .86 for "identified reasons", .76 for "intrinsic reasons", .71 for "introjected reasons", .58 for "amotivation" and .66 for "caring reasons".

## Psychometric Properties of the Strategies to Sustain Discipline Scale (SSDS)

### *Principal Components Analysis*

Following a similar procedure with the previous instrument, we carried out a principal components analysis (Table 2) in order to examine the factor structure of this instrument. Items 7, 14 and 19 were excluded from the original instrument (factor loading below .40). We then computed another principal components analysis with varimax rotation without these items. Twenty four items were grouped into four factors (teacher's emphasis on caring and responsibility reasons, teacher's emphasis on intrinsic reasons, teacher's emphasis on introjected and external reasons and teacher's indifference to maintaining discipline in the physical education class) with eigenvalues above 1.00 (4.54, 4.26, 2.52 and 2.34 respectively) with a total variance explained of 56.9% (18.94%, 17.74%, 10.53% and 9.75% respectively).

**Table 2. Psychometric properties of the SSDS**

| Factors | *F1* | *F2* | F3 | F4 |
|---|---|---|---|---|
| Teacher's emphasis on caring and responsibility reasons | | | | |
| He helps us so that we do what he tells us in the end | .51 | | | |
| He helps us to be responsible for our progress | .55 | | | |
| He helps us to understand others | .53 | | | |
| He gets our attention to make us understand that it is important to do it well | .55 | | | |
| He makes us learn how to teach others | .70 | | | |
| He helps us to be responsible for our actions | .78 | | | |
| He gets our attention so that we try to improve our skills | .70 | | | |
| He helps us to co-operate and mutually understand each other | .58 | | | |
| He helps us to be responsible people | .59 | | | |
| Teacher's emphasis on intrinsic reasons | | | | |
| He makes the classes fun | | .87 | | |
| He gets our attention and makes the classes more interesting | | .84 | | |
| He gets our attention and teaches us new skills and games | | .62 | | |
| He makes us want our classmates to make progress | | .45 | | |
| He teaches the class in such a way that we pay attention and understand what we do right and/or wrong | | .47 | | |

**Table 2. (Continued)**

| Factors | *F1* | *F2* | F3 | F4 |
|---|---|---|---|---|
| He makes the classes exciting | | .68 | | |
| He makes us enjoy the classes | | .65 | | |
| Teacher's emphasis on introjected and external reasons | | | | |
| He makes us feel bad with ourselves when we misbehave | | | .73 | |
| He makes us feel uncomfortable when we misbehave | | | .79 | |
| He reminds us that only those that behave are considered good pupils | | | .56 | |
| He makes us feel ashamed if we misbehave | | | .64 | |
| He threatens us saying that we will have problems if we misbehave | | | .48 | |
| Teacher's indifference to maintaining discipline in class | | | | |
| He makes us feel that there is no discipline in the class at all | | | | .64 |
| He does not really do anything to maintain discipline | | | | .65 |
| He is not interested in discipline in the class | | | | .80 |
| Reliability | .86 | .88 | .76 | .70 |
| Explained variance | 18.94% | 17.74% | 10.53% | 9.75% |
| Total variance | | | | 56.97% |

***Analysis of Internal Consistency or Reliability***

Internal consistency analysis of the subscales of the SSDS was obtained by calculating Cronbach's alpha coefficient. The results revealed that alpha reliability was .86 for the "teacher's emphasis on caring reasons" .88 for the "teacher's emphasis on intrinsic reasons".76 for the "teacher's emphasis on introjected and external reasons" and .70 for the "teacher's indifference" subscale.

All the factors forming this scale have a Cronbach's alpha or reliability above the recommended value .70 (Nunnally, 1978).

## Descriptive and Correlational Data of All the Factors

Next the correlations among the scales adapted to the Spanish educational context were computed (Table 3). The pupils' intrinsic, identified, introjected and caring reasons for behaving were connected positively (a) between each other and, (b) with the perceptions of teacher's strategies emphasising caring and intrinsic reasons to maintain discipline in class. Amotivation reasons for behaving were positively associated with perceptions of teacher's strategies promoting introjected and external reasons to maintain discipline and with perceptions of teacher's indifference to maintain discipline in the physical education classroom.

The descriptive statistics (mean and standard deviation), indicated that for pupils there were more identified reasons for behaving ($M$ = 7.88, $SD$ = 1.45) than intrinsic reasons ($M$ = 7.44, $SD$ = 1.84), introjected reasons ($M$ = 6.18, $SD$ = 2.28), caring reasons ($M$ = 6.65, $SD$ = 2.00) and amotivation reasons ($M$ = 4.18, $SD$ = 2.34). Pupilis reported higher scores for perceptions of teaching strategies promoting intrinsic ($M$ = 7.18, $SD$ = 1.87) and caring reasons ($M$ = 7.05, $SD$ = 1.63), than introjected-external reasons ($M$ = 4.18, $SD$ = 2.33) and indifference ($M$ = 3.37, $SD$ = 2.54).

**Table 3. Mean, Standard Deviation and Correlations of all the Variables**

| | *M* | *SD* | Identif. reason | Introj. reason | Intrin. reason | Amot. reason | Caring reason | Caring emph. | Intrin. emph. | Introj. emph. | Indiff. emph. |
|---|---|---|---|---|---|---|---|---|---|---|---|
| Identified reason | 7.88 | 1.45 | - | .54** | .56** | -.17** | .57** | .53** | .50** | -.02 | -.14** |
| Introyected reasons | 6.18 | 2.28 | - | - | .32** | -.08 | .45** | .31** | .29** | .15** | .01 |
| Intrinsic reasons | 7.44 | 1.84 | - | - | - | -.07 | .44** | .54** | .66** | -.00 | -.08 |
| Amotivation reason | 4.18 | 2.34 | - | - | - | - | -.01 | .00 | -.04 | .26** | .54** |
| Caring reason | 6.65 | 2.00 | - | - | - | - | - | .36** | .36** | .11* | .02 |
| Caring emphasis | 7.05 | 1.63 | - | - | - | - | - | - | .77** | -.03 | -.08 |
| Intrinsic emphasis | 7.18 | 1.87 | - | - | - | - | - | - | - | -.14** | -.11* |
| Introyected emphasis | 4.18 | 2.33 | - | - | - | - | - | - | - | - | .55** |
| Indifference emphasis | 3.37 | 2.54 | - | - | - | - | - | - | - | - | - |

* $p < .05$; ** $p < .01$.

## DISCUSSION

After seeing the results obtained in the studies reviewed and aware of the need to validate the scales designed with samples of different populations and cultures, we decided that the objectives of our research would be to adapt two Greek discipline scales (Papaioannou, 1998) to the Spanish context in order to measure, in the first place, pupils' reasons in a sample of adolescents involved in physical education classes and secondly, the strategies used by the teacher perceived by the pupils to maintain discipline in the physical education class. Similarly, we performed a correlation analysis among the factors forming both instruments in order to check the construct validity of the scales.

Firstly, the results obtained from the exploratory factor analysis performed on the RDS scale seem to support the existence of five main factors called: identified reasons, intrinsic reasons, introjected reasons, amotivation, and caring reasons for behaving. Unlike our analysis, the original instrument created by Papaioannou (1998) was formed by 26 items (four items more than ours) grouped into 6 factors (one factor more than ours). In this respect, by means of the factor analysis of principal components, we removed one factor from the original instrument "external reasons for behaving" and we slightly modified the rest of the factors. As we have seen, there is more similarity with the original Greek scale created by Papaioannou (1998), due to both the number of items in the scale and the structure of the majority of the factors forming our Spanish version. These factors are similar to those in the original Greek version, except for the first two, since their structure has been modified slightly as a result of the factor analysis carried out, making them easier to understand and their distribution more coherent.

However, we are aware of the limitations of our research, since two factors "amotivation" and "caring reasons for behaving" show a reliability or alpha value below the recommended .70 (Nunnally, 1978). We attribute these values to the small number of items forming both factors (number of items = 3). Therefore, based on Hair, Anderson, Tatham, and Black (1998) and Nunnally and Bernstein (1994), we consider that the internal validity of both factors is accepted and we defend the need to carry out future research with samples larger than those used in order to determine whether additional items are needed in some of the factors mentioned.

As far as the SSDS is concerned, the results of the exploratory factor analysis revealed the existence of four factors. After removing three items from the original Greek version referring to the factor "teacher's emphasis on extrinsic reasons for maintaining discipline in the physical education class" we increased the instrument's validity and internal consistency substantially. Twenty-four items resulted from the final analysis grouped into four factors with a similar organisation to Spray's (2002) version, although more complete due to the fact that we eliminated only 3 items from the original Greek instrument compared with the 8 items removed by Spray. The factors are called: teacher's emphasis on caring and responsibility reasons, teacher's emphasis on intrinsic reasons, teacher's emphasis on introjected and external reasons and teacher's indifference to maintaining discipline in the physical education class.

In short, we would like to state that our Spanish version is related to both the original Greek version created by Papaioannou (1998) and the English version developed by Spray (2002), due to the fact that its organisation of the factors is similar to the second (e.g.: it eliminates part of the factor "teacher's emphasis on external reasons for maintaining discipline" and it introduces one of the items in the factor "teacher's emphasis on integrated regulation reasons") and at the same time, it keeps almost all the items in the original instrument (we eliminated only three items of the 27 in that scale). Unlike the RDS, the internal consistency or Cronbach's alpha of all the factors in this second scale showed values above the one recommended, .70 (Nunnally, 1978).

In short, our study supported, in a general view, similar factor structure of these instruments in a Spanish sample, but the results also demonstrated that there are limitations when we use different samples of different cultures. Our study indicates that some factors of these instruments can be reviewed to confirm the cross-culturally robustness of our findings. More research needs to be done to establish these cross-cultural differences.

In order to check the construct validity of the two instruments, we carried out a study of the correlations among the factors forming both scales. As Cervelló et al. (2006) stated, we believe this is one of the most important elements to bear in mind when attempting to validate a new instrument. The construct validity of a new measurement instrument involves checking its theoretical suitability by establishing relations with other theoretical constructs. The results obtained show how the pupils' identified, intrinsic, introjected and caring reasons for behaving are connected positively amongst themselves and, furthermore, with the teacher's strategies based on caring and intrinsic reasons for maintaining discipline in class. With regard to pupils' amotivation reasons for behaving, they were associated positively with the teacher's strategies based on introjected and external reasons and with the indifference shown in maintaining discipline in the physical education class.

These data coincide with the hypotheses stated at the beginning of the study and they are in line with the contributions made by Gutiérrez (2000), for whom there is a significant positive correlation between pupils' reasons and the perception they have of their physical education teachers' reasons. Similarly, different studies carried out in both the educational area (Ames, 1992; Papaioannou and Theodorakis, 1996) and in the sports area (Cervelló, Jiménez, Del Villar, Ramos, and Santos Rosa, 2004; Nicholls, 1989) have pointed out this parallelism between pupil and teacher with different study variables. As a result, according to these authors, pupils in physical education classes tend to adopt the success criteria perceived in their teacher.

Therefore, in line with the results found, those teachers concerned and intrinsically motivated to achieve good behavior from their pupils and who encourage participation in activities will develop more self-determined forms in their pupils and, as a result, more intrinsic motivation, which will make subjects take part for their own good and the satisfaction the activity generates. The rules established are internalised and more positive attitudes are shown. In other words, there is more disciplined behavior in the classroom. On the contrary, a teacher that does not care and who is not interested in maintaining order and discipline in class and who also establishes criteria based on competition and public evaluation will transfer his extrinsic motivation or amotivation for discipline to his pupils. Consequently, the pupils will not internalise the rules established, they will compete with their peers without caring about how they win and they will interrupt the smooth running of the class. This will all result in disruptive or undisciplined behavior in the class.

To sum up, this research has provided two new measurement scales: on the one hand, pupils' reasons for behaving and, on the other, the perception of the strategies used by the teacher to maintain discipline in the physical education class. However, more studies are necessary with samples from different cultures or populations in order to corroborate or refute the results obtained in this research and provide valid and reliable scales we can use to discover and determine the influence of motivation on disciplined or undisciplined behavior in the physical education class, so that we can, therefore, establish action guidelines to minimise and, as far as possible, eradicate disruptive behavior and, consequently, increase disciplined behavior in the classroom.

## REFERENCES

Anderson, C., Avery, P. G., Pederson, P. V., Smith, E. S., and Sullivan, J. L. (1997). Divergent perspectives on citizenship education: A Q-method study y survey of social studies teachers. *American Educational Research Journal, 34*, 333-364.

Ames, C. (1992). Achievement goals, motivational climate and motivational processes. In G.C. Roberts (ed.), *Motivation in sport and exercise* (pp. 161-176). Champaign,Za IL: Human Kinetics.

Cervelló, E., Jiménez, R., Del Villar, F., Ramos, L., and Santos-Rosa, F. J. (2004). Goal orientations, motivational climate, equality, and discipline of Spanish physical education students. *Perceptual and Motor Skills, 99*, 271-283.

Cervelló, E.M., Moreno, J.A., Del Villar, F., and Reina, R. (2006). Desarrollo y validación de un instrumento de medida de las estrategias motivacionales empleadas en las clases de Educación Física. *Submitted for review.*

Comrey, A. L. and Lee, H. B. (1992). *A first Course in Factor Analysis*, 2nd Edn. Mahwah, NJ: Lawrence Erlbaum Associates.

Deci, E. L. and Ryan, R.M. (1985). *Intrinsic motivation and self-determination in human behavior*. New York: Plenum.

Deci, E. L. and Ryan, R. M. (1991). A motivational approach to self: Integration in personality. In R.A. Dienstbier (Ed.), *Nebraska symposium on motivation: Perspectives on motivation* (pp. 237-288). Lincoln, NE: University of Nebraska Press.

Del Villar, F. (2001). La interacción en la Educación Física. In B. Vázquez (Ed.), *Bases educativas de la actividad física y el deporte* (pp. 199-225). Madrid: Síntesis.

Dreikurs, R., Grunwald, B., and Pepper, F. (1982). *Maintanning Sanity in the Classroom. Classroom management techniques*. New York: Haper and Row.

Edwards, C. H. (1993). *Classroom organization and management.* New York: Macmillan.

Gutiérrez, M. (2000). *Aspectos del entorno escolar y familiar que se relacionan con la práctica deportiva en la adolescencia*. Paper read it in the I Congreso Hispano-Portugués de Psicología, Santiago de Compostela.

Hair, J. F., Anderson, R. E., Tatham, R. L., and Black, W. C. (1998). *Multivariate Data Analysis*. New Jersey, Prentice-Hall: Upper Saddle River.

Hambleton, R. K. (1996). Adaptación de tests para su uso en diferentes idiomas y culturas: fuentes de error, posibles soluciones y directrices prácticas. In J. Muñiz (ed.), *Psicometría* (pp. 207-238). Madrid: Universitas.

Harrinson, J. M., Blakemore, C. L., Buck, M. M., and Pellet, T. L. (1996). *Instructional Strategies for Secondary School Physical Education*. Madison: Brown and Benchmark Publishers.

Hellinson, D. (1995). *Teaching Responsibility through Physical Activity*. Champaign, IL: Human Kinetics.

Lewis, R. (1997). Discipline in schools. In L. Saha (Ed.), *International Encyclopedia of the sociology in education* (pp. 404-411). Oxford, UK: Permagon.

Lewis, R. (2001). Classroom discipline and student responsibility: the student's view. *Teaching and Teacher Education, 17*, 307-319.

Lynn, M. (1986). Determination and quantification of content validity. *Nursing Research, 35,* 382-385.

Mieszalski, S. (1997). *About Constraint and Discipline in School Classroom*. Warsaw: WSIP.

Nicholls, J. G. (1989). *The competitive ethos and democratic education*. Cambridge, MA: Harvard University Press.

Nunnally, J. C. (1978). *Psychometric theory*. New York: McGraw-Hill.

Nunnally, J. C. and Bernstein, I. H. (1994). *Psychometric Theory*. New York, McGraw-Hill.

Papaioannou, A. (1998). Goal perspectives, reasons for being disciplined and self-reported discipline in the lesson of physical education. *Journal of Teaching in Physical Education, 17,* 421-441.

Papaioannou, A., and Theodorakis, Y. (1996). A test of three models for the prediction of intention for participation in physical education lessons. *International Journal of Sport and Exercise Psychology, 27*, 383 - 399.

Robertson, J. (1998). *Effective Classroom Control*. London: Hodder y Stoughton Limited.

Ryan, R. M. and Connell, J. P. (1989). Perceived locus of causality and internalisation: Examining reasons for acting in two domains. *Journal of Personality and Social Psychology, 57*, 749-761.

Siedentop, D. (1991). *Developing teaching skills in physical education* (3rd ed.). Mountain Views, CA: Mayfield.

Siedentop, D. and Tannehill, D. (1999). *Developing teaching skills in physical education*. Palo Alto, CA: Mayfield.

Spray, C. (2002). Motivational climate and perceived strategies to sustain pupils' discipline in physical education. *European Physical Education Review, 8*, 5-20.

Spray, C. and Wang, C.K. (2001). Goal orientations, self-determination and pupils' discipline in physical education. *Journal of Sport Sciences, 19*, 903-913.

Tinning, R. (1987). *Improving Teaching in Physical Education*. Victoria: Deakin University Press.

Vallerand, R. J., Pelletier, L. G., Blais, M. R., Briere, N. M., Senecal, C., and Vallieres, E. F. (1992). The academic motivation scale: A measure of intrinsic, extrinsic, and amotivation in education. *Education and Psychological Measurement, 52*, 1003-1017.

Vallerand, R. J., Pelletier, L. G., Blais, M. R., Briere, N. M., Senecal, C., and Vallieres, E. F. (1993). On the assessment of intrinsic, extrinsic, and amotivation in education: evidence on the concurrent and construct validity of the Academic Motivation Scale. *Education and Psychological Measurement, 53*, 160-173.

Veenman, S. (1984). Perceived problems of beginning teachers. *Review of Educational Research, 54,* 143-178.

In: Hispanic Psychology Yearbook Volume 1
Ed: Cirilo H. García pp. 101-113
ISBN: 978-1-60741-786-6


*Chapter 8*

# TREATMENT OF YOUNG ADULTS WITH GENERALIZED SOCIAL PHOBIA[*#]

***José Olivares[†], Ana Isabel Rosa-Alcázar, Pablo José Olivares-Olivares and Ángel Rosa-Alcázar***
Universidad de Murcia, Spain

## ABSTRACT

The objective of this study is to determine if the Intervention Program for Young Adults with Social Phobia/Intervención en Adultos Jóvenes con Fobia Social –IPYASP/ IAJFS- (Olivares and Rosa, 2005), is good and effective in treating this disorder. To carry it out, 20 adults, from 18 to 20 years old were selected (average: 18.8, DT: 0.83) who were randomly distributed between two experimental conditions: 1) IPYASP/ IAJFS, and 2) control group - standby. The evaluation was applied before, after and on six and twelve months after the treatment finished. The results show the program efficiency in short and medium terms of all the measurements that directly evaluate anxiety and social avoidance, as well as the correlation of self-esteem, adaptation and social abilities; on the contrary, control group subjects did not have significant statistical improvement in any of the variables measured.

**Keywords:** Generalized Social Phobia, young adults, IAJFS Program, Effectiveness, Experimental

---

[*] Research was supported by Ministerio de Educación y Ciencia (SEJ200401471/PSIC).

[#] A version of this chapter was also published in the *International Hispanic Psychology Journal, Volume 1 Issue 2*, published by Nova Science Publishers, Inc. It was submitted for appropriate modification in an effort to encourage wider dissemination of research.

[†] Address for correspondence: Facultad de Psicología, Edificio "Luis Vives", Campus Universitario de Espinardo, Universidad de Murcia, Apdo. 4021, 30080 Espinardo, Murcia (España). E-mail: jorelx@um.es; Phone: 968363976

# INTRODUCTION

Social phobia or social anxiety disorder is defined as an intense and lasting fear of one or more social situations in which the person is exposed to being observed by others and experiments fear of doing something, or fear of behaving in a manner that is humiliating or embarrassing (APA, 2000). It is distinguished from other disorders because of interpersonal situations fear and avoidance, and high interference in subjects' daily lives (Stein, Fuetsch, Müller, Höfler, Lieb and Wittchen, 2001).

It is a serious public health problem, whose prevalence is determined by the APA (2000) after a major depression and dependency on alcohol consumption. For that reason, its study, evaluation and treatment have become a clinical psychologists' priority, since it has been classified as a diagnostic category (APA, 1980). However, that preoccupation has not produced a similar development in psychological treatments that are independent from socio-economic-cultural contexts. Thus, while large epidemiological studies have been carried out among English native-speaking community (Kessler, Stang, Wittchen, Stein and Walters, 1999; Magee, Eaton, Wittchen, McGonagle and Kessler, 1996), have been designed and applied ad hoc, for the adult population (in Heimber, 1991, or Turner, Beidel, Cooley, Woody and Messer, 1994), and also for children and adolescents (see Albano, Marten and Holt, 1991, Beidel, Turner and Morris, 2000 Spence, Donovan and Brechman-Toussaint, 2000), the development of its study, evaluation and treatment in the Spanish-speaking population is still comparatively scarce in both adult populations (Mendez, Sanchez and Moreno, 2001) and in child-youth populations (Olivares, Rosa, Caballo, Garcia-Lopez and Orgiles, 2003).

The object of this study, on one hand, is to contribute to alleviating these comparative shortages, and, on the other hand, to develop our own interventions adapted to our cultural contexts. With this double purpose, some applications have already been developed for other adaptations to the Intervention in Adolescents with Social Phobia/Intervención en Adolescentes con Fobia Social (-IASP/IAFS-; Olivares, 2005) for being applied to young adult population in the treatment of individual cases (Olivares, Piqueras and Garcia Lopez, 2005), and groups using intra-subjects treatment designs for the latter case (Garcia Lopez, Ruiz, Olivares, Piqueras, Rosa and Bermejo, 2006). The following are pending: (i) the definitive summary of those adaptations in an ad hoc manuscript, which we have developed for using it in this study (Intervention Program in Young Adults with Social Phobia/Intervención en Adultos Jóvenes con Fobia Social –IPYASP/IAJFS-;Olivares and Rosa, 2005), and (ii) to get to the bottom of applications of more controlled experimental conditions. These last two themes are the core of this document: to test the effects created by IPYASP on Spanish young adult population compared with a Standby List Control Group, under basic experimental design framework.

Both, IASP/IAFS adaptations as well as previous applications to this population (Olivares, 2005) have been carried out for all cases, respecting its structure and application process (treatment units, sequence of application of strategies and treatment techniques, homework, etc.), and also updating and adjusting the contents, ranging from treatment units to the interest and needs of the young adult world.

This paper was carried out within the Detection and Intervention Program with Social Phobia general framework among the community context carried out in the Unit of

Behavioral Therapy environment, of the Applied Psychology Service at the Universidad de Murcia (Spain).

# METHOD

## Subjects

**Table 1. Measurements of other subjects variables**

| | | | IPYASP/IAJFS (n = 10) | SLCG (n =10) |
|---|---|---|---|---|
| Age | | M | 18.90 | 18.70 |
| | | T.D. | 0.87 | 0.82 |
| Gender | | Young Men | 2 (20.0) | 3 (30.0) |
| | | Young Women | 8 (80.0) | 7 (70.0) |
| Academic year | | 1° University | 4 (40.0) | 5 (50.0) |
| | | 2° University | 5 (50.0) | 3 (30.0) |
| | | 3° University | 1 (10.0) | 2 (20.0) |
| Number of phobic social situations[1] for | Relationship with others | M | 4.50 | 3.90 |
| | | T.D. | 0.53 | 0.87 |
| | Performance with others | M | 2.70 | 3.50 |
| | | T.D. | 0.95 | 1.18 |
| CO-MORBIDITY | Anguish without agoraphobia | | 0 (0.0%) | 0 (0.0%) |
| | Agoraphobia | | 0 (0.0%) | 0 (0.0%) |
| | Generalized Anxiety | | 3 (30.0%) | 1 (10.0%) |
| | Obsessive Compulsive disorder | | 0 (0.0%) | 0 (0.0%) |
| | Specific Phobia | | 5 (50.0%) | 4 (40.0%) |
| | Post-traumatic Stress disorder | | 1 (10.0%) | 0 (0.0%) |
| | Major depressive episode | | 0 (0.0%) | 1 (10.0%) |
| | Dysthymic problems | | 4 (40.0%) | 4 (40.0%)) |
| | Alcohol Consumption | | 0 (0.0%) | 0 (0.0%) |
| | Abuse of toxic substances consumption | | 2 (20.0%) | 1 (10.0%) |
| | Disorder of Personality by Avoidance | | 1 (10.0%) | 1 (10.0%) |
| | Selective Mutism | | 0 (0.0%) | 0 (0.0%) |
| | Obsessive-compulsive personality disorder | | 0 (0.0%) | 0 (0.0%) |

*IPYASP/IAJFS: Intervention in Young Adults with Social Phobia (Olivares and Rosa, 2005) *SLCG: Standby List Control Group *M: Media; *TD: Typical Deviation; *n: Number of subjects.
[1]Informed by the participants in pre-test (ADIS-IV; DiNardo, Brown and Barlow, 1994).

The participants were 20 young university students registered in Information Technology, Law, Medicine, Pedagogy, Psychology and Primary School Teaching careers that fulfilled the criteria required by DSM-IV-TR (APA, 2000) for the generalized social phobia diagnosis. The age average was 18.80 years old (SD: 0.83; range: 18-20), being most of them women (74%) in 1st and 2nd years (85%). Regarding family history, 20% had a relative in the 1st or 2nd degree that has and/or had a social phobia; 11% has relatives suffering other psychological problems. None of the participants had been treated previously for psychological problems. One hundred percent of the participants treated attended all of the program's sessions (12 sessions). Table 1 shows other relevant data related to the subjects according to their experimental status.

### Evaluation Instruments

All subjects completed the pre-test, post-test and follow-ups of the following evaluation instruments: (i) "Social Phobia and Anxiety Inventory" (SPAI; Turner, Beidel, Dancu and Stanley, 1989), which includes three scores: Social Phobia sub-scale score, Agoraphobia sub-scale score, and the Difference score; (ii) "Social Phobia Scale (SPS)" and "Social Interaction Anxiety Scale (SIAS)" by Mattick and Clarke (1998) that measure anxiety facing action and social interaction; (iii) "***Fear*** of ***Negative Evaluation Scale***" (FNES, Watson and Friend, 1969), which evaluates the cognitive component of fear to a negative evaluation; (iv) "Report of ***Confidence*** as a Speaker ***Questionnaire***" (RCSQ; Gilkinson, 1942), modified by Paul (1966), so as to evaluate both the fear and security in public speech (before, during and after action); (v) Scale for evaluating "Self-Statements during Public Speaking Scale (SSPS)" (Hofmann and DiBartolo, 2000), which is formed by two sub-scales: positive self-verbalization and negative self-verbalization; (vi) "Scale of inadaptability" (EI; Echeburua and Corral, 1987), an instrument designed to evaluate the degree in which a disorder can affect different daily life areas: work, studies, social life, leisure, couple relationships and family life; (vii) "Self-Esteem Scale" (SES; Rosenberg, 1965) developed to measure satisfaction degree with himself; (viii) the ADIS-IV:C interview (Anxiety Disorders Interview Schedule for DSM-IV Child Version; Silverman and Albano, 1996), from which it was registered the social situations number of performances and relations classified as phobic in the Social Phobia section, which was taken a dependent variable for calculating the clinical significance of treatment effect.

## PROCEDURE

Subjects were recruited as follows: (a) The SPAI was applied to a 625 voluntary participants sample, registered in the 1st, 2nd and 3rd years of the mentioned university studies, in 2 centers in the Region of Murcia and 2 in the Valencia Community, selected randomly among those existing in both autonomous Spanish communications. (b) Correction of paper and pencil tests, selection of persons starting from a previously determined cut off point of a SPAI total score (SPAI $\geq$ 98 —Olivares and Rosa, 2005—). (c) Individual interview to 87 young adults, who surpassed the established cut off point, following the ADIS-IV-L indications (DiNardo, Brown and Barlow, 1994). After the interview, only 52 fulfilled the criteria to issue the Social Phobia diagnosis (20 for Generalized Social Phobia, and 32 for Specific Social Phobia). Only the subjects with Generalized Social Phobia were selected to participate in this investigation, in order to test the IPYASP Program in the most difficult conditions; the others were selected from another treatment group. (d) Random distribution of participants in experimental conditions: 10 subjects in the IPYASP/IAJFS

Condition, and 10 participants in the Standby List Control Group. (e) Pre-test evaluation, treatment application, and later evaluations for the post-test and those for the follow-up. The evaluation was done by four collaborators (two men-women couples), specifically trained to accomplish the tasks of selection, diagnosis and pre- and post-treatment evaluation; one couple brought to the pre-test evaluation, and six month later, the follow-up; the other couple evaluated the post-test, and follow-up twelve months later. The team was informed about the data until the second follow-up was carried out; that is to say, the evaluations were disguised to avoid confusion.

## Design

An experimental design was used as an *intra* factor (pre-test, post-test and follow-ups) and another *inter* factor (IPYASP *vs*. Standby List Control Group). The integrity of treatment was controlled by developing a written manual "Intervention in Young Adults with Social Phobia" (–IPYASP/IAJFS; Olivares and Rosa, 2005). The treatment sessions were accomplished in spaces adapted for such purpose in the *campus* of two of the four universities during an accessible schedule for participants, and it was always in the morning. No experimental mortality was produced. All of the experimental conditions were found in 2 treatment groups formed by 5 participants. The subjects were randomly assigned to the two experimental groups, and evaluated before beginning the treatment (pre-test), immediately after finishing (post-test) and after 6 and 12 months (follow-up). The treatment was applied by 2 different sex therapists, with experience in treating social phobia subjects groups.

## Treatment

The program applied was IPYASP/IAJFS (Olivares and Rosa, 2005) composed of 12 treatment sessions groups, lasting 90 minutes per week. The basic program components are: (i) *Educational component.* Information concerning treatment content is given; an explicative model of Social Phobia is submitted; subject' goals to be achieved are planned (aimed behaviors) and expectations concerning treatment are examined, as well as each one of the aimed behaviors. (ii) *Training in Social Abilities.* It consists of topics such as beginning and maintaining conversations, assertiveness, living and receiving compliments, establishing and maintaining friendships, and also training in abilities and skills for public speaking; exercises in cognitive flexibility are included and directed to training the subject in developing alternatives. (iii) *Presentation.* It is the central element of the program. Almost all activities revolve around it. It is applied on live (simulated and real exhibitions) as in imaginary activities. The IPYASP/IAJFS dedicates ten of its twelve sessions to make the subject to be exposed in both training group context, in the clinical environment, and in natural situations similar to those already practiced during training. The exposition is complemented by using an audio-visual feedback in sessions aimed at training the subjects for public speaking; to which *feedback* from classmates is added (this occurs in all activities and entertainment sessions). (iv) *Cognitive re-structuring techniques.* The object of this component is that participants learn to identify automatic negative thoughts produced when past situations are evoked; they anticipate social situations which afraid them, or in which they are immersed, causing them anxiety. It is based upon Beck's cognitive therapy and it is applied by following a process that includes education, training and application stages of all the training, as well as the A-B-C Ellis form to discuss automatic and irrational thoughts. Lastly, techniques are included to strengthen the effectiveness of intervention, like training on focusing attention and on creating alternatives.

Upon finishing each one of the group sessions, the corresponding homework is provided.

IPYASP/IAJFS makes it possible to treat/orient/supervise participants in individual tutoring sessions so as to complement group work. In addition, specific instructions for preventing relapses are also included.

# RESULTS

Comparative *intra-group* and *intergroup* analysis was brought to. With respect to *intergroup*, we proceed, first, to prove in both groups, the existence of differences in the pre-test, by accomplishing a comparison of averages or frequencies of the measured variable type (Student *T* test or Pearson Chi-Square). Both results, the socio-demographic and dependent variables indicated that there were no significant statistical differences between the two groups; that is to say, the groups were initially equal (see tables 2), which allowed us to effectuate an *inter-group* evaluation of the post-test treatment and follow-up effects. For this analysis, we did a Student *T* test averages comparison. We also calculated effect scope – ES- (typified average difference, Hedges and Olkin, 1985), that came upon comparing the differences between groups in different temporary moments. Positive $d_+$ values reflect an improvement in the IPYASP group when compared to the Standby List Group. The analyses were carried out by the SSPS 14.0 (2007) statistical package and MetaWin 2.0 (Rosenberg, Adams and Gurevitch, 2000). With respect to *intra-group* comparisons, we brought to an Anova with repeated measurements of different dependent variables and later, when necessary, we proceeded *post-hoc* comparisons. Finally, we analyzed the treatment clinical meaning, using two criteria: (1) Stop fulfilling the criteria for social phobia diagnosis, and (2) partial remission of the initial number of phobic social situations indicated by the subjects in the pre-test (between 75%-99.99%). We used Pearson Chi-Square test to analyze this data.

## Inter-Group Comparisons

The averages and typical deviations are shown in table 2 together with the value of the *T* test probability for the variables which only measure anxiety and social avoidance. As we can observe, there are significant statistical differences for all of the mentioned variables (except ASPI-Difference in the post-test) between both groups of treatment in different temporal moments (post-test and follow-ups). This data was confirmed by the effect scope *(ES)* which, as we can observe, is very high after the intervention (post-test and follow-ups). In this same table, results coming from both treatment conditions from other correlatives or related variables such as self-esteem and adaptation are showed. Once again, the data indicates that there are statistically significant differences between both groups (except Self-esteem in the post-test). The *ES* are high and very high for the IPYASP/IAJFS group after the intervention (post-test and follow-ups).

**Table 2. Measurement of anxiety, social avoidance, the cognitive component and other social phobia correlative measurements**

| | | | IPYASP/IAJFS (n=10) | SLCG (n=10) | *T* | *p* | *ES* |
|---|---|---|---|---|---|---|---|
| *Measurements of anxiety and social avoidance* | | | *M (TD)* | *M (TD)* | *T* | *p* | *ES* |
| | **SPAI-Social Phobia** | Pre-test | 123.70 (11.89) | 120.90 (15.60) | 0.451 | .657 | -0.192 |
| | | Post-test | 80.20 (22.18) | 117.00 (16.68) | -4.193 | .001 | 1.785 |
| | | Follow up 6 | 57.30 (30.62) | 117.00 (16.68) | -5.414 | .000 | 2.306 |
| | | Follow up 12 | 59.60 (29.29) | 117.00 (16.68) | -5.385 | .000 | 2.293 |
| | **SPAI-Difference** | Pre-test | 104.20 (12.05) | 99.40 (11.28) | 0.919 | .370 | -0.392 |
| | | Post-test | 69.90 (19.43) | 90.10 (27.20) | -1.911 | .072 | 0.814 |
| | | Follow up 6 | 60.90 (19.47) | 90.10 (27.20) | -2.760 | .013 | 1.175 |
| | | Follow up 12 | 55.80 (26.40) | 90.10 (27.20) | -2.861 | .010 | 1.218 |
| | **SPAI-Agoraphobia** | Pre-test | 19.50 (11.66) | 21.50 (13.11) | -0.360 | .723 | 0.153 |
| | | Post-test | 10.20 (5.95) | 19.80 (11.44) | -2.352 | .030 | 1.002 |
| | | Follow up 6 | 6.40 (3.91) | 19.80 (11.44) | -3.502 | .003 | 1.492 |
| | | Follow up 12 | 3.80 (3.61) | 19.80 (11.44) | -4.214 | .001 | 1.796 |
| | **SPS** | Pre-test | 70.80 (8.95) | 69.60 (5.50) | 0.768 | .645 | -0.199 |
| | | Post-test | 40.30 (12.49) | 71.20 (3.32) | -7.560 | .000 | 3.220 |
| | | Follow up 6 | 31.10 (14.70) | 71.20 (3.32) | -8.409 | .000 | 3.583 |
| | | Follow up 12 | 27.10 (13.75) | 71.20 (3.30) | -9.854 | .000 | 4.213 |
| | **SIAS** | Pre-test | 73.90 (3.78) | 72.70 (4.03) | 0.686 | .501 | -0.293 |
| | | Post-test | 41.50 (13.93) | 63.90 (17.82) | -3.130 | .006 | 1.338 |
| | | Follow up 6 | 32.10 (15.70) | 63.90 (17.80) | -4.233 | .001 | 2.428 |
| | | Follow up 12 | 25.70 (16.99) | 63.92 (17.83) | -4.904 | .000 | 2.089 |
| | **RCSQ** | Pre-test | 60.00 (26.65) | 73.40 (4.19) | -1.570 | .134 | -0.669 |
| | | Post-test | 98.80 (11.09) | 72.60 (3.71) | 7.081 | .000 | 3.017 |
| | | Follow up 6 | 111.80 (16.64) | 72.60 (3.71) | 10.995 | .000 | 4.685 |
| | | Follow up 12 | 116.50 (9.55) | 72.62 (3.72) | 13.549 | .000 | 5.776 |
| | **Number of social phobic situations** [1] | Pre-test | 7.20 (1.03) | 7.40 (1.51) | -0.346 | .733 | 0.148 |
| | | Post-test | 0.80 (0.92) | 7.10 (0.99) | -14.719 | .000 | 6.281 |
| | | Follow up 6 | 0.40 (0.84) | 7.00 (0.94) | -16.500 | .000 | 7.027 |
| | | Follow up 12 | 0.40 (0.82) | 7.00 (0.94) | -16.500 | .000 | 7.027 |
| | **Number of social phobic situations in regard to be related to**[1] | Pre-test | 4.50 (0.52) | 3.90 (0.87) | 1.857 | .080 | -0.790 |
| | | Post-test | 0.50 (0.52) | 4.00 (0.47) | -15.652 | .000 | 6.669 |
| | | Follow up 6 | 0.20 (0.42) | 4.30 (1.05) | -10.371 | .000 | 4.844 |
| | | Follow up 12 | 0.20 (0.42) | 4.30 (1.05) | -10.371 | .000 | 4.844 |
| | **Number of social phobic situations in regard to performance** [1] | Pre-test | 2.70 (0.94) | 3.50 (1.17) | -1.672 | .112 | 0.717 |
| | | Post-test | 0.30 (0.48) | 3.10 (0.99) | -8.009 | .000 | 3.427 |
| | | Follow up 6 | 0.20 (0.42) | 3.00 (0.94) | -8.573 | .000 | 3.650 |
| | | Follow up 12 | 0.20 (0.41) | 3.01 (0.93) | -8.573 | .000 | 3.650 |
| *Cognitive component* | **SSPS** | Pre-test | 28.20 (1.93) | 27.80 (1.62) | 0.502 | .622 | -0.214 |
| | | Post-test | 16.20 (4.66) | 27.20 (1.98) | -6.863 | .000 | 2.926 |
| | | Follow up 6 | 11.10 (4.43) | 27.20 (1.98) | -10.476 | .000 | 4.468 |
| | | Follow up 12 | 7.40 (6.07) | 27.10 (1.95) | -9.792 | .000 | 4.176 |
| | **FNES** | Pre-test | 26.50 (2.22) | 26.10 (2.22) | 0.385 | .705 | -0.164 |
| | | Post-test | 15.70 (3.83) | 25.70 (2.35) | -7.028 | .000 | 2.997 |

| | | | | | | | |
|---|---|---|---|---|---|---|---|
| | | Follow up 6 | 11.50 (5.64) | 25.70 (2.35) | -7.343 | .000 | 3.130 |
| | | Follow up 12 | 9.30 (5.10) | 25.70 (2.35) | -9.229 | .000 | 3.933 |
| *Correlative* | **SELF-ESTEEM** | Pre-test | 21.20 (3.15) | 22.60 (2.27) | -1.139 | .270 | -0.185 |
| | | Post-test | 25.20 (3.19) | 22.30 (3.52) | 1.928 | .070 | 0.822 |
| | | Follow up 6 | 26.40 (3.23) | 22.30 (3.52) | 2.707 | .014 | 1.156 |
| | | Follow up 12 | 26.40 (3.13) | 22.15 (3.50) | 2.747 | .013 | 1.172 |
| | **ADAP-TATION** | Pre-test | 22.30 (4.29) | 22.30 (3.33) | .000 | .999 | 0.000 |
| | | Post-test | 12.30 (3.52) | 22.30 (3.81) | -6.071 | .000 | 2.589 |
| | | Follow up 6 | 8.60 (4.94) | 22.30 (3.80) | -6.922 | .000 | 2.952 |
| | | Follow up 12 | 7.50 (5.12) | 22.30 (3.83) | -7.313 | .000 | 3.113 |

SPAI: Social Phobia and Anxiety Inventory; SPS: Social Phobia Scale; SIAS: Social Interaction Anxiety Scale *RCSQ: Report of Confidence as a Speaker Questionnaire. *SSPS: Self-Statements during Public Speaking Scale; FNES: Fear of a Negative Evaluation Scale. *IPYASP/IAJFS: Intervention in Young Adults with Social Phobia * SLCG: Standby List Control Group; *n: Number of subjects. *M: Media; *TD: Typical Deviation; *ES: Effect Scope.
1Informed by ADIS-IV Social Phobias Section (DiNardo, Brown y Barlow, 1994) during pre-test evaluation.

## Intra-Group Comparisons

Intra-group measurements analysis (Anova with repeated measurements and Student T), carried out on both experimental groups, showed that the subjects in the IASP group lowered their scores for anxiety and social avoidance, and increased them in self-esteem variables, adaptation and number of phobic situations, founding significant differences with respect to the pre-test with a very high level of meaning (p ≤ .000). For some variables, the post-hoc differences occurred among other temporary moments (see table 3). It did not occur in the control group which did not reach statistical meaning in any of the scales.

**Table 3. Intra-group comparison and post-hoc tests**

| | | **IPYASP**/IAJFS (n=10) | | **SLCG** (n=10) | |
|---|---|---|---|---|---|
| **VDs** | *Moment Temporal* | *M (TD)* | *F; p Post-hoc comparison* | *M (TD)* | *F; p Post-hoc comparison* |
| **SPAI-Social Phobia** | Pre-test | 123.70 (11.89) | 25.534; p= .000 | 120.90 (15.60) | 1.676; p= .196 |
| | Post-test | 80.20 (22.18) | Pret-seg.1** | 117.00 (16.68) | |
| | Seg. 6 | 57.30 (30.62) | Pret-seg.2** | 117.00 (16.68) | |
| | Seg. 12 | 59.60 (29.29) | | 117.00 (16.68) | |
| **SPAI-Difference** | Pre-test | 104.20 (12.05) | 14.099; p= .000 | 99.40 (11.28) | 1.124; p= .357 |
| | Post-test | 69.90 (19.43) | Pret-post* | 90.10 (27.20) | |
| | Seg. 6 | 60.90 (19.47) | Pret-seg.1** | 90.10 (27.20) | |
| | Seg. 12 | 55.80 (26.40) | Pret-seg.2** | 90.10 (27.20) | |
| **SPAI-Agoraphobia** | Pre-test | 19.50 (11.66) | 13.292; p= .000 | 21.50 (13.11) | 1.150; p= .347 |
| | Post-test | 10.20 (5.95) | Pret-post* | 19.80 (11.44) | |
| | Seg. 6 | 6.40 (3.91) | Pret-seg.1* | 19.80 (11.44) | |
| | Seg. 12 | 3.80 (3.61) | Post-seg.2* Seg.1-seg.2* | 19.80 (11.44) | |
| **SPS** | Pre-test | 70.80 (8.95) | 57.723; p= .000 | 69.60 (5.50) | 0.767; p= .523 |
| | Post-test | 40.30 (12.49) | Pret-post** | 71.20 (3.32) | |
| | Seg. 6 | 31.10 (14.70) | Pret-seg.1** | 71.20 (3.32) | |

| | | | | | |
|---|---|---|---|---|---|
| | Seg. 12 | 27.10 (13.75) | Pret-seg.2**<br>Post-seg.1*<br>Post-seg.2*<br>Seg.1-seg.2* | 71.20 (3.30) | |
| | | **IPYASP**/IAJFS (n=10) | | **SLCG** (n=10) | |
| **SIAS** | Pre-test | 73.90 (3.78) | 52.956; p= .000 | 72.70 (4.03) | 2.760; p= .062 |
| | Post-test | 41.50 (13.93) | Pret-post** | 63.90 (17.82) | |
| | Seg. 6 | 32.10 (15.70) | Pret-seg.1** | 63.90 (17.80) | |
| | Seg. 12 | 25.70 (16.99) | Pret-seg.2**<br>Post-seg.2*<br>Seg.1-seg.2** | 63.92 (17.83) | |
| **RCSQ** | Pre-test | 60.00 (26.65) | 22.454; p= .000 | 73.40 (4.19) | 1.116; p= .360 |
| | Post-test | 98.80 (11.09) | Pret-post* | 72.60 (3.71) | |
| | Seg. 6 | 111.80 (16.64) | Pret-seg.1** | 72.60 (3.71) | |
| | Seg. 12 | 116.50 (9.55) | Pret-seg.2**<br>Post-seg.1*<br>Post-seg.2**<br>Seg.1-seg.2* | 72.62 (3.72) | |
| **Number of social phobic situations** [1] | Pre-test | 7.20 (1.03) | 114, 692; p= .000 | 7.40 (1.51) | 0.489; p= .993 |
| | Post-test | 0.80 (0.92) | Pret-post** | 7.10 (0.99) | |
| | Seg. 6 | 0.40 (0.84) | Pret-seg.1** | 7.00 (0.94) | |
| | Seg. 12 | 0.40 (0.82) | Pret-seg.2** | 7.00 (0.94) | |
| **Number of social phobic situations in regard to be related to**[1] | Pre-test | 4.50 (0.52) | 132.953; p= .000 | 3.90 (0.87) | 0.547; p= .654 |
| | Post-test | 0.50 (0.52) | Pret-post** | 4.00 (0.47) | |
| | Seg. 6 | 0.20 (0.42) | Pret-seg.1** | 4.30 (1.05) | |
| | Seg. 12 | 0.20 (0.42) | Pret-seg.2** | 4.30 (1.05) | |
| **Number of social phobic situations in regard to performance** [1] | Pre-test | 2.70 (0.94) | 14.467; p =.000 | 3.50 (1.17) | 0.824, p = .492 |
| | Post-test | 0.30 (0.48) | Pret-post** | 3.10 (0.99) | |
| | Seg. 6 | 0.20 (0.42) | Pret-seg.1** | 3.00 (0.94) | |
| | Seg. 12 | 0.20 (0.41) | Pret-seg.2** | 3.01 (0.93) | |
| **SSPS** | Pre-test | 28.20 (1.93) | 58.427; p =.000 | 27.80 (1.62) | 0.824, p = .492 |
| | Post-test | 16.20 (4.66) | Pret-post** | 27.20 (1.98) | |
| | Seg. 6 | 11.10 (4.43) | Pret-seg.1** | 27.20 (1.98) | |
| | Seg. 12 | 7.40 (6.07) | Pret-seg.2** | 27.10 (1.95) | |
| **FNES** | Pre-test | 26.50 (2.22) | 45.033; p =.000 | 26.10 (2.22) | 0.844, p = .482 |
| | Post-test | 15.70 (3.83) | Pret-post** | 25.70 (2.35) | |
| | Seg. 6 | 11.50 (5.64) | Pret-seg.1** | 25.70 (2.35) | |
| | Seg. 12 | 9.30 (5.10) | Pret-seg.2**<br>Post-seg.1*<br>Post-seg.2**<br>Seg.1-seg.2** | 25.70 (2.35) | |
| **Self-Esteem** | Pre-test | 21.20 (3.15) | 16.994; p =.000 | 22.60 (2.27) | 0.135, p = .938 |
| | Post-test | 25.20 (3.19) | Pret-post** | 22.30 (3.52) | |
| | Seg. 6 | 26.40 (3.23) | Pret-seg.1** | 22.30 (3.52) | |
| | Seg. 12 | 26.40 (3.13) | Pret-seg.2* | 22.15 (3.50) | |
| **Adaptation** | Pre-test | 22.30 (4.29) | 33.615; p =.000 | 22.30 (3.33) | 0.000; p = .999 |
| | Post-test | 12.30 (3.52) | Pret-post** | 22.30 (3.81) | |
| | Seg. 6 | 8.60 (4.94) | Pret-seg.1** | 22.30 (3.80) | |
| | Seg. 12 | 7.50 (5.12) | Pret-seg.2**<br>Post-seg.1*<br>Post-seg.2* | 22.30 (3.83) | |

The number of subjects per group is 10. * $p< .05$; ** $p< .01$. SPAI: Social Phobia and Anxiety Inventory; SPS: Social Phobia Scale; SIAS: Social Interaction Anxiety Scale *RCSQ: Report of *Confidence* as a Speaker *Questionnaire*; *SSPS: Self-Statements during Public Speaking Scale; FNE: Fear of a Negative Evaluation.

## Clinical Meaning

The clinical meaning of the changes was determined by examining subjects percentage showing a decrease in feared social situations showed in the pre-test, which implied a 100% remission (Stop meeting the criteria for social phobia diagnosis by the DSM-IV-TR –APA, 2000–), or which is found between 75% and 99.99%. For both criteria, the percentages of improvement were, respectively, 50% in the post-test, and 80% in the both, 6 and 12 months follow-up applied to IPYASP/IAJFS group, compared with 0.0% of the Standby List Control Group for the same measurements. Taking into consideration the first criteria (elimination of the problem), significant differences were found in both groups, in the post-test and during the follow-ups, favoring the IPYASP group [$\chi 2(1) = 6.667$, $p = .010$; $\chi^2(1) = 13.333$, $p = .000$; $\chi^2(1) = 13.333$, $p = .000$]. Regarding second criteria (remission between 75% and 99.99%), only significant statistical differences were found in the post-test [$\chi 2(1) = 6.667$, $p = .010$] since the number of participants that improved in this range, the Standby List Control Group rose to 20.0% and none of the subjects in the IPYASP/IAJFS group showed improvement within this interval [$\chi^2(1) = 2.222$, $p = .136$, for the 6 month follow-up, and $\chi^2(1) = 2.222$, $p = .136$ for the measurement after 12 months].

# Discussion

The results found show a significant statistical decrease in the anxiety and social avoidance responses of the group treated in comparison with the control group, both, in post-test and in the follow-ups. These results coincide with those found in adolescent and adult populations (Garcia-Lopez et al., 2006; Hayward et al., 2000; Olivares and Garcia-Lopez; 2001; Taylor, 1996).

On the other hand, the results have also allowed us to prove that in the post-test, 50% of the subjects treated did no longer inform us any phobic social situation; in other words, they no longer fulfilled the criteria required for social phobia diagnosis, and the other 50% had reduced the number of phobic social situations informed in the pre-test above 75%. This data improved in the follow-up, exactly as occurred in other studies in which presentation techniques and cognitive restructuring have been applied (see Mendez, Sanchez and Moreno, 2001) and in those obtained by our own group upon applying the IASP (for example, see Olivares, Rosa and Olivares-Olivares, 2006 or Olivares-Olivares, Rosa and Olivares, 2007).

On the other hand and due to "self-esteem" and "adaptation" variables, the results also showed higher scores for the subjects treated when compared with those who were not treated (control group). This data coincides with the adult Spanish population ones, provided by Salaberria and Echeburua (1995).

Concerning effect scope, we proved that this is very high for the post-test as well as during follow-ups, once again corroborating improvement in subjects treated when compared to those not treated, and these are consistent with those found by our group in previous investigations about the treatment of adolescents from 14 to 17 years old (according to Olivares, Rosa and Piqueras, 2005). The effect scope allows us to conclude that the IPYASP/IAJFS Program is likely effective (see Cohen, 1988).

With respect to intra-group comparisons, it must be indicated that the treated group reached significant improvement in both, post-test and follow-up for all variables measured, while the Standby List Control Group did not show improvement any improvement in none of the pre-test or post-test variables.

In reference to future investigations, we feel that it would be important to consider the following, among other aspects: To increase the number of subjects participating in order to increase the size of the experimental groups, including new experimental conditions to allow us to test new hypotheses; to present observational measurements to evaluate the effect of more objective treatments, to use parents (couples, friends, etc.) as informers about the changes produced in the subjects, so as to study the social validity IPYASP/IAJFS effects; to analyze the degree of effectiveness upon considering the degree of generalization of the disturbance (see Piqueras, Olivares and Lopez-Pina, 2007); to investigate under controlled conditions the contribution of different components of the IPYASP/IAJFS Program to determine which are more effective for provoking therapeutic change, as well as for analyzing if these are additional or interactive acts in order to try to understand and to explain the reasons under this proved change operates; to study if the effects of this Program are more influenced when applied to a group or to an individual; to analyze the use of audiovisual feedback as compared to peers feedback, etc.

Finally, we would like to state that in our case, we have proceeded as opposed to the way previously used for adaptation of psychological treatment in the English-speaking environment: First, the effectiveness was tested in the adult population, and later the protocol was modified for application on the child-young population. Thus, to mention only two meaningful examples: Social Effectiveness Therapy for Children –SET-C– (Beidel, Turner and Morris, 2000) was derived from Social Effectiveness Therapy –SET– (Turner, Beidel, Cooley, Woody and Messer, 1994) and the Cognitive Behavioral Group Therapy for Adolescents –CBGT-A– (Albano, Marten and Holt, 1991) from the Cognitive Behavioral Group Therapy –CBGT– (Heimberg, 1991). We developed a specific program for the adolescent population between from 14 to 18 years old, and now we are verifying the validity of our adaptation to young adult population, in other words, the next age generation.

## REFERENCES

Albano, A.M., Marten, P.A. & Holt, C.S. (1991). Therapist's manual for cognitive-behavioral group therapy for adolescent social phobia. Unpublished manuscript.

American Psychiatric Association. (2000). Diagnostic and Statistical Manual of Mental Disorders (4th. Ed. Reviewed text). Washington, DC: APA

Beidel, D. C., Turner, S. M. & Morris, T. L. (2000). Behavioral treatment of childhood social phobia. Journal of Consulting and Clinical Psychology, 68, 1072-1080.

Cohen, J. (1988). Statistical power analysis for the behavioral sciences (2nd. Ed.). Hillsdale, NJ: Erlbaum.

DiNardo, P. A., Brown, T. A. & Barlow, D. H. (1994). Anxiety Disorders Interview Schedule for DSM-IV (Lifetime version). San Antonio, TX: Psychological Corporation

Echeburúa, E. & Corral, P. (1987). Escala de Inadaptación. Unpublished manuscript.

García-López, L. J., Ruiz, J., Olivares, J., Piqueras, J. A., Rosa, A. I. & Bermejo, R. (2006). Aplicación de un programa de tratamiento multicomponente para adolescentes con ansiedad social en población joven adulta: Un estudio piloto. Psicología Conductual, 14, 63-73.

Gilkinson, H. (1942). Social fears as reported by students in college speech classes. Speech Monographs, 9, 141-160.

Hayward, C., Varady, S., Albano, A. M., Thienemann, M., Henderson, L. & Schatzberg, A. F. (2000). Cognitive-behavioral group therapy for social phobia in female adolescents: Results of a pilot study. Journal of American Academy of Child and Adolescent Psychiatry, 39, 721-726

Hedges, L. V. & Olkin, I. (1985). Statistical methods for meta-analysis. Orlando, FL: Academic Press.

Heimberg, R.G. (1991). Cognitive-behavioral treatment of social phobia in a group setting: A treatment manual (2nd. Ed.). Unpublished manuscript. University at Albany-State University of New York.

Hofmann, S. G. & DiBartolo, P. M. (2000). An instrument to assess self-statements during public speaking: Scale development and preliminary psychometric properties. Behavior Therapy, 31, 499-515.

Kessler, R.C., Stang, P., Wittchen, H-U., Stein, M.B. & Walters, E.E. (1999). Lifetime comorbidities between social phobia and mood disorders in the United States National Comorbidity Survey. Psychological Medicine, 29, 555-567

Magee, W.J., Eaton, W.W., Wittchen, H.U., McGonagle, K.A. & Kessler, R.C. (1996). Agoraphobia, simple phobia and social phobia in the National Comorbidity Survey. Archives of General Psychiatry, 53, 159-168

Mattick, R. P. & Clarke, J. C. (1998). Development and validation of measures of social phobia scrutinity fear and social interaction anxiety. Behaviour Research and Therapy, 36, 455-470.

Méndez, F. X., Sánchez, J. & Moreno, P. (2001). Eficacia de los tratamientos psicológicos para la fobia social: un estudio meta-analítico. Psicología Conductual, 9, 39-59.

Moreno, P. J., Méndez, F. X. & Sánchez, J., (2000). Effectiviness of cognitive-behavioural treatment in social phobia: a meta-analytic review. Psicothema, 12, 246-352

Olivares, J. (Ed.) (2005). Programa IAFS. Protocolo para el tratamiento de la fobia social en adolescentes. Madrid: Pirámide.

Olivares, J. & García-López, L. J. (2001). Un nuevo tratamiento multicomponente para adolescentes con fobia social generalizada: Resultados de un estudio piloto. Psicología Conductual, 9, 247-254.

Olivares, J. & Rosa, A. I. (2005). Un estudio sobre los datos normativos del "Social Phobia and Anxiety Inventory" en su aplicación a adultos jóvenes españoles. Departamento de Personalidad, Evaluación y Tratamiento Psicológicos. Facultad de Psicología. Universidad de Murcia (España). Unpublished paper.

Olivares, J., Piqueras, J. A. & García-López, L. J. (2005). Tratamiento de un adulto joven con fobia social generalizada. In J. P. Espada, J. Olivares & F. X. Méndez (Eds.), Terapia Psicológica. Casos prácticos (67-91). Madrid: Pirámide.

Olivares, J. & Rosa, A. I. (2005). Programa "Intervención en Adultos Jóvenes con Fobia Social". Departamento de Personalidad, Evaluación y Tratamiento Psicológicos. Facultad de Psicología. Universidad de Murcia (España). Unpublished manuscript.

Olivares, J., Rosa, A. I., Caballo, V., García-López, L. J. & Orgilés, M. (2003). El tratamiento psicológico de la fobia social en niños y adolescentes: una revisión meta-analítica. Psicología Conductual, 11, 599-622.

Olivares, J., Rosa, A. I. & Olivares-Olivares, P. J. (2006). Atención individualizada y tratamiento en grupo de adolescentes con fobia social generalizada. International Journal of Clinical and Health Psychology, 6, 565-580.

Olivares, J., Rosa, A. I. & Piqueras, J. A. (2005). Detección temprana y tratamiento de adolescentes con fobia social generalizada. Psicothema, 17, 1-8.

Olivares-Olivares, P. J., Rosa, A. I. & Olivares, J. (2007). Validez social de la intervención en adolescentes con fobia social: padres frente a profesores. Terapia Psicológica, 25, 63-71.

Piqueras, J. A., Olivares, J. & López-Pina, J. A. (2007, en prensa). Empirical validation of a new proposal about delimitation and operationalisation of the subtypes of social phobia in a sample of Spanish adolescents. Journal of Anxiety Disorders,

Rosenberg, M. (1965). Society and the Adolescent Self Image. Princeton: Princeton University Press.

Rosenberg, M. S., Adams, D.C. & Gurevitch, J. (2000). MetaWin 2.0: Statistical software for meta-analysis. Sunderland, MA: Sinauer Assoc.

Spence, S. H., Donovan, C. & Brechman-Toussaint, M. (2000). The treatment of childhood social phobia: The effectiveness of a social skills training based cognitive-behavioral intervention, with and without parental involvement. Journal of Child Psychology and Psychiatry, 41, 713-726.

SPSS 14.0 (2007). Statistical Package for the Social Sciences. SPSS Inc.

Taylor, S. (1996). Meta-analysis of cognitive-behavioral treatments for social phobia. Journal of Behavioral Therapy and Experimental Psychiatry, 27, 1-9.

Turner, S. M., Beidel, D. C., Dancu, C. V. & Stanley, M. A. (1989). An empirically derived inventory to measure social fears and anxiety: The Social Phobia and Anxiety Inventory. Psychological Assessment, 1, 35-40.

Turner, S.M., Beidel, D.C, Cooley, M.R., Woody, S.R. & Messer, S.C. (1994). A multicomponent behavioral treatment for social phobia: Social effectiveness Therapy. Behaviour Research and Therapy, 32, 381-390

Watson, D. & Friend, R. (1969). Measurement of social-evaluative anxiety. Journal of Consulting and Clinical Psychology, 33, 448-45.

In: Hispanic Psychology Yearbook Volume 1
Ed: Cirilo H. García pp. 115-123
ISBN: 978-1-60741-786-6


*Chapter 9*

# CONTINGENCY CONTRAST IN MATCHING TO SAMPLE WITH UNIVERSITY STUDENTS*

***Isaac Camacho***[a]***, Mario Serrano***[b] ***& Claudio Carpio***[c]
[a]Instituto Politécnico Nacional. CICS- UST
[b]Universidad de Guadalajara. CEIC
[c]Universidad Nacional Autónoma de México (FES, Iztacala)

## ABSTRACT

To evaluate the effect of the difference in response morphology emitted to sample (SS1 and SS2) and comparison stimuli (COS1 and COS2) on the accuracy index, four groups of university students participated in a successive symbolic matching to sample task. The groups were unequal among them by the morphological difference of the response to SS and COS stimuli. The results showed than in the conditions of similarity between SS1-COS1 and SS2-COS2, but with differences between SS1-SS2 and COS1-COS2, the participant's accuracy was greatly enhanced as opposed to any other type of difference between the stimuli. Results are discussed by the analysis of the role of the difference in the contingency structures in the development of conditional stimulus control.

**Keywords:** Matching to sample, contingency structures, university students.

## INTRODUCTION

Conditional discrimination is a particular type of conditional probability arrangement, which is generally presented in a matching to sample task. In such a task, the discriminative or delta properties of stimuli vary given other stimuli occurring before or simultaneously.

---

* A version of this chapter was also published in the *International Hispanic Psychology Journal, Volume 1 Issue 2*, published by Nova Science Publishers, Inc. It was submitted for appropriate modification in an effort to encourage wider dissemination of research.

Figure 1 represents an outline of the contingency structures, which are the conditional relationships between sample (SS), comparison (CoS), their responses (r), reinforcement ($E^R$) and a time interval between each trial (ITI) that define the task.

Learning under such conditionalities is regarded as the degree in which a SS controls the presence or absence of responses given to one of the CoS, this phenomenon is known as conditional control.

The development of conditional control has been evaluated by systematically manipulating the value of some variables of interest (inter trial interval duration or response number to sample stimuli). Such variations can be grouped under one of the following criteria: a) between phases (Holt & Shafer 1973; Nelson & Wasserman, 1978; Pilgrim, Jackson & Galizio, 2000; Weavers, Foster & Temple, 1998; Wilkie & Spetch, 1978), b) between groups (Cooper, 1989; Lionello & Urcuioli, 1998; Lionello-DeNolf & Urcuioli, 2000; Santi, 1982) and c) between groups and phases (Zentall, Sherburne & Urcuioli, 1993). A constant factor in these studies is that, independently of the criteria, the value of the independent variable remains the same for the contingency structures in effect during the task.

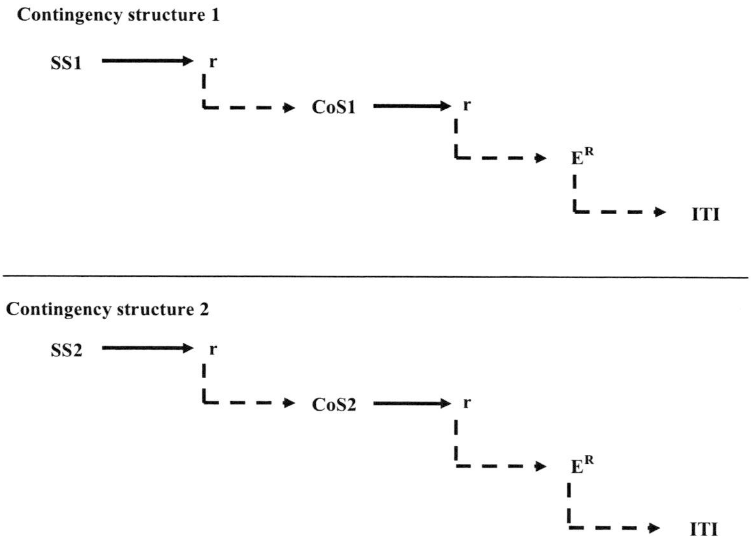


Figure 1.

However, difference between the elements that constitute the contingency structures of the task is a condition which has been reported as positive in the development of conditional control, for example when deferential outcomes (Brodigan & Peterson, 1976; Cohen, Looney, Brady & Aucella, 1976; DeLong & Wasserman, 1981) or when different sample response requirements are used (Eckerman, 1970; Lyndersen & Perkins, 1974).

In their studies, Eckerman (1970), Lydersen & Perkins (1974) y Cohen, Looney, Brady & Aucella (1976), showed that difference between conditional arrangements established by different sample responding had an important effect on conditional control. Even Eckerman (1970) proposed a model which was based upon differential sample responding.

To extend the knowledge on the role of the contingency structure difference given differential sample responding, now by morphology difference, the present study evaluated the effect of morphologically different sample and comparison responding on precision index in a matching to sample task with human participants.

# METHOD

## Subjects

Twenty students from the second semester in the psychology school of Iztacala College of Superior Studies (UNAM).

## Instruments

A four- responses device was used. Their dimensions were: 52 cm. long by 16 cm. high and 16 cm. wide. The central panel of the device was divided into four 13 cm. portions. At the center of each one of them was a 12 cm. diameter hole and the response device was found at the bottom thereof: In the first hole, there was a button; in the second one, a lever; in the third one, a chain, and in the fourth hole, there was a movement sensor. To record the answers and the stimuli programming, a Pentium II computer was used along with a SuperLab Pro Beta 2.1 program.

## Procedure

Four groups were formed with five persons each. The assignment of a person in each group was randomly done. The groups differed between themselves from the differentiation of contingency structures. Differentiating conditions refer to the assignment of the same response device or a different device for each stimulus to be used in the task of matching the sample, which necessarily implies an equal or different coordination of the body's reactive systems as a response to each stimulus.

The subjects of each group were exposed during the same session to two phases: 1) The phase for establishing the response, which consisted in the successive and random presentation of all of the stimuli to be used in the experiment and the specification of the response device corresponding to each one, and 2) the training phase, during which a task for equaling the successive sample was implemented.

Group 1. Phase one began with the presentation of the following instructions on the monitor screen:

*"Hello. The first thing you have to do is get to know the response console in front of you. On the front side of the console there are four holes, inside of each one there is a response device. Each device is marked by its generic name.*

*Now, activate each one with one hand: move the lever, press the button, touch the sensor and pull the chain. When you are familiar with each one, inform the researcher so that the session may begin. During the session different symbols will be presented on the screen of the monitor and what you have to do is to discover which device must be activated when each symbol appears. This is very important because your success on the experiment depends on this. Ready?"*

Afterwards, the four stimuli to be used were presented at random. The criterion for cancellation of each one was the manipulation of a response device. After each activation of the device, one of the following texts appeared on the monitor screen: a) "CORRECT, YOU USED THE CORRECT DEVICE" or b) "INCORRECT, YOU DID NOT USE THE CORRECT DEVICE" according to the following arrangement: SS1 – press the button, SS2 - press the button, CoS1 – press the button, CoS2– press the button. Under this programming, 12 tests were carried out (3 presentations for each stimulus). Immediately afterwards, the following instructions appeared on the monitor screen: "NOW YOU MUST RESPOND MORE QUICKLY". Once again at random, the same stimuli were presented, but now the criterion for their cancellation was the response device activation or a 3 sec time lap. If there was no response during this period of time, a message appeared: "YOU MUST RESPOND MORE QUICKLY" and the trial was repeated. Without considering the repetition trials, this phase lasted another 12 trials, making a total of 24 trials.

Next, phase two started. At the beginning the following instructions were displayed:

*"Good. Now your task will be to identify which symbol matches other symbols; in other words, which ones are pairs. You must remember which device must be used to respond to each symbol, but now the most important task is to identify the pairs.*

*First, you will see a symbol. Examine it and activate the corresponding device. When this is done, the symbol will disappear and another one will appear. Look at it rapidly (it will only last for a few seconds) and then decide if this second one matches the first one. If you think it does, activate the corresponding device, if you do not think so, do not do anything and it will disappear automatically. In the beginning you will have to guess, but as you progress, the correct answers and errors will be indicated to you upon searching for pairs. Ready?*

These instructions were followed by the presentation of one of two possible stimuli displayed on the monitor screen, SS1 or SS2 (two arbitrary symbols); the frequency of presentation of each stimulus was 50% of the trials. The response requirement for termination of this stimulus and the presentation of the comparative stimulus was to push the button. If a different device was activated, the following message will appear: "YOU ACTIVATED THE WRONG DEVICE" and the trial was restarted. As a comparison stimulus any of the following stimuli appeared on the monitor: CoS1 or CoS2 (two arbitrary symbols different from SS1 and SS2). The response requirement for the comparison stimuli was to press the button. Sample and comparison stimuli participated in two types of trials: negative (SS1 – CoS2 y SS2 – CoS1) and positive (SS1 – CoS1 y SS2 – CoS2). If response requirement was not accomplished during the first 3 sec of stimuli presentation, it was cancelled and a 2 seconds inter-trial interval would immediately begin (ITI). The presentation of each comparison was done randomly to avoid bias due to the frequency of positive and negative trial presentation.

Four types of response were established: 1) accuracy in performance (AP) when a response to the CoS occurred on positive trials, 2) accuracy by omission (AO) when a response to the CoS on negative trials was not emitted, 3) mistake in performance (MP) when the subject responded to the CoS on negative trials, and lastly 4) mistake by omission (MO) when the CoS response on positive trials did not occur.

Once comparison response was issued (only accuracies and mistakes in performance), the consequences were displayed on the monitor screen: 1) "CORRECT: IT MATCHED", for positive trials and 2) "WRONG: IT DID NOT MATCH" for negative trials. Consequences lasted 3 seconds. Trials with correct answers by omission and mistakes by omission did not have programmed consequences, and immediately after the comparison cancellation the ITI began.

During the ITI the monitor screen remained in blank and then a new test began. This phase consisted of 64 trials.

Group 2. Programmed experimental conditions for this group were the same as for the previous group, except that during phase one, pressing the button (SS1 and CoS1), and moving the lever (SS2 and CoS2) were established as response morphologies, this made contingency structures differ due to the response morphology between them, but remained the same inside each one (See Table 1).

Group 3. Programmed experimental conditions for this group were the same as for group one, except that during phase one, pressing the button (SS1 and SS2) and moving the lever (CoS1 and CoS2) were established as response morphologies, so that contingency structures did not differ between themselves but they did differ inside each one (See Table 1).

Group 4. Programmed experimental conditions for this group were the same as for group one, except that during phase one, pressing the button (SS1) and moving the lever (SS2), activating the sensor (CoS1) and pulling the chain (CoS2), were established as response morphologies. In such an arrangement contingency structures differed between themselves and inside each one (See Table 1)

For a synthetic design display, see Table 1.

**Table 1.**

| GROUP | PHASE 1 | PHASE 2 |
|---|---|---|
| **G1**= intra and between similarity | SS1-a, CoS1-a<br>SS2-a, CoS2- | SS1---**a**----CoS1-----**a**-------ER<br>SS2---**a**----CoS2-----**a**-------<br>-- |
| **G2**= differentiation in between/intra similarity | SS1-a, CoS1-a<br>SS2-b, CoS2- | SS1--**a**-----CoS1-----**a**-------ER<br>SS2--**b**-----CoS2-----**b**-------ER |
| **G3**= intra differentiation /between similarity | SS1-a, CoS1-b<br>SS2-a, CoS2- | SS1---**a**-----CoS1-----**b**------ER<br>SS2---**a**-----CoS2-----**b**------ER |
| **G4**= intra and between differentiation | SS1-a, CoS1-b<br>SS2-c, CoS2- | SS1---**a**---CoS1------**b**-------ER<br>SS2---**c**---CoS2------**d**------<br>-- |

## Measurements

The measurement to estimate the performance of subjects was the precision index. This was calculated by using the two possible types of accuracies and mistakes, by applying the following formula: Precision index = AP+AO/AP+AO+MP+MO.

# Results

The objective of this study was to evaluate the effect of the different response morphology to sample and comparison stimuli on the precision index in a symbolic matching to sample task with human participants. This objective's guiding axis was: in matching to sample tasks, the precision index's value depends on the difference between contingency structures.

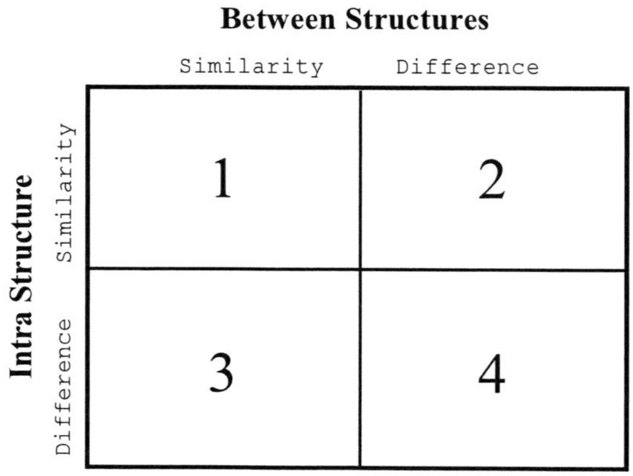


Figure 2.

Figure 3 presents the precision index for each group. Group 2 had the highest precision index (1.0), meanwhile Groups 1 and 4 followed showing a 0.838 and a 0.83 index, respectively. Lastly, Group 3 obtained the lowest precision index with a value of 0.64.

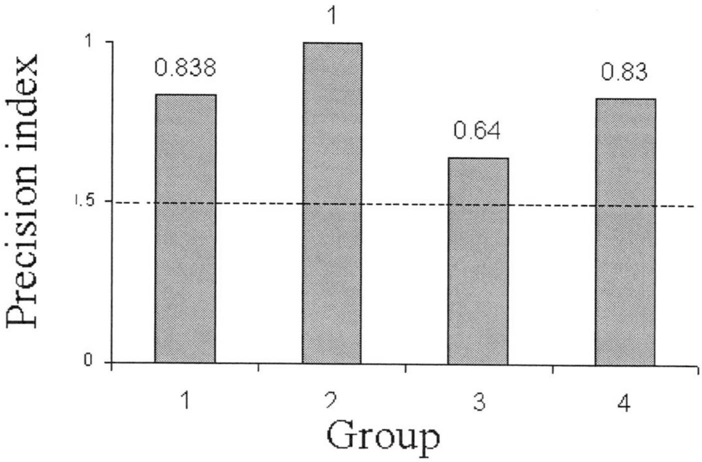


Figure 3

In regard to the speed of acquisition, Figure 4 displays precision index for each group according to 8 tests blocks. Group 2 obtained a 1.0 perfect acquisition on all blocks. The next ones were Group 1 and 4 with similar acquisition speed. Lastly, figure shows that Group 3 had the lowest acquisition speed.

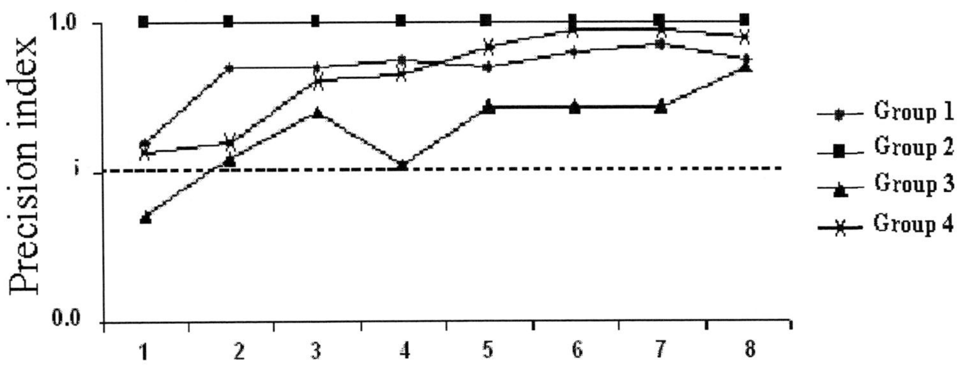


Figure 4

One ANOVA 4 (groups) x 8 (blocks) revealed that there is a main effect in all of the groups [$F(3,159)=30.250$, $p<0.001$]. Differences were also found during the training period [$F(7,159)=6.726$, $p<.001$], but there were no significant differences found in interaction Group x Block [$F(21,159)=1.362$, $p=0.150$]. The main group effects showed that there were no differences in the precision index between Groups 1 and 4; Group 2 obtained the highest index; Group 3, the lowest one.

## DISCUSSION

Studies concerning both differential responses and differential outcomes in conjunction with this study, allows for the proposition that the difference in contingency structures affects the development of conditional control.

However, to estimate the total results of this study, it is necessary to make an additional distinction in the contingency structure analysis.

Just as it is possible that a certain difference between contingency structures 1 and 2 exists, it is also possible that inside each one certain parametric properties (*e.g.* physical dimension, duration, position, etc.) of the stimulus and response events that constitute them make another difference. From now on, this difference inside each structure will be called intra structure contingency differentiation and the first one the between contingency structures difference.

Taking these two types of differentiations into account, experimental analysis can rest in the following propositions: a) Conditional relationships between the elements in a task are unified conditional structures and are analytically distinguishable, and b) the differentiation between or intra contingency structures in a task, are conditions that affect conditional control development in specific ways. Both constitute the bases for a Contingency Contrast Model, whose paradigmatic cases of empirical exploration are represented through the following contingency contrast matrix:

An advantage of this model is that it allows the integration of variables previously manipulated by other authors. For example, the SS's physical dimension in regard to CoS (Santi, 1978); the response requirement to CoS (Wilkie & Spetch, 1978); SS duration with respect to the CoS's (Cooper, 1989), or the duration of the inter trial interval (Serrano, Camacho & Carpio, 2006) can be variables from which investigations derived from the Contingency Contrast Model may be done. In addition, this model can make it possible to recognize a functional general continuum, independently of the variable manipulated, instead of favoring micro-theories construction (Cabrer, Daza & Ribes, 1975).

From this model and this study's data, it is possible to recognize, first, that there is a specific conditional control effect by the differentiation between/intra contingency structures. Groups 2 (differentiation in between/intra similarity) and 3 (intra differentiation /between similarity) can be considered as extreme cases, while groups 1 (intra and between similarity) and 4 (intra and between differentiation) can be considered to be intermediate cases. In the second place, the differentiation or similarity between and intra contingency structures are conditions whose effects are not isolated but interactive.

The results of this study suggest that differentiation between and intra contingency structure similarity are favorable conditions for conditional control development, more so than conditions of between structure similarity and intra structure differentiation and of course more than between-intra similarity and intra-between structure differentiation.

Even though this study included all four cases identified in the matrix of contingency contrast, it is necessary that in future studies a detailed evaluation of the specific participation of each of the elements composing the structures is conducted (*e.g.* differentiation due to duration of the sample, due to delay between sample and comparison, etc.). In addition, a promising route of inquiry could be the systematical exploration of variables whose effects are well known in literature (e.g., reinforcement delay). All of this may be seen in the future, for the time being the data in this study ratifies the basic suppositions the contingency contrast model, and, in general, the study presents it as a viable alternative for future conditional control development research.

## References

Brodigan, D. L., & Peterson, G. B.(1976). Two-choice conditional discrimination performance of pigeons as a function of reward expectancy, prechoice delay and domesticity. *Animal Learning and Behavior. 4,* 121-124.

Cabrer F., Daza, B. C., & Ribes I. E. (1975). Teoría de la conducta: ¿Nuevos conceptos o nuevos parámetros? *Revista Mexicana de Análisis de la Conducta.* 1, 191-212.

Cohen, L. R., Looney, T. A., Brady, J. H., & Aucella, A. F. (1976). Differential sample response schedules in the acquisition of conditional discriminations by pigeons. *Journal of the Experimental Analysis of Behavior.* 26, 301-314.

Cooper D. L. (1989). Some temporal factors affecting conditional discrimination. *Animal Learning & Behavior.* 17, 21-30.

DeLong, E. R., & Wasserman, E. A. (1981) Effects of differential reinforcement expectancies on successive matching to sample performance in pigeons. *Journal of Experimental Psychology: Animal Behavior Processes.* 7, 394-412.

Eckerman, D. A. (1970). Generalization and response mediation of a conditional discrimination. *Journal of the Experimental Analysis of Behavior.* 13, 301-316.

Holt, L. G., & Shafer, N. J. (1973). Function of intertrial interval in matching to sample. *Journal of the Experimental Analysis of Behavior.* 19, 181-186.

Goeters, S., Blakely, E., & Poling, A. (1992). The differential outcomes effect. *The Psychological Record.* 42, 389-411.

Lionello, M. K. & Urcuioli, P. J. (1998). Control by sample location in pigeons' matching to sample. *Journal of the Experimental Analysis of Behavior.* 70, 235-251.

Lionello-DeNolf, M. K., & Urcuioli, P. J. (2000). Transfer of pigeons' matching to sample to novel sample locations. *Journal of the Experimental Analysis of Behavior.* 73, 141-161.

Lyndersen, T.,& Perkins, D.(1974). Effects of response-produced stimuli upon conditional discrimination performance. *Journal of the Experimental Analysis of Behavior.* 21, 307-314.

Nelson, R. K., & Wasserman, E. A. (1978). Temporal factors influencing the pigeon's successive matching to sample performance: Sample duration, intertrial interval and retention interval. *Journal of the Experimental Analysis of Behavior.* 30, 153-162.

Pilgrim, C., Jackson, J. & Galizio, M. (2000). Acquisition of arbitrary conditional discriminations by young normally developing children. *Journal of the Experimental Analysis of Behavior.* 73, 177-193.

Santi, A. (1978). The role of physical identity of the sample and correct comparison stimulus in matching to sample paradigms. *Journal of the Experimental Analysis of Behavior.* 29, 511-516.

Santi, A. (1982). Hue matching and hue oddity in pigeons: Is explicit training not to peck incorrect hue combinations a sufficient condition for transfer? *The Psychological Record.* 32, 61-73.

Serrano, M., Camacho, I. & Carpio, C. (2006). Intervalos entre ensayos de distinta duración en Igualación de la muestra demorada. *Revista Mexicana_de Análisis de la Conducta*, 32, 1-12.

Weavers, R., Foster, M. T., & Temple, W. (1998). Reinforcer efficacy in a delayed matching to sample task. *Journal of the Experimental Analysis of_Behavior.* 69, 77-85.

Wilkie, M. D. & Spetch, L. M. (1978). The effects of sample and comparison ratio schedules on delayed matching to sample in the pigeon. *Animal Learning & Behavior.* 6, 273-278.

Zentall, R. T., Sherburne, M. L. & Urcuioli, J. P. (1993). Common coding by pigeons in a many to one delayed matching to sample as evidenced by facilitation and interference effects. *Animal Learning and Behavior.* 21, 233-237.

In: Hispanic Psychology Yearbook Volume 1
Ed: Cirilo H. García pp. 125-136

ISBN: 978-1-60741-786-6


*Chapter 10*

# EFFECTS OF COUPLE THERAPY ON DYSFUNCTIONAL FAMILY STRUCTURE[1*]

***Jaime Montalvo Reyna, Carlos García Mondragón***
***Israel Velasco Jiménez, Maria Rosario Espinosa Salcido, &***
***C. Susana González Montoya***
Universidad Nacional Autónoma de México (FES, Iztacala)

## ABSTRACT

This paper employs a quasi-experimental ABA design to analyze the implementation of Communicative Restructuring (CR) in 15 cases of couple therapy. A semi-structured interview format with a guide was used to measure family dysfunction (FD) before and after the application of the CR. Even though the therapy only targeted the marital holon, the effects of CR seem to have influenced family structure at large, since the degree of FD decreased significantly after the implementation of the technique. The affected boundaries changed from the diffuse to the clear or partially clear, and conflicts tended to disappear. The paper also emphasizes the importance of the systemic principle of totality (if an element in the system is modified this will alter or affect the other elements) and the need to take it into account.

**Keywords**: Communicative restructuring, couple problems, family dysfunction, family structure, boundaries, conflicts.

---

[1] Research supported by the PAPIME program, DGAPA UNAM.
Address for correspondence: Jaime Montalvo Reyna-Ezequiel Chavez No. 8, Colonia Magisterial Vista bella Tlalnepantla, Estado de México, CP.54050, México.
E-mail: mrjaimemx@hotmail.com, mrj@servidor.unam.mx

[*] A version of this chapter was also published in the *International Hispanic Psychology Journal, Volume 1 Issue 2*, published by Nova Science Publishers, Inc. It was submitted for appropriate modification in an effort to encourage wider dissemination of research.

# Introduction

The couple is generally seen as the basis of the family, while the latter is considered the fundamental cell of society. The structures and processes that originate it are as multifarious as those that take place after its foundation, shaping it through time and in response to specific experiences. Overall, these phenomena constitute types of human interaction and organization.

But why is it that human beings (as well as some other animal species) pair up in couples? This question has been historically explored by many disciplines and the conclusions have been varied. From a biological perspective, the goal is that of procreation and, by extension, the preservation of the species; according to economics, societies seek to share resources and increase benefits at the same time that they reduce risks. Some psychologists, on the other hand, have portrayed the couple as a vehicle through which partners are able to get around each other and express freely, without limitations. According to this theory, the couple eases the individual wounds caused by an individual's exposure to daily life and interaction with the world, providing a physical and emotional space that enables restoration or, as some authors call it, "sacrifice" (Stanley, Whitton, Sadberry, Clements, and Markman, 2006).

The definitions of "couple" can be highly varied and cover all practical possibilities, but the concept implies a union between individuals who, even if they belong to the same social group and therefore share a number of characteristics, are still distinct people with very subjective and particular experiences, knowledge, and beliefs. And yet this does not stop individuals from pairing up, at least not on a general basis. This could be the reason why some theoreticians have suggested that factors such as choice of partners, interaction patterns, and development processes determine a couple's breakup or end.

According to Kershaw (1994), the words and behaviors used by a couple during interaction constitute a kind of hypnotic dance where the behavior of each partner condenses the other's focus of attention (p. 19). This process can awaken memories and result in feelings of vulnerability associated to the past. That is, the partners mutually stimulate each other into states akin to trance: attention is singly focused and there is dissociation between thought, feeling, and action. The author maintains that any kind of hypnosis is self-hypnosis and that, for this reason, interaction serves as a catalyst that induces a hypnotic state in each partner. Their attention narrows and this is followed by an interactive sequence in which each partner's state of consciousness leads to automatic behaviors that link to those of their counterpart, resulting in reciprocal progressions.

Döring (2000) points to the eminently human need to enjoy intimate company, share likes and dislikes, and have a physical and temporal space for personal and emotional life (p. 37), but warns about the risks of basing such goals on fantasies and self-deception, as this can lead to disillusionment. When speaking of a couple, the author does not only refer to partners who live together or share a life, but also those who have a relationship based on mutual support and growth. Those who are more capable of confronting their existential commitment and taking responsibility for it will be the most likely to establish a partnership and, generally, engage in more fulfilling, less dependent relationships that promote the constant growth of those involved.

When speaking of couple interaction we must inevitably address the vast amount of infor

-mation exchanged by partners, which is why we think it necessary to address the topic of communication.

## What is Communication?

Much is being written nowadays on the issue of communication and the subject very popular. When we meet teenagers who do not speak to their parents we say that they have "communication problems"; we apply this same criterion to a problematic marriage. Every single individual has a personal communication system based on certain fundamental attitudes, stances toward self and others, work, life, and a series of other factors. An individual's capacity to communicate can go beyond the ability to speak or write well. On the other hand, it is important to point out that a person's virtues and overall possibilities of success and self-realization appear to be directly linked to the ability to communicate (Vilchez, 1985).

To communicate means to take the other into consideration. This is not about doing one thing or another, speaking or remaining silent; rather, it is an attitude, a basic process we continually implement, an evolutionary reality subject to change, and a learning process. This is why an educated approach to communication plays a fundamental role in a couple's process. Communication must be understood as a part of the vast spectrum of human expressiveness that is, in turn, part of our nature. We communicate what and how we are while referencing the culture and social groups to which we belong (Vilchez, 1985).

Bornstein and Bornstein (1998) have pointed out that communication among partners can be defined as the set of symbolic means people use to transmit messages. Words and verbal behavior are usually the most common form of communication, but non-verbal behaviors (e.g., tone of voice, body language, posture, gestures) comprise a most important part of this process. Regardless of the type of communication or its content, the symbols must be shared by both parties if the message is to be understood on its own terms. Simply put, misunderstandings are likely to arise if meanings are not shared, as in the case of couples suffering from communication problems. In short, the generic term "communication problems" actually refers to the inadequate transmission of symbolic messages. There is no doubt that insufficient communication presents a fundamental problem in relationships among partners. That which couples choose to talk about and the way in which they do it affect the perceived level of satisfaction in the relationship (Bornstein & Bornstein, 1998).

For these authors, communication between partners occurs when the two people involved express attitudes of protectiveness or love toward the relationship they maintain. They also distinguish two types of partner communication: intimate and economic. Intimate communication is related to verbal and non-verbal behaviors employed by one partner in order to send messages to the other; they can include smiles, winks, hugs, and many other ways of expressing love. For most couples without communication problems the intent of the messages is quite clear, but those experiencing problems will often profoundly disagree on the "intention" behind the message and its impact.

Rage (1996) has described some of the communicative differences between harmonious couples and those at odds:

- Although there is no difference in regards to the intent behind the messages, partners who are at odds will perceive each others' messages in a less positive light than those who are in harmony.
- The rate of agreements vis-à-vis disagreements is much higher among harmonious couples.
- Non-verbal behavior marks a very significant difference between harmonious couples and those at odds, and the latter show significantly more non-verbal negative behaviors than the former.
- Partners at odds tend to pay more attention to cross-complaints and the messages they send themselves than to the messages sent by the other member.
- Completely open and unrestricted communication has been observed more frequently among couples at odds than among those living in harmony.

## Structural Family Therapy (STF)

Structural Family Therapy (or STF) was created and pioneered by therapist Salvador Minuchin. Instead of approaching the family as a set of individual aspects belonging to each of the members, Minuchin interprets it as a system where each member can relate to the others in accordance with certain rules, thus constituting the family structure (Minuchin, 1986). Family structure is defined as the "invisible set of functional demands that organize the ways in which every member of a family interacts. The family is a system that operates through given transaction guidelines and in which repeated transactions establish guidelines regarding how, when, and with whom to interact. These guidelines underpin the system. For example, when a mother tells her son to drink his juice and he obeys, this interaction defines who she is in relation to him and who he is in relation to her in that very context and during that moment" (Minuchin, 1986 p. 86). Transaction guidelines regulate the conduct of the family members and are maintained by a pair of joint systems: the first is generic and encompasses the rules that govern family organization (e.g., a power hierarchy in which parents and children possess different levels of authority); the second is idiosyncratic and encompasses the mutual expectations of the different family members.

A family's structure must be able to adapt to changing circumstances. The continued existence of the family as a system depends on a range of [extant?] guidelines, the availability of alternative transaction guidelines, and the flexibility required to implement them whenever necessary (Minuchin,1986). Minuchin also mentions boundaries between the family subsystems or holons, and these are constituted by rules that decree who participates and how. The function of the boundaries is to protect the system's differentiation, as every family subsystem has specific functions and places specific demands on each family member. Minuchin differentiates between internal and external boundaries: the former are those that can be identified by the rules governing the members of the family subsystems, while the latter comprise the rules governing the interaction between the family and the external environment (e.g., other families).

Minuchin also distinguishes four types of boundaries:

a) Clear: these are suitably precise and allow subsystem members to develop their role without improper interference; they also enable contact between members of one subsystem and another.
b) Diffuse: these characterize a family whose members do not know exactly who should participate, how, and when. When something needs to be done, the relationships between members are found to be lacking in autonomy; there is a lot of resonance (the behavior of one person overly affects others) and an exalted sense of belonging among members (barring a search for autonomy); members avoid confronting problems and display excessive "loyalty," while some holons are invaded by others.
c) Rigid: these are inflexible and adamantly opposed to necessary change. This type of boundary results in highly disconnected family subsystems, and members are too independent to display loyalty or belonging.
d) Flexible: these are malleable and adapt to the needs posed by the development of the system as a whole, as well as the diverse subsystems (e.g., a crisis or the move from one stage of the family life cycle to another).

Minuchin has pointed out that the presence of diffuse or rigid boundaries can be an indication of psychological problems in one or several of the family members, whereas clear and flexible boundaries are less likely to foster problems.

Montalvo (2000) has studied the ways in which interaction between family members is established; that is, the types of communication that link not only the different holons or subsystems, but also the whole family and external systems. One of his proposed concepts is that of "hierarchy," or the implementation of power: the establishment of rules under which family interaction takes place, the application of these rules, and the consequences arising from their being followed or broken. Ideally, parents should be in charge of the hierarchy; otherwise, family dysfunction problems could arise. This happens, for example, when a son or daughter is in charge or carries out activities belonging to the parental subsystem, a case usually known as "parentified child."

Another component of interaction structure is that of "centrality": that is, the monopolizing or agglutination of most family exchanges. A single member could become the center of family interaction for positive or negative reasons. Negative centrality takes place when the person at the hub of the system is in said position because of a problem, either physical (e.g., illness, disability) or psychological (e.g., cases of identified patient or "black sheep," criminality, drug addiction). Positive centrality, on the other hand, is characterized by the central member's valued accomplishments (e.g., being the best sportsman, student, artist; being well-behaved, etc.). Commonly, the existence of a central member is accompanied by the presence of a peripheral one, someone with the least amount of participation in family interaction and organization. This can be due to absence (the person is hardly ever at home), lack of involvement on the part of the individual, or the individual being barred from interacting by other members.

An "alliance" involves the union of two or more family members who join in order to obtain benefits. "Coalitions," on the other hand, entail conflict and are meant to describe the union of two or more family members seeking to damage another. While alliances are relatively harmless, coalitions create problems—especially if they are permanent or intergenerational. According to Umbarger (1987), coalitions are specific forms of "triangulation." An example of the latter takes place when parents who are simultaneously present but in conflict communicate or send messages to each other through a child.

"Overinvolvement," another possible type of family interaction, is characterized by emotional interdependence, which could also have elements of overprotectiveness (e.g., one or both parents being overly concerned about a child) and results in diffuse boundaries between subsystems, to the point of almost erasing personal independence. A number of clinical cases have revealed an interactive phenomenon that could also be seen as a structural element and which Montalvo (2000) has classified as "parent as child." As the name implies, this type of interaction is characterized by a parent who behaves as a sibling to her or his children, lacks hierarchy, and is under the control of the partner or even another child.

The purpose of this study is to test the effectiveness of the Communicative Restructuring (CR) technique in the solving of couple conflicts and establish whether the dysfunctional elements present in the couples' families undergo any changes.

## METHOD

**Sample**: 15 couples who stated that their main reason for seeking treatment involved partnership problems at different stages of the family life cycle.

**Setting**: cubicles in the Clinical Psychology facilities at FES Iztacala.

**Materials:** notebooks, pens, pencils, and an audio recorder.

**Instruments:** interview guide, Scale of Individual Psychological Wellbeing and Scale of Couple Psychological Wellbeing.

**Dependent variables:** individual and couple psychological wellbeing, degree of family dysfunction, and complaints.

**Independent variable**: Communicative Restructuring technique

**Indicators:** psychological problems, family structure (centrality, periphery, boundaries, hierarchy, alliances, coalitions, triangulations), dysfunction, stage of the family life cycle, preferred representational systems (PRS), and type of client.

### Design

The study followed a quasi-experimental ABA design. Phase A: identification of the structure, gathering of demographic data, administration of the scales of individual and couple psychological wellbeing. Phase B: Implementation of the CR technique. Phase A: Examination of the effects of the CR technique.

### Procedure

#### *Phase A.*

During the first session the patients were informed about the working procedure (the length of the sessions), and it was explained that two therapists would be present in order to provide better attention. A semi-structured interview based on Montalvo and Soria's (1997)

guide was administered, and the degree of dysfunction was established by adding up the elements of the structure (Montalvo 2006). This enabled the detection of problematic (dysfunctional) interactions: diffuse or rigid boundaries between holons and/or the external world, hierarchies that were not shared by both parents, coalitions, parentified children, peripheral members, negative centrality, overinvolvement, triangulations, presence or lack of parental alliances.

***Phase B.***

**Implementation Of The Communicative Restructuring Technique.**

During the second session the couples were introduced to the CR technique: it was explained to them how reality is constructed, how it can be of either first or second order, and how it is built based on preferred representational systems (PRS). They were also given rules with which to improve their communication. Explanations included examples meant to improve understanding. The concepts of first and second order reality were illustrated by the using the word "facts" to describe the former and "reflection" (perception, idea, interpretation) for the latter, thus avoiding technical terms and replacing them with common words. The patients were also provided with examples or situations that illustrated these concepts using drawings or vignettes.

**Representational Systems and the Conception of Reality**

In order to explain how preferred representational systems are at the basis of the construction of reality, the couples were given simple illustrations and drawings depicting the representational systems taken into account by Neuro-Linguistic Programming (NLP): the visual, the auditory, and the kinesthetic. The clients were then asked to start a conversation while looking each other in the eye and trying to maintain eye contact. The purpose was for them to identify their partner's representational system. If only one member was present, they were asked to remember a conversation with their partner and focus on their eye movements and frequently used words. This led to a hypothesis regarding the other partner's representational system, which could be tested later.

The next step in the CR technique was to suggest some rules meant to improve interaction and problem discussion. Communicative behavior was emphasized, since it involves words, gestures, and postures. The rules were as follows:

- Avoid bringing up past arguments when trying to solve a [present?] conflict. This was meant to show couples that there is no point in talking about the past or past events, helping them realize that the present and the future are more important.
- Attempt to communicate without becoming emotionally upset (angry). This did not mean the clients should remain immune to anger, but that they should avoid arguing when they noticed the first physiological signs of ire. That is, individuals had to identify this initial response in themselves and then ask their partner to postpone communication until they had clamed down.
- Avoid arguments from spouse's family.

- Once these steps had been explained, the couples were asked to return fifteen days later. In the meantime, they were told to discuss their conflicts and reach an agreement following the previously established rules of interaction.

***Phase C.***

This phase comprised a new evaluation of the couple in order to chart any potential changes in the structure (degree of dysfunction).

# RESULTS

## Classification of Complaints

The types of complaints reported during the first sessions were briefly classified. Some couples reported more than one type (see Table 1).

Twelve cases (80%) showed at least one change in structure, while the remaining 3 (20%) registered none.

**Table 1. Complaint Type Classification**

| Complaint type | Frequency |
|---|---|
| Communication problems | 8 |
| Jealousy | 4 |
| Differences regarding the children's education | 3 |
| Separation | 2 |
| Addictions | 1 |

***Changes Involving Boundaries in The Marital Subsystem***

Out of 15 cases that showed diffuse or rigid boundaries, 11 (73.3%) changed to clear boundaries and 1 (6.7%) showed a change from rigid to partially flexible boundaries. That is, 12 of these cases (80%) showed some type of change. The remaining 3 (20%) showed none.

***Changes Involving Boundaries in The Parental Subsystem***

Four of the 15 cases had no children while 8 (100%) had dysfunctional boundaries. Three (37.5%) of them changed to clear boundaries and 5 (62.5%) did not show any change at all.

***Changes Involving Boundaries in The Fraternal Subsystem***

The 3 cases (20%) that had initially shown dysfunctional boundaries registered no change. The rest of the cases showed clear boundaries from the start or did not involve any siblings.

***Changes Involving Exterior Boundaries***

Out of the 7 cases (100%) that initially showed diffuse boundaries, 1 (14.28%) changed to clear boundaries, 3 (42.85%) went from diffuse to partially clear, and the remaining 3 (42.85%) showed no change at all.

***Changes Involving Hierarchy***

Initially, 8 cases (100%) showed that hierarchy was not shared by both parents. In 2 of them (25%) hierarchy moved from one to both parents, while the remaining 6 (75%) showed no change.

***Changes Involving Coalitions***

The one case (100%) that had initially shown the presence of coalitions showed no change.

***Changes Involving Parentified Children***

The one case (100%) that had initially shown the presence a parentified child showed no change.

***Changes Involving Negative Centrality***

Out of the 8 cases (100%) displaying negative centrality, 5 (61.53%) no longer showed it and the remaining 5 (38.47%) registered no change.

***Changes Involving Periphery***

Out of the 8 cases (100%) displaying a peripheral family member, 4 (50%) no longer showed it and the remaining 4 (50%) registered no change.

***Changes Involving Alliances***

Out of the 11 cases (100%) displaying no alliances, 2 (18.19%) developed new parental alliances while the remaining 9 (81.81%) showed no change.

***Changes Involving Overinvolvement***

Out of the 3 cases (100%) displaying overinvolvement, 1 (33.3%) no longer showed it while the remaining 2 (66.6%) registered no change.

***Changes Involving Triangulations***

Triangulation disappeared from the one case (100%) that had initially shown its presence.

***Changes Involving Conflicts***

Out of the 15 cases (100%) displaying at least one conflict, 6 (40%) no longer showed any, 6 (40%) showed the disappearance of at least one conflict, and the remaining 3 (20%) showed no change.

## Stages of the Family Life Cycle

An analysis of the stages of the family life cycle in relation to dysfunctional markers before and after the implementation of the CR technique (see Figure 1) shows that, initially, couples with adult children had the highest degree of dysfunction (7). They were followed, in decreasing order, by marriages with small children (6.5), marriages with school-aged children (6.33) and, finally, couples who were still in the courtship stage (4). After the implementation of the CR technique, dating couples showed the most significant decrease in the degree of dysfunction, which went down to 0.25 and showed an overall 3.75 point reduction. Marriages with school-aged children went down to 4.33, showing an overall reduction of 2 points, while marriages with adult children went down to 6, showing a 1 point reduction.

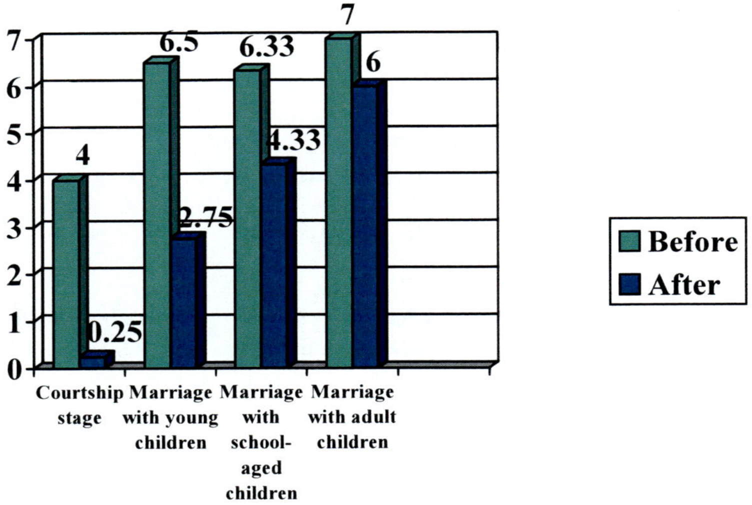


Figure 1. Dysfunction before and after the implementation of CR according to stages of the family life cycle.

### *Type of Client.*

Dysfunction measurements based on type of client were analyzed before and after the implementation of CR: A-type clients showed the most significant difference, followed by C-types and then B-types, who showed a difference of 1 point after CR. It must be pointed out that the sample was small and that over 70% of the participants were A-type clients.

**Table 2. Dysfunction Level Measurements According to Type of Client Before and After the Implementation of CR.**

| Type of Client | Dysfunction Before CR | Dysfunction After CR | Difference |
|---|---|---|---|
| A (N = 11) | 5.73 | 2.64 | 3.09 |
| B (N = 2) | 7.5 | 6.5 | 1 |
| C (N = 2) | 5.5 | 3.5 | 2 |

## Changes in Complaints

In most cases, complaints underwent positive changes (see Table 3).

**Table 3. Changes in Complaints**

| Categories | Frequency | Percentage |
|---|---|---|
| Positive modification | 10 | 66.6 |
| Disappearance | 2 | 13.4 |
| No change | 3 | 20 |

## Discussion

The purpose of this research was to prove the efficacy of the Communicative Restructuring (CR) technique, and the results show that it led to changes in the family structure, promoting new and more functional behavior patterns.

The changes involving major or outstanding complaints are notable since, out of 15 cases, 10 reported positive changes after CR, 2 reported their disappearance, and only 3 remained unchanged. When speaking of "positive changes" we are referring to cases in which clients stated that, even if the main complaint or problem remained unsolved, the couple's disposition and readiness to discuss the issue while remaining on good terms had improved, as had their willingness to find a solution. "Disappearance of complaints" refers to those clients who reported that the problem that had led them to seek therapy had been completely resolved. In these cases, focus was placed on the ways in which their agreement could be preserved.

Most of the cases showed diffuse family subsystem boundaries before the implementation of CR, which was also the case in Montalvo's (2000) study. The stage of the family life cycle that showed the highest degree of dysfunction was that of marriages with adult children, although the differences between this and the other two stages involving children were not statistically significant. This might be due to the reduced size of the sample and could warrant further, future research.

Three of the couples showed none of the expected changes after the implementation of CR. In one of these cases, the woman reported she had been having many problems with her partner and always cried when talking about her issues, but her partner did not cooperate: he did not attend any of the sessions and did not agree to follow any of the steps required by the technique. Another couple with communication problems attended only two sessions, during which they were interviewed and informed about the technique. They did not return because a strong episode of intrafamilial violence led to their separation. This might suggest that, when there is evidence of intrafamilial violence, the technique could fail to have the desired effects if the violence itself is not directly addressed.

Finally, it must be pointed out that this study does view the CR technique as a solution to all possible structural family dysfunctions. Rather, it recommends it as a basis for future intervention. The technique is meant to create and strengthen a favorable environment where the couple can discuss their problems and search for solutions.

## REFERENCES


Bornstein, P. H. & Bornstein, M. T. (1998). *Terapia de pareja. Enfoque conductual-sistémico*. Madrid: Ediciones Pirámide.

Döring, M. T. (2000). Elección de pareja. In M. T. Döring,. (Ed.). *La pareja: ¿Un sueño imposible?* México: Distribuciones Fontamara.

Kershaw, C. J. (1994). *La danza hipnótica de la pareja*. Buenos Aires: Amorrortu.

Minuchin, S. (1986). *Familias y Terapia Familiar*. México: Gedisa.

Montalvo Reyna, J. (2000). *Los efectos del uso de la retroalimentación estructural familiar en varias etapas del ciclo vital*. Ph.D thesis. Universidad Iberoamericana.

Montalvo Reyna, J. (2006). *Terapia Sistémica Breve Estructural: teoría, investigación y aplicaciones*. Monterrey: Ediciones Cree-Ser.

Montalvo Reyna,. J. & Soria, T. M. R. (1997). Estructura familiar y problemas psicológicos. *Psicología y Ciencia Social, 1,* 32-37.

Rage, E. (1996) *La pareja. Elección, problemática y desarrollo*. México: Plaza y Valdés & Universidad Iberoamericana.

Stanley M. S., Whitton S, Sadberry S., Clements M. L., & Markman H. J. (2006) Sacrifice as a Predictor of Marital Outcomes. *Family Process, 45*, 3, 289-303.

Vilchez, L. F. (1985). *Conflictos matrimoniales y comunicación*. Madrid: Ediciones Madrid.

In: Hispanic Psychology Yearbook Volume 1
Ed: Cirilo H. García pp. 137-153
ISBN: 978-1-60741-786-6


*Chapter 11*

# MODEL FOR HIV/AIDS PREVENTION BY FORMING PSYCHOSOCIAL COMPETENCIES*

***Ariel César Núñez Rojas[a1], Sergio Tobón[b], Diana Arias Henao[a], and Stefano Vinaccia[c]***
[a]Universidad de Manizales, Colombia
[b]Universidad Complutense de Madrid, Spain
[c]Universidad de San Buenaventura, Mexico

## ABSTRACT

In this chapter, we will analyze the strategies for HIV/AIDS prevention, especially on young people, since they are the riskiest group to be infected, due to their life style and practices in today's situations and contexts. From the experience of working with young people in the promotion of health, the authors propose a model for HIV/AIDS prevention, based on psychological competencies development and strengthening, which, at a time, is based on the following: (1) to transmit clear and true information concerning HIV/AIDS and preventions methods; (2) to develop high motivation for the use of prevention methods; (3) to develop the necessary abilities to handle risky situations and to put them into practice when necessary; and (4) to confront the environments that favor or block young people from practicing prevention. To undertake these aspects, it is necessary to evaluate the development state of young people's psychosocial competencies; to understand and intervene from young culture's point of view, and to tackle the dynamics of living with health and illness processes, incorporating prevention as an academic course, as well as parent education.

**Keywords:** Prevention, promotion, psychosocial competencies, HIV, AIDS.

---

* A version of this chapter was also published in the *International Hispanic Psychology Journal, Volume 1 Issue 2*, published by Nova Science Publishers, Inc. It was submitted for appropriate modification in an effort to encourage wider dissemination of research.

## INTRODUCTION

Infection by the human immunodeficiency virus (HIV) is increasing. According to the latest data, it has been found that between 34.1 and 47.1 million people in the world are infected (ONUSIDA,2006); 17.7 million of those infected are women, while 2.3 million are children under 15 years. In the year 2006, there were close to 4.3 million new persons infected, and approximately 530,000 were young people under 15 years.

Since the discovery of this virus in 1983, it is calculated that almost 20 million persons have died, an alarming number that demonstrates this illness is a central public health problem which must be given utmost attention. The regions with the highest number of infected persons are: Sub-Saharan Africa (24.7 million), Southern and Southeastern Asia (7.8 million), Latin America (1.7 million), Eastern Europe and Central Asia (1.7 million), and North America (1.4 million). This shows that the infection mainly affects people in developing countries.

Lately, young people are one of the populations at greatest risk for infection, which is mainly due to the lifestyles in which risky behavior occurs, even though there is information in reference to the possible consequences, as it is mentioned by Nuñez, Tobon and Arias (2006a) and Vallejo; Nuñez, Escobar, Ramirez, Velez and Gallego (2007). It is calculated that young people between 15 and 24 years are the half of the population that has recently been infected by HIV in the world, and more than 6000 young people are infected each day (ONUSIDA, 2004). In 2006, there were more than 380,000 deaths of young people under 15 years old due to the infection (ONUSIDA, 2006).

There are diverse reasons why young people are at high risk: early sexual relations initiation (Mejia, 2000; Profamilia, 2005); use of intravenous drugs; lack of information about the virus; poverty and lack of access to protection resources, and especially the feeling that health is an intrinsic and natural process that is part of living the moment, by using the body as a tool and psychological ling to pleasure (Nuñez, Tobon and Arias, 2006a).

So far, it is known that this virus is transmitted by bodily fluids, especially blood (blood transfusions and organ transplants) and semen (during unprotected sexual contact) (Ballester, 1997, ONUSIDA, 2006). HIV is also found present in other fluids such as saliva, perspiration and tears, but the amounts found are not sufficient to transmit the infection to other human beings.

Taking into account that there has been very important progress in the analysis of blood reserves used for transfusions around the world, the main risk factor for transmitting the disease is by having sexual relations without using condoms; having contact with blood from infected persons and by consuming drugs intravenously with non-sterile syringe.

Due to the continuous growth of HIV infection cases, and AIDS development during the last decade, different prevention projects and programs were implemented among the general population, especially young people. However, it seems that those programs have not yet achieved a significant impact in promoting healthy behaviors. For that reason, in spite of preventing campaigns and strategies, young people continue to have risky behavior, increasing the probability of HIV/AIDS infection; for example, sharing syringes, having sexual relations without using condoms, etc. (More examples on Meekers, Klein and Foyet, 2003). Even among university students, risky behavior that may lead to infection by HIV/AIDS is frequent, in spite of the fact that this group supposedly has an adequate information level concerning the matter (Piña, 2004), which has to do with pleasant sexual experiences, which postpone the assumption of risk as something negative (Nuñez, 2002; Nuñez, Tobon and Arias, 2006a; Vallejo et al, 207). This is related to the results of previous studies carried out in Mexico. An important percentage of young people with risky behavior was found, which coincides with other studies carried out in this country (Villagran and Diaz-Loving, 1999).

In this article, a general model is presented to orient the design of HIV/AIDS prevention programs among the young population. This model is based on acquiring and strengthening psychosocial competencies, which are characterized as effective behaviors for dealing with certain situations, such as sexuality, so that they can be practiced by the young with the smallest possible risk to health. An approach from competencies allows having a common language in educational system, organizations and institutions committed to young health and, in this manner, to integrate promotional activities within the academic program (Tobon, 2004), by focusing on illness prevention and health promotion, taking into account young's cultural and social dynamics, and in addition to conditions, practices and beliefs in the area of the health of young people, which is exactly as Nuñez and Zambrano (2002) state, it deals with the promotion of health and the prevention of illness as processes that run from individuals to socio-cultural internalization. Without a doubt, this implies to visualize the need to focus on Intervention Procedural Models in human health, in pandemic nature problems, such as HIV/AIDS, exactly as it is established by Nuñez and Tobon (2005b); Tobon and Nuñez (2005); Nuñez, Tobon, Vinaccia and Arias (2006), and Nuñez, Tobon, Bañol and Arias (2006).

## Effective Interventions in Hiv/Aids Prevention

According to Tundra, Izquierdo, Fumaz and Ferrer (2003), up to now, the following conclusions can be reached with respect to HIV prevention effective programs:

1. Traditionally, prevention programs have emphasized on communicating information in educational environments. Basically, the majority of studies indicate that, on this matter, information is efficient, nevertheless only for a better knowledge in the infection of HIV and in the creation of favorable attitudes towards the practice of safe sex.
2. The combination of information and training in abilities development creates major changes on human behavior's three levels: cognitive, affective-attitudinal and behavioral levels.
3. In young populations in several countries, the greatest way to be infected is by sharing hypodermic injection. Here, there is a double risk for infection: sharing needles and having unsafe sex under drugs effect. With respect to prevention, it has been found that combining information and developing abilities is useful (for example, clean needles and the use of condoms) to decrease the HIV infection risks. However, there is still no concluding information about its effectiveness in decreasing the risk of unsafe sexual practices in this group of drug users.

According to this, we can therefore say there is evidence showing that this combination of information with the development of abilities is the best strategy for preventing HIV infection in young people. However, new studies are necessary to establish the efficacy, efficiency and effectiveness of specific components in the intervention. The mentioned combination, as a mechanism for HIV prevention is an important support for introducing the prevention model based on competencies formation, which, even though they are composed of these two elements, have other components that potentially make them more pertinent in working with young people. For this, it is necessary to keep in mind that the competencies of human beings are constructed from basic nerve processes, which after going through psychological processes such as memory, learning, perception, thought and language, evolve into complex processes such as intelligence, creativity, behavior and personality. Competencies are not permanent and they are not universal, they are developed according to social, cultural and economic contexts. For that reason, it is necessary to recognize individual differences between young people and those who pretend to develop a competence.

## Hiv/Aids Psychosocial Competencies Approach

Different studies and programs for young's HIV/AIDS can be grouped into three essential models. The first one corresponds to Bandura's self-efficacy theory (1997). In this approach, the main objective is to determine how effectiveness beliefs have an influence on risky behaviors, and promotes appropriate self-effective behaviors, allowing reducing risky activities (Lopez, Salinas and Landero, 1999).

The second model deals with reasoned action theory by Ajzen and Fishbein (1980); Fishbein and Azjen (1975). This model involves studying basic attitudes and beliefs for risky behaviors in order to carry out actions to modify and implement new attitudes, searching for a reasoned action of the person who takes risks (Perello and Villagran, 2000).

Lastly, we have the psychological model of biological health by Bayes and Ribes (1992). From this approach, some HIV/AIDS risk factors have been evaluated (Piña, Gonzalez, Molina and Cota, 2003). Especially, it has been tried to determine which are the social circumstances and reasons that have an influence on risky behaviors, so as to modify strategies.

The psychological model of biological health is considered as a relevant base for the prevention of risk factors associated with HIV/AIDS. Succinctly, the model establishes a psychological health dimension based on three factors: (1) biological states modulated by behavior; (2) people's interactive behavior styles, and (3) functional competencies to interact with diverse situations.

Within this model, competencies are understood as the abilities possessed by individuals to effectively interact according to requirements established by a situation (Bayes, 1992). This is related to the ability of persons to successfully confront challenges imposed by daily life, which, according to Mantilla (2002), has to do with human development promotion and prevention of psycho-social problems related to the health of young people's practices and lifestyles. In this manner, competencies are capacities effectively placed into action due to environment circumstances in which they interact. From this point, it is found that in an analysis of competencies, in order to make a person to confront certain situation, it is necessary to establish the social environment in which the competency will take place, as well as the person's internal factors related to that competency, such as knowledge, attitudes, motives, and the procedures execution.

Traditionally, in the study of psychosocial risk factors, aspects such as stress, social support, self-esteem and personality have been emphasized. In general, this latter point refers to consistent modes of behavior that are placed into action in certain situations, but that have no explicit effectiveness criteria for the person. Competencies, on the other hand, are performances people possess when interacting with their environment, which are formed in the self-organizing process of human behavior, interacting with the environment; they are used for reacting in an effective manner to certain situations based on explicit criteria. (Bayes, 1992; Piña, 2003)

The model of competencies, which in the case of prevention of sexually transmitted diseases, would be placed in the psychosocial area because it links the cognitive-affective aspects (psychological) with social interaction (social), it also allows to direct systematically, preventive actions to concrete fields of behavior, taking into account the wide rank of behaviors in interaction with the context in which they occur, and where health and risk experiences are carried out by young people.

## Essential Axis of an Hiv/Aids Prevention Model Based on Development of Competencies

The approach on competencies is of psycho-social order because it links the psychic (cognitive-affective-behavioral) to social relations and cultural devices that are meaningful for health. This model pretends to develop and strength competencies in young people to handle their own sexuality with responsibility, preventing sexually transmitted diseases and HIV/AIDS. Thus, according to Restrepo (non published data), in young people's process of developing psychosocial competencies, it is necessary to keep in mind, according to constructivist approach contributions to the psycho-social competency theory, three basic ideas: the importance of collaboration between couples as the core of mechanisms for resolving problems; the importance that the cultural context has for developing relevant learning, and the importance of social interaction in individual abilities development.

A program focused on competences formation must (1) intervene in the contexts in which young people live to favor prevention; (2) to offer information about this topic (HIV/AIDS nature, transmission mechanisms, condoms use, etc.); (3) to motivate prevention; and (4) to support abilities (condoms use; postponement of sexual relations when no condoms are available; to say no when the person does not want to have sexual relations, etc.), and to promote people to put those abilities in practice, according to effective criteria. This last aspect is what characterizes any topic based in competencies formation. It is not enough to transmit information and to develop abilities; it is essential to create mechanisms so that certain information and abilities are put into practice in interacting contexts, under certain circumstances and environmental and biological events (Nuñez, Tobon, Vinaccia y Arias, 2006).

All of this is related to the concept of life abilities that is proposed by the OMS (1998), and worked on by Mangrulkar, Vincent and Posner (2001), and Mantilla (2002), which explains how adolescents and young people can best confront the situations which can potentially affect their daily life. Those abilities are: knowledge of oneself, empathy, effective communication, interpersonal relationships, decision-making, problems and conflicts solutions, creative and critical thought, feelings and emotions dealings, tension and stress handling.

Psychosocial competencies and abilities work for life is based on action plans and strategies development that have been developed in Latin American countries, regarding an integral care program to adolescents and young people (OPS, 1998), emphasizing on sexual and reproductive health (OPS, 1995). Under the criteria of integral intervention in young people's health, Nuñez and Tobon (2005a) have constructed a care model for young health, based on health re-conceptualization from human development point of view. That model has the following axis of action: Axis 1: To establish government policies for prevention and promotion. Axis 2: To provide integral health services. Axis 3: To form health competencies. Axis 4: To offer friendly and simple access health services. Axis 5: To empower young people to be the authors of the conditions that guarantee their own health. This model is correlated to the articulation logic proposed by Nuñez and Tobon (2005b) and Nuñez and Tobon (2006) in the Mental Health Procedural Model as the path for the integration, research and the clinical practice from a psychological intervention point of view in front of the complex human health problems. The axes previously exposed, must be integrated under the following criteria:

## To Communicate a Clear and Truthful Information

Psychosocial competencies formation for preventing HIV/AIDS requires young people to structure and to know, in a clear and precise manner, which is the nature of this infection, its risk factors and control mechanisms. Although there has been progress and better information within the community, more information on the topic is still lacking, which must be coming from trustworthy sources that are close to and legitimated for young people. .

In HIV/AIDS prevention we have had important progress in establishment disclosing strategies (although a lot is still missing from this field), but we must develop preventive abilities as such, that are put into practice by young people in an effective manner. In Colombia, many of the difficulties of current prevention programs reside in this hollow, since it emphasizes on offering information and not on working on behavior execution as such, under a context of certain reinforcing and facilitating environmental situational risk behaviors.

It is necessary to continue giving information. However, such information must be easily understood by young; it must be in comprehensive reading, but specially, it must be reliable. This implies developing interactive, dynamic activities close to their imaginary activities, beliefs and health practices (Orozco y Nuñez, 2001), in which they are brought up to date as to the latest discoveries about the infection, as well as all that concerns the preventive behavior to be followed. Regarding prevention behaviors, young people should not only know which behaviors to follow, but also how to follow them; although sometimes this seems to be obvious, at times. In this sense, it is not sufficient to advise the condom use, but how and why to use it.

## To Induce a Strong Motivation Towards Preventive Behaviors

Motive is a central component for all behavior, constituting a compelling factor for behavior so as to obtain an immediate or later goal. As stated by Piña et al. (2003), the reasons are manifested by selections and preferences of objects and events. Such selections and preferences increase the probability of risky behaviors for HIV/AIDS infection.

HIV/AIDS prevention programs must determine the main reasons for risky behaviors and young prevention, in order to take them into account in the activities. Prevention programs in this field must motivate young people to put on practice healthy behaviors, including two aspects. One is to look for external motivators which compel them towards those behaviors (externally reinforced), and the other is to orient them towards self-motivation in order to have a healthy life.

Motivation has an essential role in competencies and studies indicate that the best persons for preventing risky behaviors against HIV/AIDS are generally motivated to take care of their health and to prevent infection. This is proved by a research carried out by Piña (2004) among young university students in México. In this study, the predictability was evaluated under several aspects of competencies (knowledge, beliefs, motives and circumstances), concerning four risky behaviors: a) Sexual relations with different couples; b) Frequency of condoms use throughout life ; c) Sexual relations with sporadic couples; and d) the condom use with sporadic partners. Logistic regression proved that motives were the competency factor that predicted these four behaviors. Upon analyzing only one of the risky behaviors studied, it was found that the main reasons for "not consistently using a condom" risky conduct, were the following: a) their partner does not like to use one; b) they did not have a condom with them; c) they have never known how to use one, and d) it makes sex less pleasant. Other researchers have obtained similar results (Anderson, Wilson, Doll, Jones and Barker, 1999; Brigham et al., 2002).

The reasons are central axes that measure the risky behavior for HIV/AIDS infection, in addition to health promotion and disease prevention. In this sense, in order for young people to be competent in HIV/AIDS prevention, they must have solid reasons for doing so, and block the possible reasons for not doing it, such as the fact that condom use decreases pleasure. Programs in this filed must be focused on dealing with the reasons which block a healthy life style, and on promoting the reasons that lead to prevent infection behaviors. This implies sensitizing young people about the disease and about how to have safe and pleasant sex.

## To Develop and to Strength Abilities for Handling Sexual Behavior

It is not enough to intervene in transmitting information or creating motivation contexts for provoking effective prevention behaviors; it is also necessary to possess habits to prevent infection and to use them according to effectiveness criteria. Therefore, the programs in this area must establish mechanisms so that young people may develop necessary habits and act effectively.

For example, one practice is the use of condom. It involves knowing how to use it, knowing that it can be used only once, and knowing that vaginal penetration condoms are not the same as those for anal penetration (it requires a finer one). Likewise, it is required that young use it at the right moment.

Prevention programs must take action on abilities development. It needs workshops where young people learn to follow prevention behaviors by observing models in videos and in dramatizations. Then, it is essential to ask young people to practice those preventive behaviors. It is also very important for young people to be conscious of likely risky behavior contexts in order to be alert before going to such contexts. This consciousness implies having knowledge about the possible reinforcement of environmental factors, in which probability of risky behaviors increases. For example, many times, condom is not used due to the immediate pleasure of ejaculating within the vagina. Risky behaviors such as rectal coitus or coitus with prostitutes also constitutes significant levels of risk for young people, as determined by Alvarez, Gil, Ramirez and Restrepo (2002) in a study done among university students.

## To Intervene in Risky Situations

They are situations in which a person interacts with his/her natural and social environment, giving a bi-directional feedback. In the case of HIV/AIDS, the situations related to the infection are, in general, the relationships of friendship, "courtship", recreation and the search for sexual satisfaction with prostitutes or with strangers. These are the risky behavior contexts in which prevention must be put in practice.

In this case, prevention must be based on spaces for interaction which make risky behaviors more probable as well as for situations control, so in this way, the strategies to be implemented must be taken into account. It requires knowing about young people culture, their customs and places where they socialize.

Academic environment must carry out a detailed analysis of all possible situations likely to be risky for VIH/AIDS transmission. School-aged adolescents and young people are the greatest risky infection group, (Bayes, 1995). Consequently, mechanisms must be established so that they show preventive behaviors and be able to have access to condoms and to necessary information for practicing safe sex.

Risky situations intervention involves research processes and integral systematization, which from qualitative and quantitative tendencies allow a deep and contextual approach to the problems related to young health. There are examples of studies carried out that come from knowledge of the dynamics and meanings of juvenile sexuality (Mejia, 2000) and up to biological and psycho-social factors related to young university students health conditions (Nuñez, Arias and Tobon, 2005), and work systematization processes with abilities for living (Nuñez, 2002; Nuñez, Tobon and Arias, 2006a; Nuñez, Tobon and Arias, 2006b; Nuñez, Castaño and Aristizabal, 2006c); and Botero, Gonzales and Valencia (2002).

## General Guidelines for Prevention Programs Implementation

### *To Carry Out a Psycho-Social Competencies Diagnosis*

To implement an HIV/AIDS prevention project for young people requires knowing exactly the psycho-social skills and the competencies formation in this population related to the infection prevention. This permits to know about aspects to be emphasized, and also the impact coming from other actions of the community, through educational processes, media massive campaigns, family education and information received from groups of couples.

For diagnosis, it is important to use qualitative as well as quantitative instruments which facilitate to determine the level of the young person's psycho-social competencies and abilities for living, in addition to their comprehension, meanings and accounts respecting these ones, exactly as is shown by Nuñez (2002), Nuñez, Arias and Tobon (2006b). In the qualitative part, young people will be asked to provide certain data concerning their risky behavior as well as prevention measures to be used to confront this health problem, since it will allow them to participate and to be responsible for the prevention processes of the disease and to promote health.

In the quantitative part, it is important to use instruments designed to evaluate competencies, which have characteristics that are different from traditional questionnaires for evaluating psychological factors. Although there is still little progress in this area, important contributions have begun to occur, such as the instrument for evaluation of risk factors in infected persons by Piña (2003) or the questionnaire developed by Torres (1994) that was redesigned and validated by Piña, Molina and Cota (at the press). The latter questionnaire contains 29 items, with adequate reliability (alpha of 0,754) and validity (it has a two factors and two indexes structure which explain the 54.26% of the variance). This instrument has been used with young people and it evaluates the following competency factors: knowledge with respect to HIV/AIDS, beliefs, motives, circumstances and risk behaviors (see Table 1).

**Table 1. Examples of risk factors analysis in a psycho-social competency framework.**

| | |
|---|---|
| Knowledge<br>-Has the idea that HIV is an uncommon virus.<br>-Does not know about HIV/AIDS.<br>-Knows how HIV can be prevented.<br>-Has sufficient trust in the other person. | Motives:<br>-To have sexual relations with different partners: physical attraction, opportunity, curiosity, excitement, drugs/alcohol.<br>-For not using the condom consistently: he does not like to use it; his/her partner does not like it; he doesn't use it for religious or other reasons.. |
| Sexual Abilities:<br>- He does not know how to use a condom.<br>- He/ she is not careful and does not buy a sufficient number of condoms for all sexual relations with the same person or with different persons.<br>-The condom slips off sometimes or it breaks. | Social situations in which sexual relations can take place without protection:<br>-Possibility of several sexual partners.<br>-Several sexual relationships with the same partner.<br>-Parties, trips, etc.<br>-Relations with unknown persons. |

*Note*: some common examples of risk factors following the psycho-social competencies model are shown.

## To Understand Juvenile Cultures and The Inclusion of Young People in Prevention Programs

The definition of what the young population is has several variations according to the approach to be followed. Generally, it is understood that this population is from 14 to 24 years old, although in many cases it includes 12 years old boys and girls, and also persons between 25 to 29 years old. The lower limit is related to sexual and reproductive functions development and the beginning of formal thought. On the other hand, the upper limit has to do with the end of the academic and occupational preparation process which allows people to start working in a determined field of work. In addition, this last limit involves full consciousness maturity as a citizen with rights and duties; the establishment of a solid identity and the mature formation of a family. Thus, this concept can be understood as a period and vital process that runs from physiological maturity to social maturity.

Prevention programs focused on forming psycho-social competencies must be based on the knowledge of social and personal concepts that young people have about their body, their sexuality and young culture in which they live and which defines and redefines their life experience. Many prevention programs fail because they neglect this part. This is discussed by Nuñez (2002), upon stating that in young people's life and their health, things are complicated by collective and individual appropriations of meanings and attitudes towards healthy practices and disease, in which the image of a healthy and vital body is exchanged, but in it is included the acceptance of risk as the mediator of pleasant practices under novelty criteria, experimentation and intensity of them; and this is something almost naturally associated to risky sexual practices and substances use and abuse, all of them considered to be in high correlation with HIV/AIDS infection.

With respect to what was previously mentioned, an investigation was carried out among university students based on the depth and establishment of approaching groups (Nuñez, Tobon and Arias, 2006a); its goal was to understand the meaning of health for the students, which included interpreting the meaning of university experiences and health practices, as well as to understand the relationship existing between health and disease, and the meaning of health practices for university students compared with adult models.

The study established that health practices and strategies for young university students means living at the university, experimenting with their sexuality, drugs, their body, pleasure and enjoyment; where friendship bonds and closeness are, at the same time, an affinity, complicity and appearance for men and women. Living as a university student is to be in and to live the present. Health is the place to look at your image, to experiment and, at the same time, to take risks that cause pleasure and enjoyment with a young and vital body in action, a body that does not need care. Feeling and living life to the limit of the moment; health is a temporary place and a temporary finding; not something searched for. The soften boundary between care and risky life is crossed, where living the moment is something natural for young people. From the institutional point of view, an external reading, different and far from university students reality is made, blocking their strategies, still assumed as close to adults and family members with a protecting and prohibitive sense anchored in old traditions, customs, careful behaviors, criteria of prejudice and control, being necessary a two-faced strategy is necessary, one for showing and another for being.

From this study, it is concluded that it is necessary to establish prevention programs with young people, taking into account their autonomy, their freedom, their life experiences and their own motivation. The language must be constructed from their own language and references, with the goal of finding the best way to orient their own behavior, without imposing outside patterns, which are related to that set forth by Nuñez (2002), regarding the need for recognizing processes of attitudes and behavior symbolic appropriation related to young people health. We face, then, the need to address self-consciousness and offer young people spaces so that they may self-regulate their behavior, far from the control society wishes to impose on them, which they resist, allowing them to assume aspects such as pleasure, adventure and risk, frequently not taken into account in the "adult" language of prevention nor in behavioral technology programs. On the other hand, HIV/AIDS prevention activities for young people require professional psychologists interacting continuously with them and negotiating meanings, goals, strategies and objectives, since psycho-social competencies and abilities development for life is inscribed on their vital process (Nuñez, Castrillon y Bañol, 2002b).

All prevention programs must involve the same young people carrying out different activities, as has been set forth in different social programs (Senderowitz, 1997). This can be, for example, providing information in mass communication media (radio, newspapers, Internet and television) and establishing contact with other young people to motivate the condom use to prevent sharing needles.

In accordance with this, it is necessary to propose more integral work models to young people who are able to articulate human development dimension regarding health processes, on the individual and collective levels (POH, 1995, 1998, 2000) in which it is proposed that for having a healthy development, young people needs: to have had a healthy infancy; to live in safe environments which encourage them and offer opportunities through the family, couples and other social institutions; to have access to information and opportunities so as to develop a wide range of practical vocational and life abilities; to have equal access to a wide range of services, education, employment, health, justice and well-being. In addition, the POH adds the need for a macro-environment that supports them, created by policies and legislation, values of society, models of positive roles and standards of conduct, supported by media.

The previously mentioned criteria as regards to the HIV/ AIDS complex problem, and the necessity to consider of young people psycho-social competencies implies thinking, exactly as it is proposed by Tobon and Nuñez (2000), that individual and community health depends on the intervention of multiple hereditary biological factors, social relations, beliefs and symbolic representations facing health and illness, social expectations, housing, food, safety, availability and accessibility to health services, among others.

## To Incorporate HIV Prevention as an Academic Program

Young people spend an important part of their lives in educational institutions acquiring the necessary knowledge and abilities to live in society and to perform a determined occupation. Consequently, the HIV and AIDS infection topic, and also that of sexually transmitted diseases must be discussed and have an important space as an academic course of study, so that this question can be dealt with and planned by teachers and carried out in a systematic manner. It requires taking into account the fact that infection is a question that transcends the health limits, and it is framed in diverse biological, sociological, economic and political questions. This places the topic in an interdisciplinary level requiring diverse disciplines contributions in which the study plan has been traditionally organized, such as: natural sciences, mathematics, social sciences, ethics, physical education, linguistics and the arts areas.

On the other hand, it is important to take into consideration that the psycho-social competency model that we have presented, also requires an academic program to be based on competencies formation from a complex and interdisciplinary perspective. Experience shows that prevention activities using traditional educational approaches based on communicated information and abilities formation, without taking into account context, make difficult to carry out efficient activities for HIV/AIDS prevention, since they do not enact young's abilities in real daily life situations in daily life with effectiveness criteria. Readers interested in academic programs designed by competencies can refer to Works by Tobon (2004), in which a series of methodological elements are proposed to carry out this process.

In general, competencies formation as an academic course implies to clearly identify and to describe those supporting competencies for young people, parents and experts; to establish the contribution of each area to their formation; to identify how its progressive development will be carried out in different academic levels; to establish standards for evaluating and constructing activities for forming them. It must be promoted teamwork among teachers, as well as meaningful interdisciplinary projects for students. In reference to this, it is interesting to summarize an important project that has been applied in Spain as to this subject. It is "AIDS: to know how to help" program that is focused on students, attempting to offer information and prevent contagion through interdisciplinary activities (Prats, 2002).

## To Train and to Involve Parents

Family and home environments are very important for developing young people psycho-social competencies, in order to prevent HIV infection. Some studies show young who achieve positive, solid and supporting relationships with their parents are less likely to be involved in risky situations (Blum, Beuhring and Rinehart, 2000; Lammers, Ireland, Resnick and Blum, 2000). For example, in a study accomplished in a USA school, sixth and seventh grade students whose relation with their parents was strong, show to be less likely to use drugs, and also to delay sexual activity. (Turner, Irwin, Tschann and Millstein, 1993).

Parents' participation in sexual education is sometimes hard because of bad communication with young people and due to the lack of training on the topic. Frequently, parents and children try to avoid the sexual topic since for them is uncomfortable (Weiss, Whelan and Rao Gupta, 1996; Bumpas, 1999). Often, young people feel their parents are only concentrated on warning them about sexual relations risk, and many young people do not get along enough with their parents to be able to talk about these topics. In addition, many parents, repeatedly, do not have necessary and adequate information concerning sexually transmitted diseases and AIDS.

As a result, it is necessary for parents to be trained in two aspects: (1) the development and solidification of the relationship with their children through respect, understanding, affection and authority; (2) contribution to psycho-social competencies formation of their children by adequate information, motivation, daily abilities, and practices development. The best way for training parents is through formal education, that is, conferences and workshops.

Besides that, it must be included pamphlets, manuals and books which clearly describes how to act and react in different situations in reference to this subject. It is important to warn that conferences and workshops and also the documents given to parents must be developed by specialized professionals on sexual education and HIV prevention, so as to avoid social prejudices, taboos, and moral questions influences, which frequently are more harmful than beneficial.

## CONCLUSIONS

HIV/AIDS prevention programs design must begin with clear theoretical models oriented towards diagnosis as well as implementation of strategies within the population and the evaluation of results. In this sense, the approach on prevention based on psycho-social competencies, according to orientation of the psychological health model developed by Bayes (1995) offers a set of orientations aimed at detecting prevention behaviors, their structural axes (knowledge, motivations and abilities), the likely environments and effectiveness criteria. In this manner, a program based on this model will be focused on forming young people able not just for practicing a profession, but also for life, which must be systemized in concrete projects related to the promotion of health and integral prevention, emphasized on parallel processes for psycho-social competencies development and the abilities to live, which include HIV/AIDS prevention activities (Nuñez, Castrillon y Bañol, 2002b). This agrees with Burt (2000) with respect to psycho-social, biological and cultural readings, taking into account protection, risk and vulnerability factors. Facing this, it must be considered, as determined by POH (1996) that tasks applied to young people and adolescents, it must be included the family, the group of couples, the neighborhood and potential social opportunities. Finally, exactly as it is suggested by Nuñez and Tobon (2005a) and 2005b); Nuñez, Tobon, Bañol and Arias (2006), and Nuñez and Tobon (2006), it must be taken care of constructing integrated models of intervention directed towards today's huge human health problems, such as pandemic HIV/AIDS around the world.

## REFERENCES

Álvarez, C., Gil, P., Ramírez, M., & Restrepo, J. (2002). Conducta sexual en estudiantes solteros de primer semestre de la Universidad de Caldas y la Universidad Manizales. In A.C. Núñez, M. Ramírez, L. Jurado, P. Gil, y J. Restrepo (Eds.), *Promoción de la salud: experiencias universitarias* (pp. 159-163). Manizales: Alcaldía de Manizales, Grupo Interinstitucional de Programas para Adolescentes, Universidad de Manizales, Universidad de Caldas.

Ajzen, I., & Fishbein, M. (1980). *Understanding attitudes and predicting social behavior.* Englewood Cliffs, NJ: Prentice- Hall.

Anderson, J.E., Wilson, R., Doll, L., Jones, T.S., & Barker, P. (1999). Condom use and HIV risk behaviors among U.S. adults: Data from a national survey. *Family Planning Perspectives, 31*, 24-28.

Ballester, R. (1997). Intervención psicológica en SIDA y VHI: Prevención y tratamiento. In Pascual, L.M., y R. Ballester (Eds.), *La práctica de la psicología de la salud: Programas de intervención* (pp. 207-248). Valencia: Promolibro.

Bandura, A. (1977). Self-efficacy: Toward a unifying theory of behavioral change. *Psychological Review*, *84*, 191-215.

Bayés, R. (1992). Variaciones sobre un modelo de prevención de enfermedad y su aplicación al caso del SIDA. *Acta Comportamentalia*, *0*, 33-50.

Bayés, R. (1995). *SIDA y psicología*. Barcelona: Martínez Roca.

Bayés, R., & Ribes, E. (1992). Un modelo psicológico de enfermedad: su aplicación al caso del SIDA. In J.A. Piña (Ed.), *Psicología y Salud: aportes del análisis de la conducta* (pp. 1-21). Hermosillo, México: Editorial UNISON.

Blum, R., Beuhring, T., & Rinehart, P. (2000). *Protecting teens: Beyond race, income and family structure*. St. Paul: University of Minnesotta.

Brigham, T.A., Donahoe, P., Gilbert, B.J., Thomas, N., Zemke, S., Koonce, D., & Horn, P. (2002). Psychology and AIDS education: Reducing high-risk sexual behavior. *Behavior and Social Issues, 12*, 10-18.

Botero, B., Gonzáles, M., & Valencia, P. (2002). La experiencia de habilidades para vivir en el ámbito universitario. In Nuñez, A., C., M. Ramírez, L. Jurado, P. Gil, y &. Restrepo (Eds.), *Promoción de la salud: experiencias universitarias* (pp. 59-70). Manizales: Alcaldía de Manizales, Grupo Interinstitucional de Programas para Adolescentes, Universidad de Manizales, Universidad de Caldas.

Bumpas, K. (1999). *Parent-child communication: Promoting healthy youth*. Washington, D.C.: Advocates for Youth.

Godoy, J.F. (1999). Psicología de la salud: Delimitación conceptual. In M.A. Simon (Ed.), *Manual de psicología de la salud* (pp. 77-114). Madrid: Biblioteca Nueva.

Lammers, S., Ireland, M., Resnick, M., & Blum, R. (2000). Influences on adolescents' decision to postpone onset of sexual intercourse: A survival analysis of virginity among youths aged 13 to 18 years. *Journal of Adolescent Health*, *26*, 42-48.

López, F., Salinas, M.C., & Landero, R. (1999). Se perciben más autoeficaces las mujeres en la prevención de conductas de riesgo sexual. *Perspectivas Sociales*, *2,* 77-86.

Mangrulkar, L., Vincent, W., & Posner, M. (2001). Enfoque de habilidades para la vida para un desarrollo saludable de niños y adolescentes. Washington: OPS-Fundación Kellogg.

Mantilla, C.L. (2002). *Habilidades para vivir: una propuesta educativa para la promoción del desarrollo humano y la prevención de problemas psicosociales.* Bogotá: Fundación Fé y Alegría.

Meekers, D., Klein, M., & Foyet, L. (2003). Patterns of HIV risk behaviors and condom use among youth in Yadoundé and Doula, Cameroon. *AIDS and Behavior, 7,* 413-420.

Mejía, I. (2000). *Dinámica, ritmos y significados de la sexualidad juvenil.* Bogotá: Universidad de los Andes, Programa La Casa (Fundación Antonio Restrepo Barco, Ministerio de Educación Nacional y Bienestar Familiar).

Nuñez, A.C., Castrillón, M.D., & Bañol. R.J. (2002a). Hacia una lectura de vivencias, relatos juveniles y habilidades para vivir en estudiantes, desde el proyecto para la promoción de la salud y prevención integral de la Universidad de Manizales. In A.C. Nuñez, M. Ramírez, L. Jurado, P. Gil, & J. Restrepo (Eds.), *Promoción de la salud: experiencias universitarias* (pp. 133-150). Manizales: Alcaldía de Manizales, Grupo Interinstitucional de Programas para Adolescentes, Universidad de Manizales, Universidad de Caldas.

Nuñez, R., Castrillón, D., & Bañol, R. (2002b). Promoción de la salud en la Universidad de Manizales: gestión y consolidación de un proyecto. In Nuñez, R., A., Ramírez, M., Jurado, L., Gil, P., Restrepo, J. (Eds.). Promoción de la salud: experiencias universitarias (págs. 27 – 43). Manizales: Alcaldía de Manizales, Grupo Interinstitucional de Programas para Adolescentes, Universidad de Manizales, Universidad de Caldas.

Nuñez, R., A. (2002). La interacción simbólica y la salud en jóvenes. In Nuñez, A.,C., Ramírez, L. Jurado, P. Gil, & J. Restrepo (Eds.), *Promoción de la salud: experiencias universitarias* (pp. 71-79). Manizales: Alcaldía de Manizales, Grupo Interinstitucional de Programas para Adolescentes, Universidad de Manizales, Universidad de Caldas.

Nuñez, R., A., & Tobón, S. (2005a). Construcción de un modelo de atención en salud para jóvenes: un enfoque desde el desarrollo humano. In *Cuadernos de línea, Línea de Investigación en Familia, Identidad y Cultura*. Universidad de Manizales, Facultad de Psicología: Manizales. 2, 75 – 95.

Nuñez, R., A. & Tobón, S. (2005b). Terapia cognitivo-conductual. El modelo procesual de la salud mental como camino para integración, la investigación y la clínica. Manizales: Universidad de Manizales.

Nuñez, R., A., & Tobón, S. (2006). La integración en la terapia cognitivo – conductual desde el modelo procesual de la salud mental. *Humanitas Revista de Investigación Universidad Católica de Costa Rica,* 3, 3, pp. 59-60.

Núñez, R., A., Tobón, s., & Arias, H., D. (2006a). *Jóvenes universitarios y salud: vivir la universidad. Investigación sobre la salud y sus significados para jóvenes estudiantes universitarios.* In Revista Hacia la Promoción de la Salud. Manizales: Universidad de Caldas Facultad de ciencias para la salud (En proceso de publicación)

Nuñez, R., A., Arias, H., D., & Tobón, S. (2006b). *Conceptuación de habilidades para vivir y monitoreo sobre el nivel de manejo de las mismas en estudiantes universitarios.* Manizales: Universidad de Manizales, Facultad de Psicología Grupo de Investigación en Psicología Clínica y Procesos de Salud.

Nuñez, R. A., Castaño, G., R., & Aristizabal, O. (2006c). Factores biológicos y psicosociales relacionados con las condiciones de salud: una aproximación al perfil de salud de jóvenes estudiantes universitarios. *Revista Proyecciones.* Centro de Investigaciones de la Universidad de Manizales. Manizales. 8, 51 - 71.

Nuñez, R., A. Tobón, S., Bañol, R., J., & Arias, H., D. (2006).Sistema articulado de bienestar universitario. En: *Revista hacia la promoción de la salud.* Manizales: Universidad de Caldas, Facultad de Ciencias de la Salud. 11, 61 – 71.

Nuñez, R., A., Tobón, S., Vinaccia, S. & Arias, H., D. (2006) Diseño de un modelo de intervención psicoterapéutica en el VIH/SIDA a partir del enfoque procesual del estrés. In *Revista Suma Psicológica. Bogota: Fundación Universitaria Konrrad Lorenz Facultad de Psicología.* 13, 2, pp. 105 – 116.

Organización de las Naciones Unidas-SIDA (ONUSIDA 2004). *Informe sobre la epidemia mundial de SIDA. Cuarto informe mundial.* Ginebra: ONUSIDA.

Organización de las Naciones Unidas-SIDA (ONUSIDA (2006). *Situación de la epidemia de SIDA.* Ginebra: ONUSIDA.

Organización Mundial de la Salud (OMS) (1998). *Habilidades para vivir.* Bogotá: Ministerio de Salud.

Organización Panamericana de la Salud (OPS)- Fondo de Población de las Naciones Unidas (1995). *Guía para abogar por la salud integral de los/las adolescentes con énfasis en salud sexual y reproductiva*. Washington: OPS.

Organización Panamericana de la Salud (OPS) (1996). *Promoción de la Salud: Una Antología*. Washington: OPS.

Organización Panamericana de la Salud (OPS) (1998). Plan de acción de desarrollo y de salud de adolescentes y jóvenes en las Américas 1998-2001. Washington.

Orozco, C., & Núñez, A.C. (2001). Modelo integrado de interacción con jóvenes. Evaluación de necesidades versus opciones de intervención. In *Memorias del Diplomado en Dinámicas y Significados de la Realidad Juvenil* (pp. 203-211). Manizales: Alcaldía de Manizales, Grupo Interinstitucional de Programas para Adolescentes GIPA.

Perelló, M., & Villagrán, G. (2000). Predictores del uso del condón en hombres. In *La Psicología Social en México, Vol. VIII* (pp. 741-747). México: Asociación Mexicana de Psicología Social.

Piña, J.A. (2003). Validación de un instrumento para medir competencias conductuales en personas VIH positivas. *Salud Pública de México*, *45*, 293-297.

Piña, J.A. (2004). Eventos disposicionales que probabilizan la práctica de conductas de riesgo para el VIH/SIDA. *Anales de Psicología*, *20*, 23-32.

Piña, J.A., González, D., Molina, C., & Cota, M (2003). Variables psicológicas y VIH/SIDA en estudiantes de nivel superior: estudio comparativo en función del sexo y la edad. *Revista Colombiana de Psicología, 12,* 19-27.

Piña, J.A., Molina, C. & Cota, M. (in press). Validación de un instrumento que mide eventos psicológicos relacionados con el VIH/sida. *Revista Iberoamericana de Comportamiento y Salud.*

Prats, J. (2002). Sida: saber ayuda. Un programa interdisciplinario para la educación secundaria. Ginebra: Oficina Internacional de Educación.

Senderowitz, J. (1997). *Involving young people in reproductive health programs.* Washington, D.C.: FOCUS.

Profamilia (2005). *Encuesta Nacional de Demografía y Salud*. Bogotá: Profamilia.

Restrepo, Jaime. Desarrollo humano y competencias psicosociales. Universidad de Manizales, Facultad de Psicología Grupo de Investigación en Familia identidad y Cultura, Bienestar Universitario, Equipo para la Promoción de la Salud y Prevención Integral. Manizales (documento no publicado).

Sattler, C. (1997). Descubriendo mis habilidades. Trabajando en el salón de clases. Lima, Perú: CEDRO, Centro de Información y educación para la prevención de drogas.

Tobón, S. (2004). *Formación basada en competencias: Pensamiento complejo, diseño curricular y didáctica*. Bogotá: ECOE.

Tobón, S., & Núñez, R.A. (2000). Psicología y sistema de salud en Latinoamérica. *Perspectivas en Psicología, 3*, 21-40.

Tobón, S., & Nuñez, A., C. (2005). Antecedentes, filosofía y dimensiones centrales del modelo procesual de la salud mental. In Nuñez, R., A. y Tobón, S. *Terapia cognitivo-conductual. El modelo procesual de la salud mental como camino para la integración, la investigación y la clínica (99-132)*. Manizales: Universidad de Manizales

Torres, C.J. (1994). *Aplicación de un modelo psicológico de salud biológica al problema del SIDA*. TUnpublished thesis. Guadalajara, México: Universidad de Guadalajara.

Tuldra, A., Izquierdo, I., Fumaz, C., & Ferrer, M.J. (2003). Guía de tratamientos psicológicos eficaces en la infección por el virus de la inmunodeficiencia humana (VIH). In M. Pérez, J.R. Fernández, C. Fernández & I. Amigo (Eds.), *Guía de tratamientos psicológicos eficaces 2. Psicología de la salud.* Madrid: Pirámide.

Turner, R., Irwin, C., Tschann, J., & Millstein, S. (1993). Autonomy, relatedness, and the initiation of health risk behaviors in early adolescence. *Health Psychology*, *12*, 200-208.

Vallejo, G., T., Nuñez, R., A., Escobar, V., G., Ramírez, D., M., Vélez, C., & Gallego, P. (2007). Factores asociados con la aparición de lesiones neoplásicas del tracto genital inferior femenino en una población adolescente del departamento de Caldas, Colombia. Convenio interinstitucional Universidad de Caldas, Departamento de Ciencias Básicas de la Salud, Grupo de Investigación de cáncer de cuello uterino y de mama y la Universidad de Manizales, Facultad de Psicología, Grupos de Investigación en Psicología Clínica y Procesos de Salud y Familia, Identidad y Cultura. Manizales.

Villagrán, G., & Díaz-Loving, R. (1999). Conocimientos sobre sida, prácticas sexuales y actitudes y creencias hacia el uso de condón en estudiantes universitarios. In R. Díaz-Loving y M.K. Torres (Eds.), *Juventud y sida: una visión psicosocial* (pp. 83-92). México, D.F.: UNAM/Grupo Editorial Porrúa.

Weiss, E., Whelan, D., & Rao Gupta, G. (1996). Vulnerability and opportunity: Adolescents and HIV/AIDS in the developing world. Findings from the women and AIDS research program. Washington, D.C.: International Center for Research on Women.

In: Hispanic Psychology Yearbook Volume 1
Ed: Cirilo H. García pp. 155-166
ISBN: 978-1-60741-786-6


*Chapter 12*

# RELEVANT FACTORS FOR OBJECTIVES EFFECTIVENESS ACCOMPLISHMENT IN COMPENSATION PAYMENTS: THE USE OF BONUSES AS A PAYMENT FOR PERFORMANCE*

***Sergio Manuel Madero Gómez[a] and Amaia Arizkuren Eleta[b]***
[a]Instituto Tecnológico y de Estudios Superiores de Monterrey, *Campus* Monterrey, Mexico
[b]Universidad de Deusto, San Sebastián, Spain

## ABSTRACT

This study describes and explains how the interest of companies in paying performance bonus (PPB) and information of the current process has an impact on the payment objectives' effectiveness (POE). The research was carried out between 419 persons who are executives (11.5%); managers (41.1%), and administrators (47.5%), from which 213 do receive performance bonus (50.8%), and 206 do not receive it (49.2%). Regarding sex, the sample is divided into 66.6% male and 33.4% female. Concerning age, 202 persons are under 30 years old; 141 persons are between 31 and 40 years old, and the other 76 are over the age of 40. The object of the article is to find out if POE shows significant differences between people who do receive the PPB and those who do not. By using variance analyses, there were found significant statistical differences between variables. In addition, to test the hypotheses presented, the results obtained are analyzed from their management's point of view.

**Keywords:** Compensation, Performance Bonuses, Monetary Incentives, Variable Compensation, Human Resources.

* A version of this chapter was also published in the *International Hispanic Psychology Journal, Volume 1 Issue 2*, published by Nova Science Publishers, Inc. It was submitted for appropriate modification in an effort to encourage wider dissemination of research.

## INTRODUCTION

A relevant factor for reaching compensations objectives' effectiveness: Performance bonus.

In the XXI Century, a great number of companies are realizing the structures, objectives and methods used for their operation were designed in a historical time which is coming to an end. Time for supporting companies has started, so that they may be highly competitive, improve their processes and be prepared to face the inherent challenges of the new millennium.

The environment in which businesses participate at this time is focused on competitiveness, fulfillment and accomplishment in results, as well as efficiency, diversity in the use of tools for improvement1, for correct use of technology (Ulrich, 2000), for environment concern and consciousness of the importance of social responsibility2.

For that reason, we feel that now is the right time. It is a great opportunity for compensation area specialists to propose, create and develop clear, efficient, novel, applicable and innovative administration structures that can be adapted to current market demands, which has been called "the employee decade" (Jamrog, 2002).

Compensations' administration has undergone a series of changes and questions that have been very relevant throughout history, having, in some cases, a strategic perspective as indicated by Gomez- Mejia and Welbourne (1988); Gomez-Mejia and Welbourne (1991), upon comparing several factors related to payments' structure, questioning if it is the position or the person that should be rewarded; the performance or experience that should be taken into account for evaluating the achievement of certain goals; if programs are designed for individual or team incentives; if internal equity or external competitiveness are important or not, or if fixed or variable payments need to be focused on.

Taking into account the need to know about and design variables in programs for human resources management in the enterprises -such as payments based on yields, also known as monetary incentives, since they are related to performance, productivity and quality- we have been led to reflect and confirm the importance of investigating and knowing what are the most relevant factors in compensation management, so as to take them into account and use them in the best possible manner. In order to develop this article, we have considered that PPB refers to a variable reward based on the evaluation of the performance a person receives at work.

Under this wide variety of changes, of enterprising strategies, of the use of different tools for business administration, of intercultural and generation aspects, of attitudes, values and interests, companies are understanding that variable payment systems implementation is becoming more and more commonly used in the daily practice of human resources management (Deckop, Merriman and Blau, 2004).

---

[1] http://www.spri.es/aSW/web/cas/servicios/publicaciones/index.jsp, revised on December 12, 2007

[2] http://cemefi.org/spanish/content/view/632/19/, revised on December 12, 2007

# The Importance of Payments

In the world of business, very concrete changes have occurred concerning different forms for personnel rewarding, which today are developed in our reality, causing a deep transformation in the payment systems management. For that reason, it is important to analyze and review, in detail, the different applications of performance payments. The goal is to support individual and/or team growth, so as to achieve the objectives.

Taking into consideration the fact that compensation management is a key and essential element for the good run of the business, without allowing for the industrial activity, or size, it is important to point out "an appropriate salary structure reflects the company's philosophy on rewards", since it shows the importance that must be given to a company's salary system. (Stoskopf, 2002),

The ways to reward people in companies must be focused on developing a pleasant and positive work atmosphere; its implementation must be designed to bring about constant communication between those involved in the process, from both, employer's and employees' points of view.

Of course, the efficient use of compensations has a basic and important role in the structure of company's culture, since it changes the way of doing things, of working and even the way of being and thinking.

According to Fusco (2003), presently, business administrators need five tools related to personnel administration. We can mention three of them: (1) "To access to information related to payments which reflect the current market value situation of company's positions; (2) To make the necessary decisions to keep internal equity and external competitiveness; (3) To develop an incentive program to reward work teams for improving the critical objectives of the company".

## Payment Programs for Performance

There is a series of authors showing which payment practices based on performance have been used recently, Aguilar Pastor (2000); Allen and Helms (2001); Ivancevich (2005); Lawler (2003); Scott, McMullen, Wallace and Morajda (2004); Van Neck and Smilko (2002), among which can be pointed out: (1) individual compensations incentives; (2) work teams or groups incentives, standing out those who share savings or benefits obtained from workers' active participation in any specific process improvement, also known as gain sharing"; and (3) those common awarded incentives, reached for all the workers of the company such as: profit sharing obtained in a determined period of time called "profit-sharing"; there are also plans for stocks purchasing or acquisition, both, for executives- "stock-options"- and for any hierarchical level employees, "employee stock-ownership"; and, lastly, non-monetary recognition.

In a compensations study carried out in Latin America, Uzcategui and Diez (2005) mentioned that Mexico is the country which awarded the most short-term incentives in 2001 and 2002; it also shows there are different elements interacting in compensations management, having different implications. For example, in a country level there are economic, political and socio-cultural aspects, while on a company level there are corporate culture and organizational challenges.

Table 1, showed in the attachments, presents a series of aspects involved in performance measurement process, which are a relevant part of performance bonus payment system. In such model, the importance of keeping a close relationship between performance measurement and incentives programs implementation can be observed. (Rynes, Gerhart and Parks, 2005; Werner and Ward, 2001).

**Table 1. Demographic characteristics of the sample**

| | | Gender | | Age | | | Antiquity in the company (years) | | |
|---|---|---|---|---|---|---|---|---|---|
| | | Masculine | Feminine | Less than 30 | Between 30 & 40 | More than 40 | Less than 5 | Between 6 & 10 | More than 10 |
| **Receive PPB** | 213 | 146 | 67 | 79 | 88 | 46 | 105 | 62 | 46 |
| | 51% | 52% | 48% | 37% | 41% | 22% | 49% | 29% | 22% |
| | | | | | | | | | |
| **Not receive PPB** | 206 | 133 | 73 | 123 | 53 | 30 | 124 | 43 | 39 |
| | 49% | 48% | 52% | 60% | 26% | 15% | 60% | 21% | 19% |
| | | | | | | | | | |
| **TOTAL** | 419 | 279 | 140 | 202 | 141 | 76 | 229 | 105 | 85 |
| | 100% | 67% | 33% | 48% | 34% | 18% | 55% | 25% | 20% |
| Chi Square | | 0.746 | | 21.529 | | | 5.476 | | |
| df | | 1 | | 2 | | | 2 | | |
| Probability level | | 0.388 | | 0.000 | | | 0.064 | | |

| | | Antiquity on the position (years) | | | Hierarchic Level | | |
|---|---|---|---|---|---|---|---|
| | | Less than 5 | Between 6 & 10 | More than 10 | High Direction | Management | Administrative |
| **Receive PPB** | 213 | 161 | 35 | 17 | 33 | 113 | 67 |
| | 51% | 76% | 16% | 8% | 15% | 53% | 31% |
| **Not receive PPB** | 206 | 168 | 29 | 9 | 15 | 59 | 132 |
| | 49% | 82% | 14% | 4% | 7 | 29% | 64% |
| **TOTAL** | 419 | 329 | 64 | 26 | 48 | 172 | 199 |
| | 100% | 79% | 15% | 6% | 11% | 41% | 47% |
| Chi Square | | 3.056 | | | 44.83 | | |
| df | | 2 | | | 2 | | |
| Probability level | | 0.217 | | | 0.000 | | |

In the performance evaluation schemes it is necessary to first include measurements or indicators of performance and later, to keep in mind a very clear idea of the process to be followed for different payment schemes implementation. Regarding performance process evaluation, we can mention the importance of a clear and transparent development of the basis used in measuring, as well the procedure to be followed, the personnel involved and responsible to carry it out. It is also necessary to take into account the main factors to be evaluated as well as their respective indicators. In addition, it is always convenient to keep in mind the communication processes used in performance measurement, since they are the core in boss-collaborator relationship when evaluation is carried out, or when pertaining feedback is given for each worker. We find that communication plays a very important role in the development of the process, since it has direct impact on different levels of the company with respect to the action plans that can come forth; it can also affect improvement programs or programs for professional development. Furthermore, it must have performance evaluation method; for example, if evaluation is made under 360 ° scheme, or under 180° methodology, or of it is a unidirectional evaluation3.

Today, monetary rewards strongly influence job's appeal for a person. That is why, there are many companies which partially base their compensation systems on salary incentives, as a way to motivate their employees to reach a greater yield and efficiency. Because of that, (Zingheim and Schuster, 2001) state that in the near future it will be possible to find a good relationship between companies and workers in order to help compensation systems be the motor of the success formula. Companies will offer better working conditions and a series of challenging activities, while workers will develop abilities and competencies to be considered during hiring and developing processes, giving them the possibility to perform, in the best possible way, the roles assigned them in different company's positions.

## THE OBJECTIVES OF COMPENSATIONS

Bohlander, Snell and Sherman (2001); Ellig (2002); Fay and Thompson (2001); Lawler (1995); Newman and Krzystofiak (1998); Werther and Davis (2000) point out so as to design compensation systems, there must be certain main objectives: (a) to maintain and retain personnel; (b) to motivate personnel to a better performance in order to achieve their goals; (c) to improve procedures and activities so as to achieve goals and commitment; and (d) to achieve the employee growth to link payments to the development of abilities and knowledge". The objectives considered to be analyzed in this article are: (1) to improve labor performance, Werner and Ward (2001); (2) to help in developing competencies and abilities, Lawler and Ledford Jr.(1987); Levy-Leboyer (1997); Murray and Gerhart (1998); St-Onge, Haines III and Klarsfeld (2004); and (3) to help worker labor careers, Judge, Cable, Boudreau and Bretz Jr. (1995).

The effectiveness of compensation objectives (POE) will be considered according to associates' perception based on the help they received to fulfill each one of their objects from the payment they have. Table 2, from attachments, shows the model used to develop his research.

---

[3]Levy-Leboyer (2000) presents how 360° evaluations can be developed and implemented.
On the other hand, Alles (2002) works on his own, by considering competence performance.

**Table 2. Affective / Attitudinal Commitment variable analysis**

| Variables / Questions | | Receive bono[1] | Not receive bono[2] | | |
|---|---|---|---|---|---|
| | | Mean | | F ratio | Significance |
| **Affective / Attitudinal Commitment** | Alpha Cronbach: 0.945 | 3.889671 s=0.0738 | 3.665049 s=0.0750 | 4.56 | 0.033375** |
| 1.- I feel like "part of the family" in the organization. | Factor loading -0.775740 | 3.821596 s=0.0793 | 3.650486 s=0.0806 | 2.29 | 0.130874 |
| 2.- The organization has a great personal significance for me. | Factor loading -0.889943 | 3.948357 s=0.0780 | 3.771845 s=0.0793 | 2.52 | 0.113436 |
| 3.- I feel emotionally attached to the organization. | Factor loading -0.893725 | 3.849765 s=0.0799 | 3.587379 s=0.0813 | 5.30 | 0.021802** |
| 4.- I have a great sense of membership in the organization. | Factor loading -0.879225 | 3.938967 s=0.0815 | 3.653659 s=0.0831 | 6.01 | 0.014638** |

[1] n=213 [2] n=206
*significant at a level of 0.01%
**significant at a level of 0.05%

# METHOD

Next, we will focus on demonstrating the activities from a methodological point of view that are related to the development of this work. The research carried out is not an experimental one; the population includes all those people working in high management, intermediate and administrative positions4, of companies belonging to Monterrey, Nuevo Leon Metropolitan zone, in Mexico. They are from commercial, industrial and service sectors. Without taking into account if they receive or not performance bonus, a favorable sample was taken. Information was obtained by filling out a questionnaire. The scales used to score each variable is Likert scale, from 1 to 5, where "1" pertains to the phrase "I totally disagree with", and "5" pertains to "I totally agree with". 213 questionnaires were answered by people who do receive PPB, which is 50.8% of our sample, and 206 questionnaires were answered by people who do not receive PPB, being 49.2% of the sample; a total of 419 questionnaires.

## Participants

We immediately analyze the data for the people who answered the instrument, which was given to 419 persons, pointing out that 66.6% are male and 33.4% are female. On the other hand, 48.2% are under 30 years old, 33.6% are between 30 and 40 years old, and 18.1% are older than 40. On respect to the experience or seniority, 54.6% have been working in the

---

[4] "High Management" pertains to "General Management" of the business and "Operational Management" (including hierarchical second level). "Intermediate hierarchy" are those depending on High Management ; they belong to the third or fourth hierarchical level.

company for less than 5 years; 25.1% for 6 to 10 years, and at last, 20.2% for more than 10 years. Regarding position seniority, 78.5% has less than 5 years in the position; 15.3% has been in the same position for 6 to 10 years, and the rest, 6.2%, has been during more than 10 years. Concerning position level, 11.5% belong to High Management; 41.1% is hired in Operational Positions, and 47.5% belongs to Administrative level.

The comparison allows observing differences expected due to the population. Regarding gender, both groups are predominately male; those who do not receive bonus are younger (60% under 30 years old) than those who do receive it (37%). Concerning seniority, the proportion is the same as age, since personnel who do not receive bonus (60%) have less than 5 years in the company, meanwhile, those who do receive it (49%) have more than 5 years. In addition to seniority in the position, the number of people who do not receive bonus is higher (82%) having less than 5 years than those who do receive it (76%). Fifteen percent of High Management personnel receive the bonus, and 7% do not receive it. This data can be observed in Table 3 in the attachments.

**Table 3. Continuative / Calculative Commitment variable analysis**

| Variables / Questions | | Receive bono[1] | Not receive bono[2] | | |
|---|---|---|---|---|---|
| | | Mean | | F ratio | Significance |
| **Continuative / Calculative Commitment** | Alpha Cronbach: 0.743 | 2.728873 s=0.0642 | 3.199029 s=0.0653 | 26.39 | 0.000000* |
| | | | | | |
| 1.- In this moment, being a member of the organization is a necessity, not a desire. | Factor loading 0.579454 | 2.957747 s=0.0861 | 3.446602 s=0.08762 | 15.82 | 0.000082* |
| 2.- I feel I have low possibilities of having another job if I leave the organization. | Factor loading 0.693384 | 2.29108 s=0.0874 | 2.737864 s=0.0889 | 12.82 | 0.000383* |
| 3.- I consider that one of the serious causes of not leaving the organization are the few alternatives of getting another job. | Factor loading 0.813691 | 2.784038 s=0.0851 | 3.398058 s=0.0865 | 25.59 | 0.000001* |
| 4.- It is going to be very difficult to leave the organization in this moment; even though I would like to do it. | Factor loading 0.487776 | 2.882629 s=0.0869 | 3.213592 s=0.0884 | 7.13 | 0.007868* |

[1] n=213 [2] n=206
*significant at a level of 0.01%
**significant at a level of 0.05%

## RESULTS

For each one of the items used in reward objectives measurement, a confirming factorial analysis was carried out to simplify the variables used in the instrument, with factorial loads >

than 0.80 which allows us to group them into a new variable, which is POE, resulting in a .9176 Cronbach alpha. The first factor in our model is related to monetary compensation, that is, a performance bonus payment received by the workers in a company, for which Gomez-Mejia, Balkin and Cardy (2001) mention that there are 3 elements upon considering a total reward package that people have when they provide their services for a company, which are: basic salary, benefits and incentives.

The first hypothesis of the research establishes that there is a significant difference in the POE between people who do receive a performance bonus and those who do not.

POE average indicator for people who do receive PPB is 3.374 compared with the one of those who do not receive it, which is 3.029. That is why we observe there is a difference between both populations, and according to the F statistics (9.54) and $p<0.005$, it is estimated the difference between both groups is statistically significant. For that reason we find PPB does help to improve performance, acquire abilities and competencies as well as to promote people's stay with the companies.

Another factor considered in our model is related to workers' perception about company's interest on PPB systems; they point out the interest in developing, fulfilling and supporting PPB systems follow-up, in order to support workers who obtain better incomes, as well as to establish PPB clear standards and policies. We realized there is not enough literature about that particular matter; that is why it is a relevant factor for this study.

The second hypothesis establishes there is a significant difference in the POE between people indicating enterprises do really have interest on PPB systems and those who do not.

According to the results obtained, we observe POE average of people indicating that companies are not interested in PPB is 2.571, while those indicating companies are interested in PPB is 3.896. A difference is found between both, and we can prove it by the F statistic (104.17) and $p<0.001$. Therefore, we realize that there is a significant statistical difference. It is understood that those enterprises showing interest in developing, fulfilling and following up their compensation systems, shall help to make them be more productive, acquire more abilities, as well as to make them remain in the company, developing and growing as professionals.

Taking into consideration some of the different aspects that Hale and Bailey (1998); Mulvey, LeBlanc, Heneman and McInerney (2002) show in their research model how important is for each of the employees to know, to understand, and to possess the different aspects related to payment systems, as satisfaction, commitment and reliability makers. We have included in our model the information factor, which we focus on PPB system. Heneman, Mulvey and LeBlanc (2002); Mulvey, LeBlanc, Heneman and McInerney (2002); St- Onge (2000); Mulvey, Ledford Jr. and LeBlanc (2000) indicate that wide information about payment programs in companies is a strong personnel satisfaction predictor. It also shows it is closely related to retention aspects. The phrase they present is the following: "Employees know much less about payment processes than the structure itself and its results". For that reason, the following hypothesis is related to the PPB process information people is concerned, which mainly consists of understanding and comprehending different aspects related to PPB; PPB operational rules; activities to be carried out to reach PPB, and the follow-up plan. Therefore, the third hypothesis establishes there is a significant difference in the POE between those who do not know about PPB process, and those who really do.

For all of the above, we can realized POE average persons indicating they do know PPB system process is 3.771; while the average of those indicating they do not know PPB system process is 2.546, which can be proved by F statistic (73.73) and $p<0.001$, and for that reason there is a significant statistical difference. This demonstrates the relevance of the processes the company has to develop so that PPB can be successful and the expected results can be obtained.

The next component is related to the performance measurement process, standing out the importance of the different criteria used to measure performance, the unambiguity of the performance evaluation process, provoking the fourth hypothesis which establishes there is a significant difference in the POE between those who do not know about the performance measurement process who really know it.

We observe POE average of people indicating they do know about the process of the measurement of performance is 3.557, while the average of those indicating they do not know the performance measurement process is 2.644 and, for that reason, we can prove by statistical F (72.96) and $p<0.001$, there is a significant statistical difference. By this, we realized it is relevant to take into account the clear explanation of the processes in the different enterprise activities related to performance measurement and compensation system.

## DISCUSSION

According to the results obtained during this research development, we can indicate PPB is an auxiliary tool which helps to fulfill with the compensation objectives; however, it is necessary to manage pertinently a series of factors interrelated between themselves so it can be attractive to workers and, therefore, they develop their labor tasks efficiently. We can also confirm that an incentive program is successful if they are taken into account, upon its design and development, company's vision, clarity in sending messages, and a philosophy focused on goals fulfillment. (Milkovich and Milkovich, 1992).

Most of the enterprises, especially small and medium-sized ones, do not possess a compensation management solid structure, reason why payment programs are developed only to fulfill labor and legal requirements, but without considering other relevant components. In addition, they ignore measurement indicators and the basis for being competitive and improving internal equity.

In addition, Hale and Bailey, (1998) indicate it is necessary to assure that employees understand and comprehend different existing company payment programs. For future research, at the time of applying a measurement instrument, it is also important to take into account and to find out if there is a PPB in the company, after identifying and differentiating if persons who take the questionnaire also participate in the PPB, and if they know people who do receive it and others who do not. Therefore, we recommend that this differentiation be made so as to obtain reliable information. On the other hand, it must be considered the fact that the progress found in studies and investigations related to human resources strategic programs, such as diversity in the current labor force management, the focus related to the goals' achievement by personnel performance and effectiveness of human resources processes, are topics which can be considered to continue researching about this subject, so interesting for some. Luthans and Sommer, (2005; Richard and Johnson (2001); Richard and Johnson (2004).

In Table 4, we show the personnel demographic characteristics from those who do receive PPB and those who do not.

**Table 4. Normative commitment variable analysis.**

| Variables / Questions | | Receive bono[1] | Do not receive bono[2] | | |
|---|---|---|---|---|---|
| | | **Mean** | | **Ratio F** | **Significance** |
| **Normative Commitment** | Alpha Cronbach: 0.712 | 3.298905 s=0.0679 | 3.147249 s=0.0691 | 2.45 | 0.118536 |
| | | | | | |
| 1.- During these days, I believe people change of organization with high frequency. | Factor loading 0.145340 | 3.638498 s=0.0758 | 3.61165 s=0.07706 | 0.06 | 0.803945 |
| 2.- From my perception, keep constantly changing of organization is non ethic. | Factor loading 0.608159 | 3.258216 s=0.0885 | 3.286408 s=0.0899 | 0.05 | 0.823268 |
| 3.- One of the principal reasons why I keep working on the organization is because I believe that loyalty is important, so I have a moral obligation feeling of permanence. | Factor loading 0.640475 | 3.361502 s=0.0864 | 3.106796 s=0.0878 | 4.27 | 0.039311** |
| 4.- Things went better when people stayed on the same organization on most of their professional trajectory. | Factor loading 0.671063 | 3.276995 s=0.0809 | 3.048544 s=0.0823 | 3.91 | 0.048521** |

[1] n=213 [2] n=206
*significant at a level of 0.01%
**significant at a level of 0.05%

## REFERENCES


Aguilar-Pastor, E. M. (2000). El diseño de la retribución de los directivos y su efecto sobre los resultados empresariales. *Economía Industrial*, 333, 131-149.

Allen, R. S. & Helms, M. M. (2001). Reward practices and organizational performance. *Compensation and Benefits Review*, 33, 4, 74-80.

Alles, M. A. (2002). *Desempeño por competencias: Evaluación de 360°*. Buenos Aires: Editorial Granica, S.A.

Bohlander, G. W., Snell, S. A., & Sherman, Jr. A. W. (2001, 12th.ed.) *Administración de Recursos Humanos*. México: Thompson Learning.

Deckop, J. R., Merriman, K. & Blau, G. K. (2004).Impact of variable risk preferences on the effectiveness of control by pay. *Journal of Occupational and Organizational Psychology*, 77, 63-80.

Ellig, B. R. (2002). Executive compensation 101: Considering the many elements. *WorldatWork Journal*, 11, 1, 11-20.

Fay, Ch. H., & Thompson, M. A. (2001). Contextual determinants of reward systems' success: An exploratory study. *Human Resource Management*, 40, 3, 213-226.

Fusco, Ch. J. (2003). Equipping company managers to attract, retain and employ human capital. *Compensation and Benefits Review*, 35, 3, 20-28.

Gomez-Mejia, L. R., Balkin, D. B., & Cardy, R. L. (2001, 3th..ed.). *Dirección y Gestión de Recursos Humanos*. Madrid: Pearson Educación.

Gomez-Mejia, L. R., & Welbourne, Th. M. (1988). Compensation Strategy: An Overview and Future Steps. *Human Resource Planning*, 11, 3, 173-187.

Gomez-Mejia, L. R., & Welbourne, Th. M. (1991). Compensation Strategies in a Global Context.. *Human Resource Planning*, 14, 1, 29-41.

Hale, J., & Bailey, G. (1998). Seven dimensions of successful rewards plans. *Compensation and Benefits Review*, 30, 4, 71-77.

Heneman, R. L., Mulvey, P. W. & LeBlanc, P.V. (2002). Improve base pay ROI by increasing employee knowledge. *Worldatwork Journal*. 11, 4, 21-27.

Ivancevich, J. M. (2005). *Administración de Recursos Humanos*. México, D.F.: McGraw Hill Interamericana.

Jamrog, J. J. (2002). Current practices: The coming decade of the employee. *Human Resource Planning,* 25, 3, 5-11.

Judge, T. A., Cable, D, M., Boudreau, J. W., & Bretz, Jr. R. D. (1995). An empirical investigation of the predictors of executive career success. *Personnel Psychology*, 48, 485-519.

Lawler III, E. E. (2003). Pay practices in Fortune 1000 corporations. *WorldatWork Journal,* 12, 4, 45- 54.

Lawler III, E. E. (1995). The new pay: A strategic approach. *Compensation and Benefits Review,* 27, 4, 14-22.

Lawler, E. III., & Ledford, G. E. (1987). Skill-Based Pay: A concept thats catching on. *Management Review,* 76, 2, 46-51.

Lévy-Leboyer, C. (1997). *Gestión de las competencias*. Barcelona: Gestión 2000.

Lévy-Leboyer, C. (2000). *Feedback de 360°*. Barcelona: Gestión 2000.

Luthans, K. W., & Sommer, S. M. (2005). The Impact of High Performance Work on Industry-level Outcomes. *Journal of Managerial Issues*, 17, 3, 327-345.

Milkovich, G., & Milkovich, C. (1992). Strengthening the pay-performance relationship: The research. *Compensation and Benefits Review*. 24, 6, 53-62.

Mulvey, P. W., LeBlanc, P. V., Heneman, R. L,. & McInerney, M. (2002). Study finds that knowledge of pay process can beat out amount of pay in employee retention, organizational effectiveness. *Journal of Organizational Excellence*, 21, 4, 29-42.

Mulvey, P. W., Ledford J.R., Gerald, E., & LeBlanc, P. V. (2000). Rewards of Work.. *WorldatWork Journal*, 9, 3, 6-18.

Murray, B., Gerhart, B. (1998). An empirical analysis of a skill-based pay program and plant performance outcome. *Academy of Management Journal*, 41, 1, 68-78.

Newman, J. M., Krzystofiak, F. J. (1998). Value-chain compensation. *Compensation and Benefits Review*, 30, 3, 60-66.

Richard, O. C. & Johnson, N. B. (2001). Undestanding the impact of human resource diversity practices on firm performance. *Journal of Managerial Issues*, 13, 2, 177-195.

Richard, O. C. & Johnson, N. B. (2004). High Performance Work Practices And Human Resource Management Effectiveness: Substitutes or Complements? *Journal of Business Strategies*, 21, 2, 133-148.

Rynes, S. L., Gerhart, B.., & Parks, L. (2005). Personnel Psychology: Performance evaluation and pay for performance. *Annual Review of Psychology*, 56, 571-600.

Scott, D., McMullen, Th. D., Wallace, M., & Morajda, D. (2004). Annual Cash Incentives for Managerial and Professional Employees. *Worldatwork Journal*, 13, 4, 6-15.

St-Onge, S. (2000). Variables Influencing the Perceived Relationship between Performance and Pay in a merit pay environment. *Journal of Business and Psychology*, 14, I3, 459-479.

St-Onge, S., Haines III, V., & Klarsfeld, A. (2004). La rémunération basée sur les compétences: Déterminant et incidences. *Relations Industrielles*, 59, 4, 651-680.

Stoskopf, G. A. (2002). Choosing the best salary structure for your organization. *WorldatWork Journal*, 11, 4, 28-36.

Ulrich, D. (2000). From eBusiness to eHR.. *HR Human Resource Planning*, 23, 2, 12-21.

Uzcategui, M.., & Diez, F.. (2005). A Journey through Compensation in Latin America. *WorldatWork Journal*, 14, 1, 59-70.

Van Neck, K. H., & Smilko, J. E. (2002). Variable pay plans creating a financial partnership with the work force. *WorldatWork Journal*, 11, 4, 74-79.

Werther, W. B., & Davis, K. (2000, 5th.Ed.). *Administración de personal y recursos humanos*. México: McGraw Hill.

Werner, S., & Ward, S. (2001) Cutting through the fog of academic writing: Ten studies worth deciphering. *WorldatWork Journal*, 10, 1, 47-55.

Zingheim, P.K., & Schuster, J.R. (2001). Winning the talent game: Total rewards and the better workforce deal. *Compensation & Benefits Management*, 17, 3, 33-39.

In: Hispanic Psychology Yearbook Volume 1
Ed: Cirilo H. García pp. 167-176
ISBN: 978-1-60741-786-6


*Chapter 13*

# SOCIAL ANXIETY ASSESSMENT THROUGH SELF-REPORT AND AUTOMATIC PROCESSING OF EMOTIONAL INFORMATION*

***María Isolde Hedlefs Aguilar[a1]***
***Ernesto Octavio López Ramírez[a], and César Jesús Antona Casas[b]***
[a] Universidad Autónoma de Nuevo León, Monterrey, México
[b] Universidad Pontificia de Salamanca, Spain

## ABSTRACT

A sample of 192 university students was divided into two groups. The first group (experimental) comprised those individuals with the highest scores on the "Fear of negative evaluation" (FNE, Watson and Friend, 1969) and the "Social avoidance and distress" scales (SAD, Watson and Friend, 1969). The second group (control) consisted of students who had obtained the lowest scores in both scales. Both groups were required to participate in one affective priming study in order to compare automatic valence recognition latencies using stressful word pairs related to social fear and social phobia, as well as positive, negative, and neutral words. Only the experimental group showed affective priming for social fear and social phobia. The control group showed no priming effect for any experimental condition. These results are discussed in terms of their implications for an integral diagnostic system of social anxiety disorder that takes into account automatic and controlled emotional appraisal of social stressful events.

**Keywords:** Social anxiety, social phobia, social anxiety disorder.

---

* A version of this chapter was also published in the *International Hispanic Psychology Journal, Volume 1 Issue 2*, published by Nova Science Publishers, Inc. It was submitted for appropriate modification in an effort to encourage wider dissemination of research.

# Introduction

Anxiety consists of a scattered feeling of fear experienced on the cognitive (e.g., thoughts, mental images, memories), physiological (e.g., heart rate increase, sweating, changes in breathing), and motor/physical (e.g., escape and avoidance reactions) levels. Anxiety in itself is neither good nor bad; it needs to be contextualized and its consequences must be assessed in order to address it. Anxiety can take many shapes and be linked to highly varied stimuli. In cases where the anxiety is derived from social situations we speak of social anxiety. Undue social anxiety greatly affects sufferers, since it usually impairs their social performance, fosters subjective unhappiness, and damages their relationships with other people. Social phobia can occur when the degree of social anxiety is such that it plainly interferes with the daily life of sufferers (APA, 2000). Although assessments of social anxiety and phobia often employ self-report instruments (e.g., interviews, scales, inventories, questionnaires) or behavioral observation, automatic cognitive processing of emotional information is also quite meaningful. The literature, in fact, confirms an automatic cognitive bias among social anxiety and phobia sufferers.

From a cognitive perspective, different emotional disorders involve different cognitive resources. Specifically, anxiety can prompt cognitive mechanisms related to fear while depression is often associated with a feeling of loss and failure (Mogg & Bradley, 2000). Cognitive literature has established a link between many preattention and selective attention information processing mechanisms and anxiety (MacLeod, 1998; Mathews & Harley, 1996; Mathews & Milrroy, 1994; Mathews & Wells, 2000a; 2000b). Depression, on the other hand, activates cognitive mechanisms of sustained attention, usually focusing on autobiographical events and mechanisms linked to the individual's memory (Dalgleish et al., 1997).

MacLeod, Mathews and Tata (1986) have conducted experimental tests in which spatial attention to emotional stimuli could be assessed through recognition latencies for visual input presented on a computer screen. Typically, the subject was presented with a series of word pairs, one word on top of the other. In the key trials, one of the words signaled a threatening event while the other one remained neutral. Each pair appeared on screen for a brief moment (500 miliseconds) and then gave way to a visual object (a black dot), which appeared where one of the words used to be. Subjects had to respond as quickly as possible by pressing one of the computer's keys to indicate the appearance of the dot. Interestingly, individuals with emotional anxiety disorders tended to respond more quickly to dots appearing right after anxiety-related words than to those that took the place of neutral words (for a summary, see Mathews & MacLeod, 1994).

Cognitive literature has also recorded biases in the automatic processing of emotional information in relation to different types of stress-inducing events (Mogg & Bradley, 2000). One of the present study's main goals is to determine if, during the automatic processing of emotional information, social situation-related words (e.g., those employed in the study's social anxiety assessment questionnaires) elicit consistent responses on the part of individuals catalogued in accordance with the scores provided by the questionnaires. If this is indeed the case, this should lead to a more comprehensive type of diagnostic. The subject's explicit and conscious responses to social anxiety questionnaires can be confirmed by a diagnostic interview (e.g., ADIS-IV in the case of social phobia; DiNardo, Brown, & Barlow, 1994) and complemented by an assessment of potential emotional cognitive dysfunctional biases that escape the individual's conscious control in social situations or events.

# METHOD

## Subjects

The sample was comprised of students at the Psychology School of the Autonomous University of Nuevo León (Mexico). Participation was voluntary. In order to be included in the high social anxiety group (experimental group from hereon) subjects had to fulfill the following criteria: a score of 19 or more points in the Fear of Negative Evaluation scale (FNE, Watson & Friend, 1969) and a score of 12 or more points in the Social Avoidance and Distress scale (SAD, Watson & Friend, 1969). In order to select those subjects with the highest social anxiety scores the established threshold was similar to or slightly below the mean score registered in other studies that tried to distinguish between subjects suffering from high levels of social anxiety and social phobia and those who did not. In terms of the FNE, Heimberg et al. (1990) and Mattick, Peters & Clarke (1989) have set a 22-24 point threshold to determine social anxiety; according to Villa, Botella, Quero, Ruipérez & Gallardo (1998), the mean for social phobia sufferers is 24,79; Oei, Kenna & Evans (1991) have indicated a score of 20,7 (5,1). Ruipérez, García-Palacios & Botella (2002) report a 26,84 (2,03) score for the generalized subtype and a 20,87 (3,87) for the nongeneral subtype. Regarding SAD, Butler, Cullington, Munby, Amies & Gelder (1984) and Heimberg et al. (1990) have indicated a 18-20 treshold. Villa et al. (1998) reported a 18,77 score among sufferers of social phobia, while Ruipérez et al. (2002) reported a 23,31 (5,29) score for the generalized subtype and 12,62 (5,58) for the nongeneral one. Our experimental group, comprised of 10 individuals, showed a mean score of 21,90 (1,66) for FNE and 17,60 (3,16) for SAD.

Our control group was comprised of 13 individuals with low scores in both scales. The threshold was 9 or fewer points for FNE and 2 or fewer points for SAD. The average scores obtained by this 13 person group were 5,69 (2, 68) for FNE and 1, 2 (0,72) for SAD.

As has been pointed out, subjects were selected after the collective administration of the FNE and SAD questionnaires. One hundred and ninety two people participated: the average age was 19,9 years (1,44; range 17-23); 158 were women (82,3%), 31 were men (16,1%), and 3 (1,6%) did not indicate their name or sex. All participants were first- to tenth-semester students. Those individuals chosen for the control and experimental groups participated in a subsequent affective priming study (see the procedure section; Fazio, 1995) that tried to assess how the emotional valence for a given word (stressing, negative, positive, or neutral) affected the recognition latency for the emotional valence of a second word. The experimental group was expected to display a greater degree of sensitivity toward words recalling social events regarded as stressing by social anxiety sufferers.

## Assessment Instruments

This study employed the FNE (Watson & Friend, 1969) and SAD scales (Watson &

Friend, 1969). These are often used together given their complementary nature (Echeburúa, 1993) and are popular measurers of social anxiety (Heimberg, Hope, Rapee & Bruch, 1988, Orsillo, 2001). FNE centers on the cognitive aspect while SAD evaluates the physiological and motor aspects. FNE comprises 30 items and SAD 28. Both scales employ a true or false answer format and take a very reasonable time span (collective administration usually takes under thirty minutes). Their authors collected data from a university student sample. After one month, the study's test-retest reliability results were 0,8 (FNE) and 0,68 (SAD), and both had a 0,94 internal consistency alpha coefficient (Watson & Friend, 1969).

According to Turner, McCanna and Beidel (1987), SAD and FNE were developed on a student population in order to asses degrees of anxiety regarding social evaluation and work well with other instruments designed to measure social anxiety, social approval, or affiliation. At the same time, they point out that, even if both scales are sensitive to anxiety, their construct validity and predictive validity have not been properly examined. Heimberg et al. (1988) sustain that they are useful tools with which to assess social anxiety or measure results in social phobia studies. Finally, both scales are characterized by good psychometric properties in adolescent and adult Spanish speaking populations (Bobes et al., 1999; García-López, Olivares, Hidalgo, Beidel & Turner, 2001; Villa et al., 1998).

Because these scales have not been validated in the context of Mexican populations, this study's construct validity must focus on convergent validity. The inventory predictions do not go beyond classifying social phobia sufferers. But if these predictions are correct, then the rigorous experimental evidence provided by the affective priming studies (see below) must corroborate the accuracy of the classifications provided by the questionnaires and demonstrate that social phobia sufferers displayed significantly greater cognitive time than non-sufferers. This would be due to a cognitive bias toward types of information relevant to selective attention-related disorders (Wells & Mathew, 1994); documented variables span from automatic rumination to the use of dysfunctional schemes kept in the long-term memory and related to traumatic life events (Williams, Watts, MacCleod & Mathews, 1997). If those individuals classified as social phobia sufferers show different results than those classified as not affected by the condition, then the information provided by the two sources will lead to the same conclusion, thus validating the inventory construct.

**Table 1. Word-pairs selected for the social anxiety group.**

| WORD PAIRS USED IN THE STUDY | | | |
|---|---|---|---|
| POSITIVE | NEGATIVE | ANXIETY | NEUTER |
| Happiness – smile | Fear – terror | People - criticize | Table - lake |
| Joy – pretty | Anger – torture | Audience - mistake | Plate – glass |
| Love – achievement | Resentment – damage | Evaluation - stupid | Window – ball |
| Enthusiasm – brilliant | Evil – weeping | Disapprove - authority | Cloud – tree |
| Hope – happy | Sadness – upset | Nervous - discussion | Bounce – tennis |
| Gift – affection | Failure – punch | Defect - discourse | Pencil – vase |
| Wish – April | Depression – death | Judgment - ridicule | Coffee - light bulb |
| Win – faithful | Aggression – defeat | Teacher - tension | Book – interview |
| Beautiful – hug | Disillusionment – blood | Group - date | Leaf – fresh |
| Generous – attention | Drown – lie | Meeting - conversation | Backpack – frog |

The emotional valence identification studies employed SuperLab Pro software, which is capable of presenting high-speed stimuli and registering recognition latencies in milliseconds. The word pairs employed in the study are shown in Table 1.

The words related to social anxiety were selected from the items presented in the social anxiety assessment questionnaires. The control was that the Spanish words could not contain more than 10 letters or fewer than 4. In the case of word pairs thought to be connected to social event-related anxiety, an effort was made to avoid any kind of associative or topical links.

## Procedure

Study participants were received in groups of 4, after which the anxiety questionnaires were administered. Once the control (low scores in both scales) and experimental (high scores in both scales) groups had been selected, participants were scheduled in groups of 5.

Each subject sat in front of a computer to take the emotional valence study, which consisted of three stages. The first stage explained the procedure to participants, who were then were allowed familiarize themselves with it during a practice session. Once this was finished, they went on to do the experimental trials. Each experimental trial involved three stages: during the first one, a black dot appeared in the middle of the computer screen to focus the participants' gaze on the place were the words would later appear. The first word was then shown for 250 milliseconds, so that they could read it in silence. After 50 milliseconds of blank screen, the second word was shown and it was up to the participant to decide if it had an emotional connotation or not and press the pertinent computer key. Once this word disappeared, the black dot came back and the sequence started all over again. This task comprised 90 random experimental trials that were completed in approximately 15 minutes.

This technique is known as affective priming with emotional identification tasks and uses a variety of stimuli, including words and nonwords (De Houwer, Hermans & Eelen, 1998), slides (Hermans, De Houwer & Eelen, 1994), drawings and pictures (Banse, 2000), and positive and negative smells (Hermans, Bayens & Eelen, 1998) among others (see also Musch & Klauer, 2003).

# Results

The average correct responses per individual were analyzed using a mixed 2x4 ANOVA. Participants with response errors greater than 20% of the total experimental trials were not processed. One of the members in the control group was eliminated because of errors in the subject's responses to the anxiety-related words. The prediction derived from the anxiety inventories was that the 13 members of the low anxiety control group had to respond differently from the high anxiety experimental group ones. Figure 1 illustrates the significant main effect for the group considered in this study.

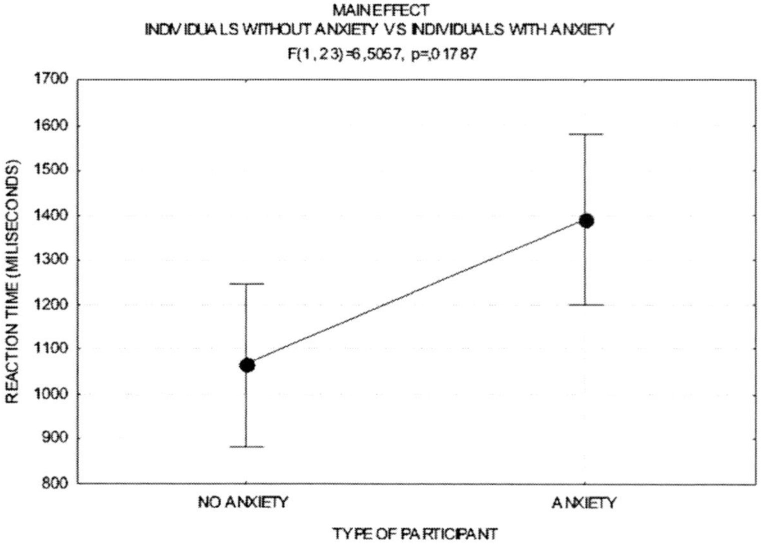


Figure 1. The group diagnosed with anxiety (right) employed more cognitive time to recognize anxiety words.

The differential effect in performance displayed by the experimental group would be explained by their susceptibility to anxiety-related words, suggesting a significant main effect given the type of relation between words. This is confirmed in Figure 2, which illustrates performance according to type of relation between words.

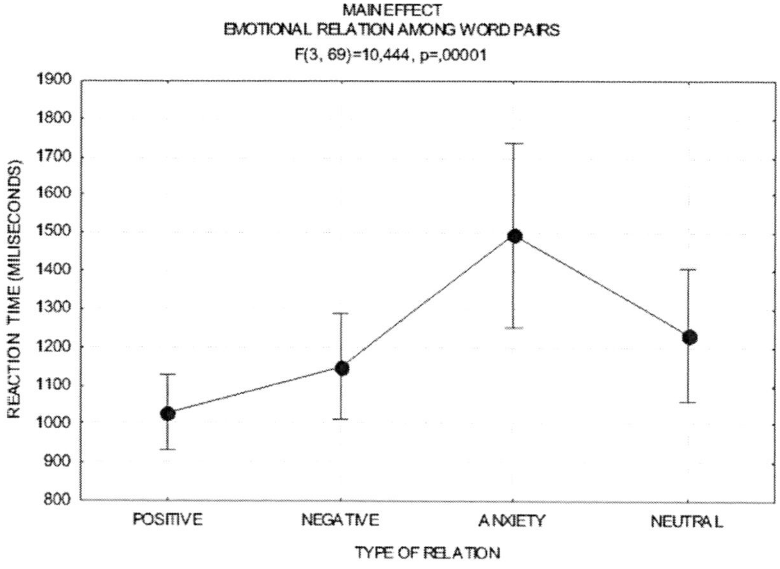


Figure 2. A significant main effect is seen when the type of relation is considered. Note that, on average, anxiety words seem to consume more of the participants' cognitive resources.

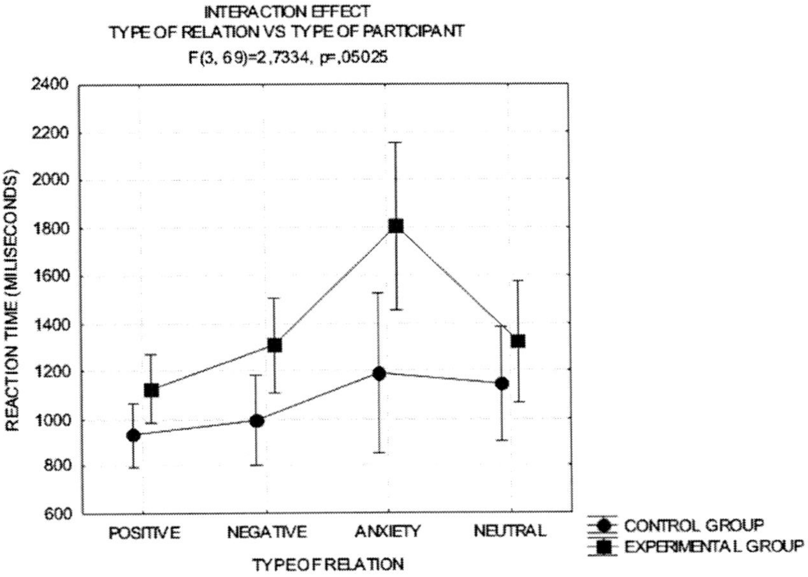


Figure 3. The maximum emotional information processing time displayed by the experimental group in regard to social anxiety-related words.

An analysis of the planned comparisons between anxiety-related and neutral words shows a significant result (F(1,23) = 4,382932, p= 0,047522). The planned comparison between the anxiety-related words and the positive and negative ones also resulted in a significant difference (F(1,23) = 23,94578, p= 0,000061). Given these differences, it becomes important to find out whether this result is related to the performance of the experimental group. Figure 3 illustrates both groups' performances according to the different experimental conditions.

A planned comparison solely between the anxiety-related words and the experimental and control groups shows a statistically significant difference (F(1,23) = 6,926400, p = 0,014907). However, when the control group's anxiety words are compared with the positive and negative ones, no significant difference can be found (F(1,23) = 3,875856, p = 0,061151). This is also the case when comparing the anxiety-related words and their neutral counterparts: F(1,23) = 3,499103, p= 0,074181. On the other hand, the experimental group shows a significant difference (F(1,23) = 4,529523, p= 0,044249) when comparing anxiety-related words with neutral ones, and also when comparing anxiety words with their positive and negative counterparts (F (1,23) = 23,95612, p= 0,000061).

It seems that only the group diagnosed as suffering from social anxiety or phobia showed a cognitive bias involving pre-attentive automatic processing. Interestingly, this group shows a link between anxiety-related words and increased cognitive time. This suggests these participants employ more cognitive resources when dealing with stressing social events.

## Discussion

The emotional identification study confirmed that those individuals with high scores in the social assessment questionnaires also showed a cognitive bias toward social anxiety-related words, using more cognitive resources on an automatic processing level. It is interesting that the control group member who was eliminated from the analysis entered the wrong responses to the anxiety-related words. Barring any other kind of explanation, this type of performance is frequent among individuals who suffer from emotional disorders but intentionally omit these sorts of stimuli as a coping strategy. A study based exclusively on the questionnaires would not have detected this condition. The individual could have also suffered from some type of emotional disorder in the past.

It should be noted that, from an integral diagnostic perspective, emotional dissociation can be diagnosed using these methods. That is, it is possible that there are patients who, both before and after therapy, will intentionally deny that stressing social situations cause them anxiety. By targeting automatic processing levels beyond conscious control, emotional valence identification studies can show whether a subject is responding truthfully or not.

## References

American Psychiatric Association (APA) (2000). Diagnostic and Statistical Manual of Mental Disorders (4th revised edition) (DSM-IV-R). Washington, DC.: APA.

Banse, R. (2000). Affective priming with liked and disliked persons: Prime vivibility determines congruency and incongruency effects. Manuscript submitted for publication, *Humbold Universität, Beerlin*, Germany.

Bobes, J., Badía, X., Luque, A., García, M., González, M. P., Dal-Ré, R., Soria, J., et al. (1999). Validación de las versiones en español de los cuestionarios Liebowitz Social Anxiety Scale, Social Anxiety and Distress Scale y Sheehan Disability Inventory para la evaluación de la fobia social. *Medical Clinical*, 112, 530-538.

Butler, G., Cullington, A., Munby, M., Amies, P. & Gelder, M. (1984). Exposure and anxiety management in the treatment of social phobia. *Journal of Consulting and Clinical Psychology*, 52, 642-650.

Dalgleish, T., Taghavi, R., Doost H.N., Moradi, A., Yule, W. & Canterbury, R. (1997). Information processing in clinically depressed and anxious children. *Journal of Child Psychology, Psychiatry,* Vol. 38, 535-541.

De Houwer, J., Hermans, D., & Eelen, P. (1998). Affectivity and identity priming with episodically associated stimuli. *Cognition and Emotion*, 12, 145-169.

DiNardo, P. A., Brown, T. A. & Barlow, D. H. (1994). A*nxiety Disorders Interview Schedule for DSM-IV (Lifetime version)*. San Antonio, TX: Psychological Corporation.

Echeburúa, E. (1993). *Fobia social. Barcelona*: Martínez Roca.

García-López, L. J., Olivares, J., Hidalgo, M. D., Beidel, D. C. & Turner, S. M. (2001). Psychometric properties of the Social Phobia and Anxiety Inventory, the Social Anxiety Scale for Adolescents, the Fear of Negative Evaluation scale and the Social Avoidance Distress scale in an adolescent Spanish speaking population. *Journal of Psychopathology and Behavioral Assessment*, 23, 51-59.

Heimberg, R. G., Dodge, C. S., Hope, D. A., Kennedy, C. R., Zollo, L. J. & Becker, R. E. (1990). Cognitive-behavioral group treatment for social phobia: Comparison to a credible placebo control. *Cognitive Therapy and Research*, 14, 1-23.

Heimberg, R. G., Hope, D. A., Rapee, R. M. & Bruch, M. A. (1988). The validity of the Social Avoidance and Distress Scale and Fear of Negative Evaluation Scale with social phobic patients. *Behaviour Research and Therapy*, 26, 407-410.

Hermans, D., Baeyens, F & Eelen, P. (1998). Odours as affective-processing context for word evaluation: A case of cross-modal affective priming. *Cognition and Emotion*, 12, 601-613.

Hermans, D., De Houwer, J. & Eelen, P. (1994). The affective priming effect: Automatic activation of evaluative information in memory. *Cognition and Emotion*, 8, 515-533.

MacLeod, C. (1998). Implicit perception: Perceptual processing without awareness. In: F. Kirsner, C. Speerman, Maybery, A.O'Brien-Malone and C. Macleod (Eds.). *Implicit and Explicit neutral processes.* Mahwah, NJ: Lawrence Erlbaum.

MacLeod, C., Mathews, A. & Tata, P. (1986). Attentional bias in emotional disorders. *Journal of Abnormal Psychology*, 95, 15-20.

Mathews, A. & MacLeod, C. (1994). Cognitive approaches to emotion and emotional disorders. *Annual Review of Psychology*, 45, 25-50.

Mathews, A. & Milroy, R. (1994). Processing of emotional meaning in anxiety. *Cognition and emotion*, 8, 535-553.

Matthews, G. & Harley, T. A. (1996) Connectionists Models of Emotional Distress and Attentional Bias. *Cognition and Emotion*,10, 5-15.

Matthews, G. & Wells, A. (2000a). Attention, Automaticity, and Affective disorder. *Behavior Modification*, 24, 52-70.

Matthews, G. & Wells, A. (2000b). The cognitive science of attention and emotion. In: Tim Dalgleish and Mick Power. *Handbook of cognition and emotion.* New York: John Wiley and Sons.

Mattick, R. P., Peters, L. & Clarke, J. (1989). Exposure and cognitive restructuring for social phobia: a controlled study. Behavior Therapy, 20, 3-23.

Mogg, K. & Bradley, B.P. (2000). Selective attention and anxiety: A cognitive-motivational perspective. In: Tim Dalgleish and Mick Power. *Handbook of cognition and emotion.* New York: John Wiley and Sons.

Musch, J. & Klauer, K. C. (2003). The psychology of evaluation: an introduction. In Jochen Musch and Karl Christoph Klauer (Eds.), *The psychology of evaluation: affective processes in Cognition and emotion*. New Jersey: LEA.

Oei, T. P., Kenna, D. & Evans, L. (1991). The reliability, validity, and utility of the SAD and FNE scales for anxiety disorders patients. *Personality and Individual Differences*, 12, 111-116.

Orsillo, S. M. (2001). Measures for social phobia. In M. M. Antony, S. M. Orsillo and L. Roemer (directors), *Practioner's guide to empirically based measures of anxiety*, (pp. 165 -187). New York: Plenum.

Ruipérez, M. A., García-Palacios, A. & Botella, C. (2002). Clinical features and treatment response in social phobia: axis II comorbidity and social phobia subtypes. *Psicothema*, 14, 426-433.

Turner, S. M., McCanna, M. & Beidel, D. C. (1987). Validity of the Social Avoidance and Distress and Fear of Negative Evaluation scales. *Behaviour Research and Therapy*, 25, 113-115.

Villa, H., Botella, C., Quero, S., Ruipérez, M. A. & Gallardo, M. (1998, noviembre). Propiedades psicométricas de dos medidas de autoinforme en fobia social: Miedo a la evaluación negativa (FNE) y escala de evitación y ansiedad social (SADS). Poster presented at the *Symposium sobre Fobias y otros Trastornos de Ansiedad*, Granada.

Watson, D. & Friend, R. (1969). Measurement of Social-Evaluative Anxiety. *Journal of Consulting and Clinical Psychology*, 33, 448-457.

Wells, A. & Mathews, G. (1994). *Attention and emotion: A clinical perspective.* Hove: Erlbaum

Williams, J. M. G., Watts, F. N., MacLeod, C. & Mathews, A. (1997). *Cognitive psychology and emotional disorders* ( 2nd.ed.). Chichester, England: Wiley.

In: Hispanic Psychology Yearbook Volume 1
Ed: Cirilo H. García pp. 177-189
ISBN: 978-1-60741-786-6


*Chapter 14*

# BURNOUT OF PUBLIC SCHOOL TEACHERS IN SAN NICOLÁS DE LOS GARZA, NUEVO LEÓN, MÉXICO*

***Laura K. Castro[1], Karla Rodríguez & Cirilo H. García***
Universidad Autónoma de Nuevo León, Monterrey, México

## ABSTRACT

The term burnout refers to a feeling of failure and to an exhausted or used-up existence, and it is considered as a three-dimensional syndrome in which feelings of emotional exhaustion, depersonalization, and lack of personal accomplishment are present. This phenomenon has become a public health concern and may turn into a menace for teams of professionals whose objective is to help others, as it is the case for the education professionals. An instrument with the aims of knowing, describing and correlating some of the models related to the presence of the burnout syndrome in primary school teachers who work in public schools, was applied in this study. This instrument was a questionnaire directed to the teachers in 123 public primary schools in the municipality of San Nicolas de los Garza, Nuevo Leon, México. The results did not evidence the presence of the syndrome in its three dimensions in the studied sample. However, it is relevant the lack of personal accomplishment in the male teachers (33.61%), while the female teachers manifested as relevant the emotional exhaustion (44.33%). The analysis of this investigation gives us an idea of the importance of preventing the burnout syndrome in teachers.

**Keywords:** teaching, burnout, emotional exhaustion, lack of personal accomplishment, depersonalization.

* A version of this chapter was also published in the *International Hispanic Psychology Journal, Volume 1 Issue 2*, published by Nova Science Publishers, Inc. It was submitted for appropriate modification in an effort to encourage wider dissemination of research.

## INTRODUCTION

It is only recently that society has begun to pay attention to the importance that stress has in public health, as well as its negative consequences in different labor sectors, Having previously often been mistaken for laziness, indifference or unwillingness, Stress is the result of the relation between individuals and an environment they perceive as threatening, surpassing their limits, an environment that places their wellbeing at risk (Lazarus, 1984). When an individual is subjected to a continuous stress process a syndrome called Burnout appears. Burnout phenomenon literally means, "being burnt". Several explanatory models have reacted to this term. Freudenberguer (1974) defined Burnout (BO) as a feeling of failure, and an exhausted or used-up life, product of an overburden of energy demand, personal resources or workers' spiritual force. For Maslach and Jackson (1981, p. 3) "It is a three-dimensional syndrome characterized by emotional exhaustion, depersonalization and personal reduced accomplishment." Emotional exhaustion relates to physical and emotional overburden produced by the continuous interaction the worker keeps with their mates and their customers; depersonalization refers to the development of attitudes and answers somewhat cynical, from the worker to his customers; and lastly, the poor personal accomplishment which leads the worker to a loss of his self-confidence and a negative self-concept of his job.

In the society, the teacher plays a very important role; in several occasions, the teacher is a role model for the student, besides the teaching of an academic level knowledge. The problem is that not all the teachers fulfill these requirements; in a classroom they do not always know how to face the emotional conflicts kids may have, or their mood changes. To fight off this insecurity, teachers center their action in discipline, meaning, in the authoritarianism, in imposing, without observing the appropriate teaching process. Sometimes, the result is emotional exhaustion, depersonalization in dealing with students, a feeling of a lack of personal accomplishment, meaning, they show a burnout syndrome characteristics, expressing symptoms like irritability, anxiety, sadness and low self-esteem. Teachers who show the burnout syndrome usually present characteristic pathological symptoms like: depression or becoming an excessive authoritarian teacher; consequences fall in absenteeism, voluntary professional abandonment or severe relationship problems with their students, among others.

The general goal of this research was: To know, to describe and to correlate some of the models related to the Burnout presence in primary school teachers in public schools, as well as to identify the prevalence of burnout dimensions in primary education teachers, such as emotional exhaustion, depersonalization and lack of personal accomplishment.

## THEORIES ABOUT TEACHERS' BURNOUT

Burnout syndrome appears in professionals categorized as of aid, those who spend a considerable time in intense implication with people who often are dealing with a problematic situation, or where the relation can be polarized with frustration feelings or desperation.

## Burnout Term Concept

Somewhere in the middle '70s, burnout phenomenon was mentioned for the first time. Freundenberguer (1974) began to observe certain exhaustion in psychotherapists of a clinic, and he used this term to describe the inappropriate treatment the professionals gave to their patients. Likewise, in 1975, the same author described burnout as a state of tiredness, frustration caused by life expectations which are not fulfilled.

Maslach (1981) made culminant researches in the Maslach Burnout Inventory and its three dimensions (MBI):

1. Emotional exhaustion.
2. Depersonalization.
3. Lack of personal accomplishment.

**Symptoms of emotional exhaustion**. It refers to the lack of emotional resources; to feel that there is nothing to offer to others, it includes feelings of depression, which, in extreme cases, can lead to the deterioration of personality, as well as negative attitudes about the person itself, the job, relations and social interaction, associated to a low self-esteem and inferiority feelings, inefficiency and incompetence. It is a burnout core component that can be physically and psychologically manifested.

The depersonalization. It is the development of negative and insensible attitudes towards the addressees of the services they render (for example, patients, students, etc.)

The lack of Personal Accomplishment. It refers to a reduction of competence and personal accomplishment feelings. It is the perception that there are no possibilities of personal achievement in their job; personal expectations are diminished; including the settlement of a negative vision, rejection of him/herself and of personal achievements; the feeling of failure is imminent, as well as a low self-esteem.

Cherniss' model (1980) proposes that an individual has to interrelate in his/her job context, his/her expectations and demands, which causes a strong stress on him/her, in different degrees and forms. This tension can be faced in two ways: the first one, planning strategies to solve it; the second one, not finding effective solutions which make the individual show a negative attitude change. This happens in different time situations, and it represents a way of adaptation to stress.

Edelwich and Brodsky propose a cyclical and progressive model constituted by four different stages. In the first stage, -"the idealism and enthusiasm"-, there are activities carried out which begin to be very important and motivating, and lead the individual to false expectations of what it can be received. The second stage "stagnation", produces an emotional shock in confirming that labor expectations are unreal; the worker is "stuck". The next phase, the very core of the burnout, is frustration: the personal effort is questioned in front of obstacles arising from his/her labor activities performance. If he/she does not have personal resources to face the situation, apathy stage finally settles in; manifested as indifference which is characterized by a feeling of emptiness that comes in an emotional isolation and self-contempt manner.

Based on the afore mentioned concepts, manifestations of burnout of teachers are presented in the following way:

1. The emotional exhaustion is a dimension experienced by the teacher mainly due to the continuous interrelation with people, including students, parents and executives.
2. The depersonalization comes from the negative manner the teacher is relating to the others and more intensely to those who share his/her profession. Negative attitudes are mostly directed to his/her students, where inappropriate comments and behaviors are done, as well as irritability and a lack of motivation for the academic tasks. Cherniss (1992), Maslach and Jackson (1981) point out that male teachers display more negative attitudes towards the students than female teachers.
3. Diminution of feeling of personal accomplishment. The teacher develops negative attitudes to him/herself and to the work; he/she avoids to get acquainted with his/her mates; his/her performance and labor productivity are reduced, and it is hard to put up with labor activities.
4. The most meaningful aspect of this syndrome is the difficulty teachers face to create new working plans, and the need of giving up their own teaching tasks.

## Intervening Factors of the Burnout

There are different factors related to the manifestation of the syndrome in different teacher's contexts.

a) Social *context.* During the last 15 or 20 years, responsibilities and demands of the teachers have been increasing. This coincides with a transformation of the teaching process and the traditional agents of social integration; the role of teachers has also been modified, and this is a situation which implies certain uneasiness for many of them, because they either have not accepted that fact or they have not wanted to do it. (Barton and Walker, 1984). Many teachers will have to change many knowledge elements they have been working with during many years and they will have to acquire other new elements they never heard of during their preparation. (Leon, 1980).
b) *Teaching practice context.* Teachers state that one of the factors that hinders the appropriate accomplishment of their job is the lack of material. They feel constricted because they do not have enough didactic material to carry out their tasks; the institution does not have the resources, and they do not have them either, their expectations start to languish, and they enter a disappointment state (Esteve, 1994).
c) Another important factor is the role conflict; according to Travers and Cooper (1997) the conflict can arise when there is no concordance between demands imposed on an individual and his/her beliefs, or when they are under demanded to perform activities they are not prepared to.
d) Interpersonal problem *context.* Caspari (1976) mentions that teachers show a greater emotional exhaustion at the end of school year; due to the exhaustion derived from the responsibility of teaching and disciplining children, than any other variable implied in the teaching level.
e) Gil-Monte and Peiro (1997) mention that continuous interactions with mates or authorities may be conflictive, and if those interactions continue for a long

period, or a lack of support from any of them can increase the risk of suffering burnout.

f) *Personality factors.* There are certain personality traits which can increase the risk of suffering burnout. According to Nagy and Davis (1985), the influence of this kind of personality is correlated with emotional exhaustion and depersonalization. Gil-Monte and Peiro (1996) mention that altruist and idealist people lead their job to the best possible development, and they feel it as a personal matter, so, when something does not result as they planned it, they feel unsuccessful, which implies a bigger susceptibility to a feeling of lack of personal accomplishment and emotional exhaustion syndrome. Another aspect is the low self-esteem; those individuals have but limited tools to face the problems as they are presented during their professional development, which provokes negative effects about their personal accomplishment feeling (Friedman y Farber, 1992). Leiter (1992) mentions that if the individual does not trust in his/her self-efficaciousness, there is a bigger risk of suffering burnout.

g) Cordes y Dougherty (1993) mention that when someone's expectations are not accomplished, he/she will feel frustrated and the risk of burnout will increase too. Finally, there are the emotional demands of the individual; according to Garden (1989) the individual will respond accordingly to his/her demand perception; if he/she perceives too much is being expected, it will be more likely he/she suffers burnout.

h) e)Demographic factors. Different authors' manifest demographic factors tend to lead to burnout. Depending on the gender, women are more prone to burnout than men, although men have a greater predisposition to depersonalization, older individuals have less risk of suffering burnout syndrome; these individuals have developed a better ability to answers, and their professional expectations have been made more realistic, according to the job they are performing. The authors also mention that younger and less experienced individuals feel more stressed than older ones; married people have fewer tendencies to suffer burnout due to the conjugal support and stability they receive and perceive (Grau y Chacon, 1998). According to Gil-Monte and Peiro (1997) persons who have children can understand others better, due to the family support they keep. Additionally, they mention people with no children are more focused on their profession, consequently, any negative effect can be perceived in a greater dimension than those with children. As stated by Grau y Chacon (1998), personnel with minimum seniority has a bigger risk to suffer burnout, due to lack of experience and expectations about the institution.

### *Burnout Consequences*

Burnout consequences affect different aspects of the individual's life.

### *Physical Consequences*

The physical consequences manifested by individuals are headache, backache or other sore muscles; gastroenteritis problems, etc. (Kahill, 1988).

### *Psychological Consequences*

Some of the emotional consequences mainly found are negative feelings emphasized on themselves (Friedman, 1991). Another consequence of negative feelings caused by burnout is mental health deterioration, since it begins with depression, irritability and anxiety (Maslach y Jackson 1982; Kahill, 1988).

### *Behavioral Consequences*

Manifestations at a behavioral level showed by individuals include behavior alterations when they interact with other persons, since they become impulsive and easily irritated. Likewise, they manifest compulsive behavior on their feeding habits, they consume drugs, and smoke and drink in excess. Cox,1985).

Maslach (1982) emphasizes the existing link between the deterioration consequence of the burnout and the extenuating family conflicts of the affected person.

### *Negative Consequences the Individual Causes on the Institution*

There are certain consequences which affect individuals who suffer burnout; the said consequences, at the same time, cause effects over the institution the individual works for. One of them which happen more frequently is absenteeism. Stern (1980) mentions that absenteeism increase is related to a low motivation the worker has to carry out his job, that and a problematic relation with his co-workers, the individual's own perception of his/her self-efficaciousness and the lack of material and didactic resources at the moment of carrying out his tasks.

## Hypothesis

Based on the literature review and the objectives proposed in the research, the hypothesis was:

The age, family demand, labor seniority, social-academic or extra labor charge have an influence on primary schools teachers of San Nicolas de los Garza when burnout syndrome is presented in light, moderate or severe way.

# METHOD

## Context

The study was carried out in primary schools of San Nicolas de los Garza, Nuevo Leon, with a sample of 687 teachers, from 123 different primary schools. On March, 2002, 50 pilot questionnaires were applied to 6 primary schools randomly chosen from the San Nicolas de los Garza, Nuevo Leon population. The instrument was applied from September to December 2002.

Data collection was made by questionnaires distribution to each teacher, according to the selected primary school, by previously requesting the Director's authorization. Approximately 1 hour was used to apply the instrument.

## Population and Sampling

A quantitative type study was used. Using the formula Hernandez and cols. formula (1998) we obtained a probabilistic sampling from primary schools of San Nicolas de los Garza, which had a population of 178, working with 123 primary schools of the study sampling, corresponding to 976 teachers, from which 687 persons – 162 men and 511 women- voluntarily participated; 14 cases were not genre analyzed. The names of the primary schools of the sampling were randomly obtained using the STATS Programs 1998) by Hernandez and cols., with a result of 377 day shift teachers; 222 from the evening shift, and 88 from both.

The formula used was the following:

$$n = \frac{400}{1+400/N}$$

### *Instrument*

The instrument used to analyze the Burnout, consisted in applying to each teacher a 44 reactives questionnaire, which was made using a combination of the collection and adaptation of two "likert" type scales, by randomly distributing the reactives. The Burnout Inventory of Maslach y Jackson (1986) is an inventory of 22 reactives in which phrases regarding thoughts related to different continuous their daily labor performance interaction situations are mentioned to the subjects (Attachment 3). Furthermore, the Brief Burnout Questionnaire (BBC), made by Moreno and cols. (1992), composed of 21 reactives which consider 7 dimensions was used: personal accomplishment, emotional exhaustion, depersonalization, boredom, task characteristics, organizational environment, and the burnout consequences in the life quality of the individual, particularly in his personal relationships.

The models used to analyze the dependent variable were classified with their indicators, as follows:

a) Age: the age of the individual;
b) Filial family demand: Number of children;
c) Labor experience: years of working in the teaching profession;
d) Seniority: years the individual has worked in the Institution;
e) Labor charge: Hours worked in the Institution;
f) social-academic labor charge: Number of students;
g) Extra-labor charge: hours worked at home.

## Data Analysis

An ***ex post facto*** type study was performed, and this is essentially an explanatory study. A factorial analysis statistics technique was used to identify if the scales used to measure the "burnout" are unifactorial o multifactorial ones. Additionally, the Alfa-Cronbach coefficient was obtained. An exploratory factorial analysis was carried out in order to observe the models contained in the scale, using, for this purpose, the main factors extraction technique known as "main axis factorization" was used, and the "varimax" rotation method", by using a selection criteria for reactives no less than .40.

Furthermore, a coefficient of the different indicators was calculated of each one of the models for the validation of the models used, and a z punctuation was obtained of each one of the grades obtained from teachers in order to carry out the comparison among them.

The statistical package for social sciences (SPSS) was used so as to help in information processing. In addition, the analysis of regression multiple method was used to determine all of the total and partial variance of the burnout explained by the models.

# RESULTS

## Descriptive Results of the Sample

The results of each model and sample indicator are shown in a general way in Table I. Sample profile shows 79% of the teachers are 36-50 years old; 62% have 2-3 children; 61% have 16-25 years of labor experience; 59.24% have 1-10 years of seniority; 52.40% works 21-25 hours per week; 61% have 21-35 students; 35% work 2 extra daily hours; 78% have a steady spouse; 72% has a Bachelor's degree, and .87% have a Master degree. The sample shows a similarity in both genders, regarding the age, filial family demand, labor experience and labor seniority models.

**Table I. Sample distribution by personal characteristics.**

| Model | Indicator | Mean | Standard deviation | Minimum | Maximum |
|---|---|---|---|---|---|
| Age | Current age | 40 | 6.44 | 19 years | 62 years |
| Filial familial demand | Number of children | 2 | 1.25 | No children | 5 children |
| Labor experience | Years of working in the area | 20.36 | 6.87 | 5 months | 43 years |
| Labor seniority | Number of years working in the institution. | 9.44 | 6.33 | 1 month | 32 years |
| Labor burden | Hour worked in the institution | 29.54 | 9.24 | 10 hours per week | 62 hours per week |
| Social-academic labor burden | Number of students | 29.42 | 8.95 | 10 students | 70 students |
| Extra labor burden | Hours worked at home | 2.52 | 1.45 | No work at home | 6 daily hours |

## Measurement Scale of the Sample

The factorial analysis of the dependent variable of the sample was made by the method of extraction "Factorization of principal axis" through which just one factor was extracted, conceptualized as "Scale of Burnout Syndrome"; the reliability was of .9103, the variance explained of 35.37%, forming a scale of 22 reactives, which were selected according to their factorial load higher than .40. (Rosenthal, 1994). The reactives of this scale with their respective factorial loads are shown in Table II. In the case of Burnout factorial analysis of the teachers, only 1 factor was identified and it was conceptualized as "Sub-scale of emotional exhaustion", with a reliability of .8747, the variance explained of 47.73% , and a 10 reactives sub-scale shown in Table III. Male Teachers and females teachers alike, had a conceptualized factor of "lack of personal accomplishment under-scale", with a reliability of .8669 and a variance explained of 36.79%. In Table IV can be observed a sub-scale composed of 14 reactives selected accordingly to the factorial load mentioned.

## Correlation Between Some of the Independent Models and the Burnout

Some explicative models were carried out, changing some of the independent models, according to the burnout dependent variable in the sub-scales of male and female teachers. For the male teachers, none of the studied models had a significant influence on the burnout; however, for the female teachers, the model had a definite impact on the social-academic labor charge model, indicating that for women, the number of students has a certain influence on the burnout (See Table V).

**Table II. "Scale of Burnout Syndrome ".**

| Items | Structure coefficients |
|---|---|
| 1. I feel used up due to my job. | .566 |
| 2. I feel I am on the limit of my possibilities in this job. | .616 |
| 3. I consider that the job I make affects my personal health (headache, insomnia, etc) | .543 |
| 4. I feel active after working with my students. | .510 |
| 5. I feel frustrated in my job. | .574 |
| 6. I feel exhausted due to my job. | .634 |
| 7. I think that I have an indifferent behavior with the people since I do this job. | .436 |
| 8. To work directly with my students makes me feel stressed. | .604 |
| 9. To assist my students all day long is a stress for me. | .695 |
| 10. I feel exhausted when I wake up in the morning, and have to face another working day. | .624 |
| 11. Frequently, my students have excessive demands and irritating behaviors. | .454 |
| 12. I feel that my students blame me for some of their problems | .450 |
| 13. I feel exhausted at the end of the working day | .666 |
| 14. In my job, I use to deal with emotional problems calmly. | .436 |
| 15. My job is repetitive. | .409 |
| 16. My job's problems reduce my efficiency | .606 |
| 17. The job I am doing is different from which I would like to do | .454 |
| 18. I feel emotionally exhausted due to my job. | .644 |
| 19. I feel very active in my job. | .540 |
| 20. I can create a relaxed environment for my students. | .455 |
| 21. When I am doing my job, I feel in bad mood | .625 |
| 22. In general, I am sick and tired of my job. | .694 |

**Table III. "Sub-scale of emotional exhaustion".**

| Items | Structure coefficients |
|---|---|
| 1. I feel "exhausted due to my job". | .713 |
| 2. I feel that I am on the limits of my possibilities in this job. | .689 |
| 3. I consider that the job I do affects my personal health (headache, insomnia, etc.). | .716 |
| 4. I feel active after working with my students. | .427 |
| 5. I feel exhausted due to my job. | .721 |
| 6. Working directly with my students, make feel stressed. | .668 |
| 7. I feel exhausted when I wake up in the morning, and have to face with working day. | .583 |
| 8. Frequently, my students have excessive demands and irritating behavior. | .472 |
| 9. I feel exhausted at the end of the working day. | .750 |
| 10. I feel emotionally exhausted due to my job. | .677 |

**Table IV. "Sub-scale of lack of personal accomplishment".**

| Items | Structure coefficients |
|---|---|
| 1. I feel that with my job, I am influencing positively in other people's life. | .562 |
| 2. I feel identified with my job. | .694 |
| 3. I believe that I have an indifferent behavior with the people since I do my job. | .534 |
| 4. I like the environment of my job. | .482 |
| 5. I think that I treat some of my students as if they were inferiors. | .505 |
| 6. I feel that my students blame me for some of their problems | .466 |
| 7. In my job I use to deal with emotional problems calmly. | .553 |
| 8. I am not interested in my current job. | .588 |
| 9. The job I am doing is different from which I would like to do. | .640 |
| 10. In reality, I am not interested in what is happening to some of my students. | .616 |
| 11. Even though the responsibility of my job, I do not know the results and scope of it. | .505 |
| 12. I feel very active in my job. | .599 |
| 13. I can easily create a relaxed environment for my students. | .618 |
| 14. I have made many things that make my job worthy. | .513 |

**Table V. Explanatory model of the sample of female teachers**

| | Adjusted $R^2$ 4.6 % | Standardized Coefficient | | |
|---|---|---|---|---|
| Models | Indicator | β (Beta) | t | Level of significance |
| Social-academic burden | Number of students | .218 | 4.87 | 0.001 |

## Teachers Burnout Grades

Finally, through the grades obtained from each questionnaire, teachers z scores were known, classifying according to Burnout degree: absent, light, moderate and severe. Z scores from -3 to 0 belongs to absence, light emotional exhaustion with a score of .1 to 1.00, from 1.01 to 2.00 moderate and 2.01; the subsequent grade is classified as severe. As it can be seen in Table VI, the degree of the analyzed dimension, more than 50% of the women did not manifest emotional exhaustion (55.67%), whereas 44.33% showed emotional exhaustion in some of the grades. For male teachers, it can be observed that they did not manifest lack of personal accomplishment with higher percentage than women (66.23%), compared with 33.77% that did presented it in some grade.

**Table VI. Sample distribution according to burnout incidence.**

| Subscale | Gender | Absent | Light | Moderate | Severe |
|---|---|---|---|---|---|
| Emotional exhaustion | Female | 55.67% | 33.61% | 6.39% | 4.33% |
| Lack of personal accomplishment | Male | 66.23% | 19.20% | 11.26% | 3.30% |

## DISCUSSION

During this research, we found some empirical evidences which confirm and/or differ from other researching about burnout. First, the teachers in San Nicolas de los Garza, Nuevo Leon did not show any significant signs of the syndrome in the three dimensions of burnout. One of the possible explanations of these findings is the one that takes into account the school period in which the research was made, since it was carried out during the first three months of the school year: emotional exhaustion, depersonalization and lack of personal accomplishment dimensions did not show up, given that indicators developing burnout were not present (factors of teachers' practice, organization, personality, etc). Caspari (1976) mentions that exhaustion manifests itself when school period is about to end.

As it can be observed, no significant differences were found in the sampling profile divided by gender, but in the indicator of the hours worked at the institution, (men work more than women) and in hours worked at home (women work more at home than men). It is considered that one of the possible differences of these results is that men work two shifts to support their families, and they are focused on their job at the institutions. Regarding female teachers, most of them work only a shift since they need to carry out other tasks, including the extra-labor tasks to prepare the school material in the institution.

In this study, it can be observed that burnout can be manifested in dimensions, as Maslach y Jackson (1986) have mentioned in their researches, but the difference in this population being that there is a relevant dimension for each gender. For men, the relevant dimension is only that of lack of personal accomplishment, whereas for women, only the dimension of emotional exhaustion. Gil Monte and Peiro (1997) results say different, since these two last ones mention that men show more depersonalization than women.

The models that were analyzed and their indicators like age, number of children, experience, labor seniority, number hours worked at the institution and number of hours worked at home do not have any explicative influence in burnout of male teachers. However, for female teachers, social-academic labor charge has an influence when trying to explain emotional exhaustion. It is considered that women have a higher emotional implication compared with male teachers, probably because women are emotionally involved with their students, meaning, they keep an intellectual and emotional relation with the students. These results confirm Gil-Monte and Peiro (1996) findings, which mention that the labor over-charge appears as a significant antecedent at an emotional exhaustion level, and their results differ regarding the lineal relation between age and emotional exhaustion.

Results for female teachers are considered an alarming figure, due to the tendency they have to show emotional exhaustion. As it can be seen, a third of the sampled individuals showed light emotional exhaustion. It is necessary to take into account the current result, to keep this figure from increasing, and to look for solution strategies to reduce Exhaustion.

There are some researches in which it is stated that some labor over-charge indicators seem to have an influence on the burnout syndrome, in any, or all of its three dimensions, as well as some aspects related to the students. Millicent y Sewell (1999) mention bad behavior of the student is a significant indicator of lack of personal accomplishment. It is important to continue researching on different indicators of social-academic labor charge, as important factors for the incidence of burnout.

It was concluded, in this research, that male and female public primary schools teachers of San Nicolas de los Garza, Nuevo Leon, do not manifest burnout syndrome due to the lack of significant signs in the three dimensions.

None of the analyzed models (age, seniority, social-academic labor charge, filial family demand, extra-labor burden) have significant and substantial statistical influence on male teachers. On the other hand, for female teachers the social-academic labor burden appears as a significant model when trying to explain the variance of the burnout. As for labor charge of female teachers, it is important to redefine the number of students in the institutions, so as to avoid Emotional Exhaustion.

Notwithstanding the low punctuation of Burnout for male teachers, there is a significant influence on the lack of personal accomplishment, in female teachers; the relevant dimension is that of emotional exhaustion.

It is recommended that future investigations evaluate the possible effects that daily interactions of the female teachers with their students have, as well as the personal models (general expectations, self- efficaciousness) in teachers.

## REFERENCES

Barton, L., & Walker, S. (1984). *Social crisis and Educational Research.* London: Croom Helm.

Caspari, I.E. (1976). *Troublesome Children in Class.* London: Routledge & Kegan Paul.

Cordes, C.L. & Dougherty, T.W. (1993). A review and an integration of research on job burnout. *Academy of Management Review*, 18, 4, 621-656.

Cherniss, C. (1980). *Professional burnout in human service organizations.* New York: Praeger.

Cherniss, C. (1992). Long-term consequences of burnout: An exploratory study. *British Journal of Orthodontics*, 26, 1, 75-76

Edelwich, J. & Brodsky, A. (1980). *Burnout.* UK: Human Sciences Press.

Esteve, J.M. (1994). *Teacher's uneasiness*. Barcelona: Paidos.

Freudenberger, H.J. (1974). Staff burnout. *The Journal of Social Issues*, 160.

Freudenberger, H.J. (1975). The staff burn-out syndrome in alternative institutions. *Psychotherapy: Theory, research and practice 12, 1, 73-82 (Reprinted by the Drug Abuse Council).* Washington, D.C.

Friedman, I.A. (1991). High and low burnout schools: School culture aspects of teacher burnout. *Journal of Educational Research*, 84, 6, 325-333.

Friedman, I.A. & Farber, B. (1992). Professional self-concept as a predictor of teacher burnout. *Journal of Educational Research*, 86, 1, 28-35.

Garden, A.M. (1989). Burnout: The effect of psychological type on research findings. *Journal of Occupational Psychology*, 62, 223-234.

Gil, P.R. & Peiro, J.M. (1996). A study over significant antecedents of "burnout syndrome" in workers occupational centers of psychological disable people. *Work and Organizations Psychology Magazine,* 12,1, 67-80.

Gil-Monte, P.R. & Peiro J.M (1997). *Work psychological weariness: burnout syndrome.* Madrid: Narcea.

Grau, A. J. & Chacon, R. M. (1998). Burnout: A threatening to health teams. A Masterly *Conference in Seminar of Colombian Sectional Association of Health Psychology.* Cali: Colombia.

Hernandez, S. R., Fernandez Collado C. & Baptista L. P. (1998). *Metodología de la investigación.* Mexico: McGraw-Hill.

Kahill, S. (1988). Interventions for burnout in the helping professions: A review of the empirical evidence. *Canadian Journal of Counseling*, 22, 3, 162-169.

Imbernon, F. (1997). *The formation and professional development of teachers to a new professional culture*. Mexico: Paidos.

Lazarus, R. & Folkman, S. (1984). *Stress, appraisal, and coping.* New York: Springer.

Leiter, M.P. (1992). Burn-out as a crisis in self-efficacy-conceptual and practical implications. *Work and Stress*, 6, 2, 107-116.

Leon, A. (1980). *Teaching profession: motivations, knowledge updating and promotion.* Barcelona: Oikos-Tau.

Maslach, C & Jackson, S.E. (1981). Maslach Burnout Inventory. Palo Alto. *Ca: Consulting Psychologists Press,*. 3.

Maslach, C & Jackson, S.E. (1982). Burnout in health professions: A social psychological analysis. In G.S. Sanders & J. Suls (Eds.). *Social psychology of health and illness.* Hillsdale: LEA.

Nagy, S. & Davis, L.G. (1985). *Burnout: A comparative analysis of personality and environmental variables*. New York: Psychological Reports.

Stern, W.A. (1980). *Teacher absenteeism at the secondary school level.* Detroit, Michigan : Michigan State University.

Travers, C.J., & Cooper, C.L. (1997). *Teachers' stress, teaching activity pressure.* Barcelona: Paidos

# INDEX

## A

## B



## C

## D



## E

## I



## J



## K

## L



## M



## N

## O



## P

## Q



## R



## S

## T



## U



## V



## W



## Y